Optimizing HPC Applications with Intel® Cluster Tools

Alexander Supalov
Andrey Semin
Michael Klemm
Christopher Dahnken

Apress
open

Optimizing HPC Applications with Intel® Cluster Tools

Alexander Supalov, Andrey Semin, Michael Klemm, and Christopher Dahnken

Copyright © 2014 by Apress Media, LLC, all rights reserved

ApressOpen Rights: You have the right to copy, use and distribute this Work in its entirety, electronically without modification, for non-commercial purposes only. However, you have the additional right to use or alter any source code in this Work for any commercial or non-commercial purpose which must be accompanied by the licenses in (2) and (3) below to distribute the source code for instances of greater than 5 lines of code. Licenses (1), (2) and (3) below and the intervening text must be provided in any use of the text of the Work and fully describes the license granted herein to the Work.

(1) **License for Distribution of the Work:** This Work is copyrighted by Apress Media, LLC, all rights reserved. Use of this Work other than as provided for in this license is prohibited. By exercising any of the rights herein, you are accepting the terms of this license. You have the non-exclusive right to copy, use and distribute this English language Work in its entirety, electronically without modification except for those modifications necessary for formatting on specific devices, for all non-commercial purposes, in all media and formats known now or hereafter. While the advice and information in this Work are believed to be true and accurate at the date of publication, neither the authors nor the editors nor the publisher can accept any legal responsibility for any errors or omissions that may be made. The publisher makes no warranty, express or implied, with respect to the material contained herein.

If your distribution is solely Apress source code or uses Apress source code intact, the following licenses (2) and (3) must accompany the source code. If your use is an adaptation of the source code provided by Apress in this Work, then you must use only license (3).

(2) **License for Direct Reproduction of Apress Source Code:** This source code, from *Optimizing HPC Applications with Intel® Cluster Tools, ISBN 978-1-4302-6496-5* is copyrighted by Apress Media, LLC, all rights reserved. Any direct reproduction of this Apress source code is permitted but must contain this license. The following license must be provided for any use of the source code from this product of greater than 5 lines wherein the code is adapted or altered from its original Apress form. This Apress code is presented AS IS and Apress makes no claims to, representations or warrantees as to the function, usability, accuracy or usefulness of this code.

(3) **License for Distribution of Adaptation of Apress Source Code:** Portions of the source code provided are used or adapted from *Optimizing HPC Applications with Intel® Cluster Tools, ISBN 978-1-4302-6496-5* copyright Apress Media LLC. Any use or reuse of this Apress source code must contain this License. This Apress code is made available at Apress.com/9781430264965 as is and Apress makes no claims to, representations or warrantees as to the function, usability, accuracy or usefulness of this code.

ISBN-13 (pbk): 978-1-4302-6496-5

ISBN-13 (electronic): 978-1-4302-6497-2

Trademarked names, logos, and images may appear in this book. Rather than use a trademark symbol with every occurrence of a trademarked name, logo, or image we use the names, logos, and images only in an editorial fashion and to the benefit of the trademark owner, with no intention of infringement of the trademark.

The use in this publication of trade names, trademarks, service marks, and similar terms, even if they are not identified as such, is not to be taken as an expression of opinion as to whether or not they are subject to proprietary rights.

While the advice and information in this book are believed to be true and accurate at the date of publication, neither the authors nor the editors nor the publisher can accept any legal responsibility for any errors or omissions that may be made. The publisher makes no warranty, express or implied, with respect to the material contained herein.

Publisher: Heinz Weinheimer
Associate Publisher: Jeffrey Pepper
Lead Editors: Steve Weiss (Apress); Stuart Douglas (Intel)
Coordinating Editor: Melissa Maldonado
Cover Designer: Anna Ishchenko

Distributed to the book trade worldwide by Springer Science+Business Media New York, 233 Spring Street, 6th Floor, New York, NY 10013. Phone 1-800-SPRINGER, fax (201) 348-4505, e-mail orders-ny@springer-sbm.com, or visit www.springeronline.com.

For information on translations, please e-mail rights@apress.com, or visit www.apress.com.

About ApressOpen

What Is ApressOpen?

- ApressOpen is an open access book program that publishes high-quality technical and business information.

- ApressOpen eBooks are available for global, free, noncommercial use.

- ApressOpen eBooks are available in PDF, ePub, and Mobi formats.

- The user-friendly ApressOpen free eBook license is presented on the copyright page of this book.

To Irina, Vladislav, and Anton, with all my love.
—Alexander Supalov

For my beautiful wife, Nadine, and for my daughters—Eva, Viktoria, and Alice.
I'm so proud of you!
—Andrey Semin

To my family.
—Michael Klemm

To Judith, Silas, and Noah.
—Christopher Dahnken

SI ENIM PLACET OPUS NOSTRUM, GAUDEBIMUS.
SI AUTEM NULLI PLACET: NOSMET IPSOS TAMEN IUVAT QUOD FECIMUS.

Contents at a Glance

Contents

About the Authors

Dr. Alexander Supalov created the Intel Cluster Tools product line, especially the Intel MPI Library that he designed and led between 2003 and 2014. Before that, he invented new finite-element mesh-generation methods, contributed to the PARMACS and PARASOL interfaces, and developed the first full MPI-2 and IMPI implementations. Alexander guided Intel efforts in the MPI Forum during development of the MPI-2.1, MPI-2.2, and MPI-3 standards. He graduated from the Moscow Institute of Physics and Technology in 1990, and in 1995 earned his Ph.D. in applied mathematics at the Institute of Numerical Mathematics of the Russian Academy of Sciences. Alexander holds 15 patents.

Andrey Semin is a Senior Engineer and HPC technology manager for Intel in Europe, the Middle East, and Africa regions. He supports the leading European high-performance computing users, helping them to deploy new and innovative HPC solutions to grand-challenge problems. Andrey's background includes extensive experience working with leading HPC software and hardware vendors. He has been instrumental in developing HPC industry innovations delivering improvements in the energy efficiency from data center to applications; his current research is focused on fine-grained HPC systems power and performance modeling and optimization. Andrey graduated from Moscow State University in Russia in 2000, specializing in possibility theory and its applications for physical experiment analysis. He is the author of over a dozen papers and patents in the area of application tuning and energy efficiency analysis, and is also a frequent speaker on topics impacting the HPC industry.

Dr.-Ing. Michael Klemm is part of Intel's Software and Services Group, Developer Relations Division. His focus is on high-performance and throughput computing. Michael received a Doctor of Engineering degree (Dr.-Ing.) in computer science from the Friedrich-Alexander-University Erlangen-Nuremberg, Germany, in 2008. His research focus was on compilers and runtime optimizations for distributed systems. Michael's areas of interest include compiler construction, design of programming languages, parallel programming, and performance analysis and tuning. Michael is Intel representative in the OpenMP Language Committee and leads the efforts to develop error-handling features.

Dr. Christopher Dahnken manages the HPC software enabling activities of Intel's Developer Relations Division in the EMEA region. He focuses on the enabling of major scientific open-source codes for new Intel technologies and the development of scalable algorithms. Chris holds a diploma and a doctoral degree in theoretical physics from the University of Würzburg, Germany.

About the Technical Reviewers

Heinz Bast has more than 20 years experience in the areas of application tuning, benchmarking, and developer support. Since joining Intel's Supercomputer Systems Division in 1993, Heinz has worked with multiple Intel software enabling teams to support software developers throughout Europe. Heinz Bast has a broad array of applications experience, including computer games, enterprise applications, and high-performance computing environments. Currently Heinz Bast is part of the Intel Developer Products Division, where he focuses on training and supporting customers with development tools and benchmarks.

Dr. Heinrich Bockhorst is a Senior HPC Technical Consulting Engineer for high-performance computing in Europe. He is member of the developer products division (DPD) within the Software & Services Group. Currently his work is focused on manycore enabling and high-scaling hybrid programming targeting Top30 accounts. He conducts four to five customer trainings on cluster tools per year and is in charge of developing new training materials for Europe. Heinrich Bockhorst received his doctoral degree in theoretical solid state physics from Göttingen University, Germany.

Dr. Clay Breshears is currently a Life Science Software Architect for Intel's Health Strategy and Solutions group. During the 30 years he has been involved with parallel computation and programming he has worked in academia (teaching multiprocessing, multi-core, and multithreaded programming), as a contractor for the U.S. Department of Defense (programming HPC platforms), and at several jobs at Intel Corporation involved with parallel computation, training, and programming tools.

Dr. Alejandro Duran has been an Application Engineer for Intel Corporation for the past two years, with a focus on HPC enabling. Previously, Alex was a senior researcher at the Barcelona Supercomputing Center in the Programming Models Group. He holds a Ph.D. from the Polytechnic University of Catalonia, Spain, in computer architecture. He has been part of the OpenMP Language committee for the past nine years.

Klaus-Dieter Oertel is a Senior HPC Technical Consulting Engineer in the Developer Products Division within Intel's Software & Services Group. He belongs to the first generation of parallelization experts in Germany, educated during the SUPRENUM project that developed a parallel computer in the second half of the 1980s. In his 25 years of experience in HPC computing, he has worked on all kinds of supercomputers, like large vector machines, shared memory systems, and clusters. In recent years he has focused on the enabling of applications for the latest HPC architecture, the Intel Xeon Phi coprocessor, and has provided related tools trainings and customer support.

Acknowledgments

Many people contributed to this book over a long period of time, so even though we will try to mention all of them, we may miss someone owing to no other reason than the fallibility of human memory. In what we hope are only rare cases, we want to apologize upfront to any who may have been inadvertently missed.

We would like to thank first and foremost our Intel lead editor Stuart Douglas, whose sharp eye selected our book proposal among so many others, and thus gave birth to this project.

The wonderfully helpful and professional staff at Apress made this publication possible. Our special thanks are due to the lead editor Steve Weiss, coordinating editor Melissa Maldonado, development editor Corbin Collins, copyeditor Carole Berglie, and their colleagues: Nyomi Anderson, Patrick Hauke, Anna Ishchenko, Dhaneesh Kumar, Jeffrey Pepper, and many others.

We would like to thank most heartily Dr. Bronis de Supinski, CTO, Lawrence Computing, LLNL, who graciously agreed to write the foreword for our book, and took his part in the effort of pressing it through the many clearance steps required by our respective employers.

Our deepest gratitude goes to our indomitable reviewers: Heinz Bast, Heinrich Bockhorst, Clay Breshears, Alejandro Duran, and Klaus-Dieter Oertel (all of Intel Corporation). They spent uncounted hours in a sea of electronic ink pondering multiple early chapter drafts and helping us stay on track.

Many examples in the book were discussed with leading HPC application experts and users. We especially are grateful to Dr. Georg Hager (Regional Computing Center Erlangen), Hinnerk Stüben (University of Hamburg), and Prof. Dr. Gerhard Wellein (University of Erlangen) for their availability and willingness to explain the complexity of their applications and research.

Finally, and by no means lastly, we would like to thank so many colleagues at Intel and elsewhere whose advice and opinions have been helpful to us, both in direct relation to this project and as a general guidance in our professional lives. Here are those whom we can recall, with the names sorted alphabetically in a vain attempt to be fair to all: Alexey Alexandrov, Pavan Balaji, Michael Brinskiy, Michael Chuvelev, Jim Cownie, Jim Dinan, Dmitry Dontsov, Dmitry Durnov, Craig Garland, Rich Graham, Bill Gropp, Evgeny Gvozdev, Thorsten Hoefler, Jay Hoeflinger, Hans-Christian Hoppe, Sergey Krylov, Oleg Loginov, Mark Lubin, Bill Magro, Larry Meadows, Susan Milbrandt, Scott McMillan, Wolfgang Petersen, Dave Poulsen, Sergey Sapronov, Gergana Slavova, Sanjiv Shah, Michael Steyer, Sayantan Sur, Andrew Tananakin, Rajeev Thakur, Joe Throop, Xinmin Tian, Vladimir Truschin, German Voronov, Thomas Willhalm, Dmitry Yulov, and Marina Zaytseva.

Foreword

Large-scale computing—also known as supercomputing—is inherently about performance. We build supercomputers in order to solve the largest possible problems in a time that allows the answers to be relevant. However, application scientists spend the bulk of their time adding functionality to their simulations and are necessarily experts in the domains covered by those simulations. They are not experts in computer science in general and code optimization in particular. Thus, a book such as this one is essential—a comprehensive but succinct guide to achieving performance across the range of architectural space covered by large-scale systems using two widely available standard programming models (OpenMP and MPI) that complement each other.

Today's large-scale systems consist of many nodes federated by a high-speed interconnect. Thus, multiprocess parallelism, as facilitated by MPI, is essential to use them well. However, individual nodes have become complex parallel systems in their own right. Each node typically consists of multiple processors, each of which has multiple cores. While applications have long treated these cores as virtual nodes, the decreasing memory capacity per core is best handled with multithreading, which is facilitated most by OpenMP. Those cores now almost universally offer some sort of parallel (Single Instruction, Multiple Data, or SIMD) floating-point unit that provides yet another level of parallelism that the application scientist must exploit in order to use the system as effectively as possible. Since performance is the ultimate purpose of large-scale systems, multi-level parallelism is essential to them. This book will help application scientists tackle that complex computer science problem.

In general, performance optimization is most easily accomplished with the right tools for the task. Intel Parallel Studio XE Cluster Edition is a collection of tools that support efficient application development and performance optimization. While many other compilers are available for Intel architectures, including one from PGI, as well as the open source GNU Compiler Collection, the Intel compilers that are included in the Parallel Studio tool suite generate particularly efficient code for them.

To optimize interprocess communication, the application scientist needs to understand which message operations are most efficient. Many tools, including Intel Trace Analyzer and Collector, use the MPI Profiling Interface to measure MPI performance and to help the application scientist identify bottlenecks between nodes. Several others are available, including Scalasca, TAU, Paraver, and Vampir, by which the Intel Trace Analyzer was inspired. The application scientist's toolbox should include several of them.

Similarly, the application scientist needs to understand how well the capabilities of the node are utilized within each MPI process in order to achieve the best overall performance. Again, a wide range of tools is available for this purpose. Many build on hardware performance monitors to measure low-level details of on-node performance. VTune Amplifier XE provides these and other detailed measurements of single-node performance and helps the application scientist identify bottlenecks between and within threads. Several other tools, again including TAU and Paraver, provide similar capabilities. A particularly useful tool in addition to those already mentioned is HPCToolkit from Rice University, which offers many useful synthesized measurements that indicate how well the node's capabilities are being used and where performance is being lost.

This book is organized in the way the successful application scientist approaches the problem of performance optimization. It starts with a brief overview of the performance optimization process. It then provides immediate assistance in addressing the most pressing optimization problems at the MPI and OpenMP levels. The following chapters take the reader on a detailed tour of performance optimization on large-scale systems, starting with an overview of the best approach for today's architectures. Next, it surveys the top-down optimization approach, which starts with identifying and addressing the most performance-limiting aspects of the application and repeats the process until sufficient performance is achieved. Then, the book discusses how to handle high-level bottlenecks, including file I/O, that are common in large-scale applications. The concluding chapters provide similar coverage of MPI, OpenMP, and SIMD bottlenecks. At the end, the authors provide general guidelines for application design that are derived from the top-down approach.

Overall, this text will prove a useful addition to the toolbox of any application scientist who understands that the goal of significant scientific achievements can be reached only with highly optimized code.

—Dr. Bronis R. de Supinski, CTO, Livermore Computing, LLNL

Introduction

Let's optimize some programs. We have been doing this for years, and we still love doing it. One day we thought, Why not share this fun with the world? And just a year later, here we are.

Oh, you just need your program to *run faster NOW*? We understand. Go to Chapter 1 and get quick tuning advice. You can return later to see how the magic works.

Are you *a student*? Perfect. This book may help you pass that "Software Optimization 101" exam. Talking seriously about programming is a cool party trick, too. Try it.

Are you a *professional*? Good. You have hit the one-stop-shopping point for Intel's proven top-down optimization methodology and Intel Cluster Studio that includes Message Passing Interface* (MPI), OpenMP, math libraries, compilers, and more.

Or are you *just curious*? Read on. You will learn how high-performance computing makes your life safer, your car faster, and your day brighter.

And, by the way: You will find all you need to carry on, including free trial software, code snippets, checklists, expert advice, fellow readers, and more at www.apress.com/source-code.

HPC: The Ever-Moving Frontier

High-performance computing, or simply HPC, is mostly concerned with floating-point operations per second, or FLOPS. The more FLOPS you get, the better. For convenience, FLOPS on large HPC systems are typically counted by the quadrillions (tera, or 10 to the power of 12) and by the quintillions (peta, or 10 to the power of 15)—hence, TeraFLOPS and PetaFLOPS. Performance of stand-alone computers is currently hovering at around 1 to 2 TeraFLOPS, which is three orders of magnitude below PetaFLOPS. In other words, you need around a thousand modern computers to get to the PetaFLOPS level for the whole system. This will not stay this way forever, for HPC is an ever-moving frontier: ExaFLOPS are three orders of magnitude above PetaFLOPS, and whole countries are setting their sights on reaching this level of performance now.

We have come a long way since the days when computing started in earnest. Back then [sigh!], just before WWII, computing speed was indicated by the two hours necessary to crack the daily key settings of the Enigma encryption machine. It is indicative that already then the computations were being done in parallel: each of the several "bombs"[1] united six reconstructed Enigma machines and reportedly relieved a hundred human operators from boring and repetitive tasks.

---

*Here and elsewhere, certain product names may be the property of their respective third parties.

Computing has progressed a lot since those heady days. There is hardly a better illustration of this than the famous TOP500 list.[2] Twice a year, the teams running the most powerful non-classified computers on earth report their performance. This data is then collated and published in time for two major annual trade shows: the International Supercomputing Conference (ISC), typically held in Europe in June; and the Supercomputing (SC), traditionally held in the United States in November.

Figure 1 shows how certain aspects of this list have changed over time.

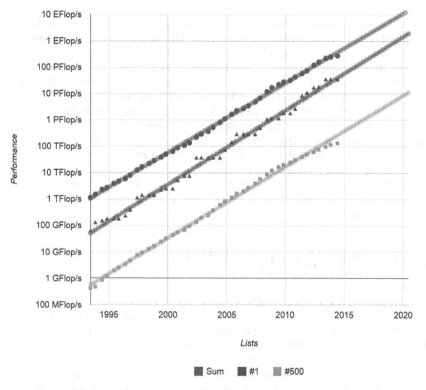

Figure 1. *Observed and projected performance of the Top 500 systems (Source: top500.org; used with permission)*

There are several observations we can make looking at this graph:[3]

1. Performance available in every represented category is growing exponentially (hence, linear graphs in this logarithmic representation).

2. Only part of this growth comes from the incessant improvement of processor technology, as represented, for example, by Moore's Law.[4] The other part is coming from putting many machines together to form still larger machines.

3. An extrapolation made on the data obtained so far predicts that an ExaFLOPS machine is likely to appear by 2018. Very soon (around 2016) there may be PetaFLOPS machines at personal disposal.

So, it's time to learn how to optimize programs for these systems.

Why Optimize?

Optimization is probably the most profitable time investment an engineer can make, as far as programming is concerned. Indeed, a day spent optimizing a program that takes an hour to complete may decrease the program turn-around time by half. This means that after 48 runs, you will recover the time invested in optimization, and then move into the black.

Optimization is also a measure of software maturity. Donald Knuth famously said, "Premature optimization is the root of all evil,"[5] and he was right in some sense. We will deal with how far this goes when we get closer to the end of this book. In any case, no one should start optimizing what has not been proven to work correctly in the first place. And a correct program is still a very rare and very satisfying piece of art.

Yes, this is not a typo: *art*. Despite zillions of thick volumes that have been written and the conferences held on a daily basis, programming is still more art than science. Likewise, for the process of program optimization. It is somewhat akin to architecture: it must include flight of fantasy, forensic attention to detail, deep knowledge of underlying materials, and wide expertise in the prior art. Only this combination—and something else, something intangible and exciting, something we call "talent"—makes a good programmer in general and a good optimizer in particular.

Finally, optimization is fun. Some 25 years later, one of us still cherishes the memories of a day when he made a certain graphical program run *300 times faster* than it used to. A screen update that had been taking half a minute in the morning became almost instantaneous by midnight. It felt almost like love.

The Top-down Optimization Method

Of course, the optimization process we mention is of the most common type—namely, performance optimization. We will be dealing with this kind of optimization almost exclusively in this book. There are other optimization targets, going beyond performance and sometimes hurting it a lot, like code size, data size, and energy.

The good news are, once you know what you want to achieve, the methodology is roughly the same. We will look into those details in Chapter 3. Briefly, you proceed in the *top-down* fashion from the higher levels of the problem under analysis (platform, distributed memory, shared memory, microarchitecture), iterate in a *closed-loop* manner until you exhaust optimization opportunities at each of these levels. Keep in mind that a problem fixed at one level may expose a problem somewhere else, so you may need to revisit those higher levels once more.

This approach crystallized quite a while ago. Its previous reincarnation was formulated by Intel application engineers working in Intel's application solution centers in the 1990's.[6] Our book builds on that solid foundation, certainly taking some things a tad further to account for the time passed.

Now, what happens when top-down optimization meets the closed-loop approach? Well, this is a happy marriage. Every single level of the top-down method can be handled by the closed-loop approach. Moreover, the top-down method itself can be enclosed in another, bigger closed loop where every iteration addresses the biggest remaining problem at any level where it has been detected. This way, you keep your priorities straight and helps you stay focused.

Intel Parallel Studio XE Cluster Edition

Let there be no mistake: the bulk of HPC is still made up by C and Fortran, MPI, OpenMP, Linux OS, and Intel Xeon processors. This is what we will focus on, with occasional excursions into several adjacent areas.

There are many good parallel programming packages around, some of them available for free, some sold commercially. However, to the best of our absolutely unbiased professional knowledge, for completeness none of them comes in anywhere close to Intel Parallel Studio XE Cluster Edition.[7]

Indeed, just look at what it has to offer—and for a very modest price that does not depend on the size of the machines you are going to use, or indeed on their number.

- Intel Parallel Studio XE Cluster Edition[8] compilers and libraries, including:

  - Intel Fortran Compiler[9]

  - Intel C++ Compiler[10]

  - Intel Cilk Plus[11]

  - Intel Math Kernel Library (MKL)[12]

  - Intel Integrated Performance Primitives (IPP)[13]

  - Intel Threading Building Blocks (TBB)[14]

- Intel MPI Benchmarks (IMB)[15]

- Intel MPI Library[16]

- Intel Trace Analyzer and Collector[17]

- Intel VTune Amplifier XE[18]

- Intel Inspector XE[18]

- Intel Advisor XE[20]

All these riches and beauty work on the Linux and Microsoft Windows OS, sometimes more; support all modern Intel platforms, including, of course, Intel Xeon processors and Intel Xeon Phi coprocessors; and come at a cumulative discount akin to the miracles of the Arabian *1001 Nights*. Best of all, Intel runtime libraries come traditionally free of charge.

Certainly, there are good tools beyond Intel Parallel Studio XE Cluster Edition, both offered by Intel and available in the world at large. Whenever possible and sensible, we employ those tools in this book, highlighting their relative advantages and drawbacks compared to those described above. Some of these tools come as open source, some come with the operating system involved; some can be evaluated for free, while others may have to be purchased. While considering the alternative tools, we focus mostly on the open-source, free alternatives that are easy to get and simple to use.

The Chapters of this Book

This is what awaits you, chapter by chapter:

1. *No Time to Read This Book?* helps you out on the burning optimization assignment by providing several proven recipes out of an Intel application engineer's magic toolbox.

2. *Overview of Platform Architectures* introduces common terminology, outlines performance features in modern processors and platforms, and shows you how to estimate peak performance for a particular target platform.

3. *Top-down Software Optimization* introduces the generic top-down software optimization process flow and the closed-loop approach that will help you keep the challenge of multilevel optimization under secure control.

4. *Addressing System Bottlenecks* demonstrates how you can utilize Intel Cluster Studio XE and other tools to discover and remove system bottlenecks as limiting factors to the maximum achievable application performance.

5. *Addressing Application Bottlenecks: Distributed Memory* shows how you can identify and remove distributed memory bottlenecks using Intel MPI Library, Intel Trace Analyzer and Collector, and other tools.

6. *Addressing Application Bottlenecks: Shared Memory* explains how you can identify and remove threading bottlenecks using Intel VTune Amplifier XE and other tools.

7. *Addressing Application Bottlenecks: Microarchitecture* demonstrates how you can identify and remove microarchitecture bottlenecks using Intel VTune Amplifier XE and Intel Composer XE, as well as other tools.

8. *Application Design Considerations* deals with the key tradeoffs guiding the design and optimization of applications. You will learn how to make your next program be fast from the start.

Most chapters are sufficiently self-contained to permit individual reading in any order. However, if you are interested in one particular optimization aspect, you may decide to go through those chapters that naturally cover that topic. Here is a recommended reading guide for several selected topics:

- *System optimization*: Chapters 2, 3, and 4.

- *Distributed memory optimization*: Chapters 2, 3, and 5.

- *Shared memory optimization*: Chapters 2, 3, and 6.

- *Microarchitecture optimization*: Chapters 2, 3, and 7.

Use your judgment and common sense to find your way around. Good luck!

References

1. "Bomba_(cryptography)," [Online]. Available: http://en.wikipedia.org/wiki/Bomba_(cryptography).

2. Top500.Org, "TOP500 Supercomputer Sites," [Online]. Available: http://www.top500.org/.

3. Top500.Org, "Performance Development TOP500 Supercomputer Sites," [Online]. Available: http://www.top500.org/statistics/perfdevel/.

4. G. E. Moore, "Cramming More Components onto Integrated Circuits," *Electronics,* p. 114–117, 19 April 1965.

5. "Knuth," [Online]. Available: http://en.wikiquote.org/wiki/Donald_Knuth.

6. Intel Corporation, "ASC Performance Methodology - Top-Down/Closed Loop Approach," 1999. [Online]. Available: http://smartdata.usbid.com/datasheets/usbid/2001/2001-q1/asc_methodology.pdf.

7. Intel Corporation, "Intel Cluster Studio XE," [Online]. Available: http://software.intel.com/en-us/intel-cluster-studio-xe.

8. Intel Corporation, "Intel Composer XE," [Online]. Available: http://software.intel.com/en-us/intel-composer-xe/.

9. Intel Corporation, "Intel Fortran Compiler," [Online]. Available: http://software.intel.com/en-us/fortran-compilers.

10. Intel Corporation, "Intel C++ Compiler," [Online]. Available: http://software.intel.com/en-us/c-compilers.

11. Intel Corporation, "Intel Cilk Plus," [Online]. Available: http://software.intel.com/en-us/intel-cilk-plus.

12. Intel Corporation, "Intel Math Kernel Library," [Online]. Available: http://software.intel.com/en-us/intel-mkl.

13. Intel Corporation, "Intel Performance Primitives," [Online]. Available: http://software.intel.com/en-us/intel-ipp.

14. Intel Corporation, "Intel Threading Building Blocks," [Online]. Available: http://software.intel.com/en-us/intel-tbb.

15. Intel Corporation, "Intel MPI Benchmarks," [Online]. Available: http://software.intel.com/en-us/articles/intel-mpi-benchmarks/.

16. Intel Corporation, "Intel MPI Library," [Online]. Available: http://software.intel.com/en-us/intel-mpi-library/.

17. Intel Corporation, "Intel Trace Analyzer and Collector," [Online]. Available: http://software.intel.com/en-us/intel-trace-analyzer/.

18. Intel Corporation, "Intel VTune Amplifier XE," [Online]. Available: http://software.intel.com/en-us/intel-vtune-amplifier-xe.

19. Intel Corporation, "Intel Inspector XE," [Online]. Available: http://software.intel.com/en-us/intel-inspector-xe/.

20. Intel Corporation, "Intel Advisor XE," [Online]. Available: http://software.intel.com/en-us/intel-advisor-xe/.

CHAPTER 1

■ ■ ■

No Time to Read This Book?

We know what it feels like to be under pressure. Try out a few quick and proven optimization stunts described below. They may provide a good enough performance gain right away.

There are several parameters that can be adjusted with relative ease. Here are the steps we follow when hard pressed:

- Use Intel MPI Library[1] and Intel Composer XE[2]
- Got more time? Tune Intel MPI:
  - Collect built-in statistics data
  - Tune Intel MPI process placement and pinning
  - Tune OpenMP thread pinning
- Got still more time? Tune Intel Composer XE:
  - Analyze optimization and vectorization reports
  - Use interprocedural optimization

Using Intel MPI Library

The Intel MPI Library delivers good out-of-the-box performance for bandwidth-bound applications. If your application belongs to this popular class, you should feel the difference immediately when switching over.

If your application has been built for Intel MPI compatible distributions like MPICH,[3] MVAPICH2,[4] or IBM POE,[5] and some others, there is no need to recompile the application. You can switch by dynamically linking the Intel MPI 5.0 libraries at runtime:

```
$ source /opt/intel/impi_latest/bin64/mpivars.sh
$ mpirun -np 16 -ppn 2 xhpl
```

If you use another MPI and have access to the application source code, you can rebuild your application using Intel MPI compiler scripts:

- Use mpicc (for C), mpicxx (for C++), and mpifc/mpif77/mpif90 (for Fortran) if you target GNU compilers.
- Use mpiicc, mpiicpc, and mpiifort if you target Intel Composer XE.

1

Using Intel Composer XE

The invocation of the Intel Composer XE is largely compatible with the widely used GNU Compiler Collection (GCC). This includes both the most commonly used command line options and the language support for C/C++ and Fortran. For many applications you can simply replace gcc with icc, g++ with icpc, and gfortran with ifort. However, be aware that although the binary code generated by Intel C/C++ Composer XE is compatible with the GCC-built executable code, the binary code generated by the Intel Fortran Composer is not.

For example:

```
$ source /opt/intel/composerxe/bin/compilervars.sh intel64
$ icc -O3 -xHost -qopenmp  -c example.o example.c
```

Revisit the compiler flags you used before the switch; you may have to remove some of them. Make sure that Intel Composer XE is invoked with the flags that give the best performance for your application (see Table 1-1). More information can be found in the Intel Composer XE documentation.[6]

Table 1-1. *Selected Intel Composer XE Optimization Flags*

GCC	ICC	Effect
-O0	-O0	Disable (almost all) optimization. Not something you want to use for performance!
-O1	-O1	Optimize for speed (no code size increase for ICC)
-O2	-O2	Optimize for speed and enable vectorization
-O3	-O3	Turn on high-level optimizations
-ftlo	-ipo	Enable interprocedural optimization
-ftree-vectorize	-vec	Enable auto-vectorization (auto-enabled with -O2 and -O3)
-fprofile-generate	-prof-gen	Generate runtime profile for optimization
-fprofile-use	-prof-use	Use runtime profile for optimization
	-parallel	Enable auto-parallelization
-fopenmp	-qopenmp	Enable OpenMP
-g	-g	Emit debugging symbols
	-qopt-report	Generate the optimization report
	-vec-report	Generate the vectorization report
	-ansi-alias	Enable ANSI aliasing rules for C/C++

(continued)

Table 1-1. (*continued*)

GCC	ICC	Effect
-msse4.1	-xSSE4.1	Generate code for Intel processors with SSE 4.1 instructions
-mavx	-xAVX	Generate code for Intel processors with AVX instructions
-mavx2	-xCORE-AVX2	Generate code for Intel processors with AVX2 instructions
-mcpu=native	-xHost	Generate code for the current machine used for compilation

For most applications, the default optimization level of -O2 will suffice. It runs fast and gives reasonable performance. If you feel adventurous, try -O3. It is more aggressive but it also increases the compilation time.

Tuning Intel MPI Library

If you have more time, you can try to tune Intel MPI parameters without changing the application source code.

Gather Built-in Statistics

Intel MPI comes with a built-in statistics-gathering mechanism. It creates a negligible runtime overhead and reports key performance metrics (for example, MPI to computation ratio, message sizes, counts, and collective operations used) in the popular IPM format.[7]

To switch the IPM statistics gathering mode on and do the measurements, enter the following commands:

```
$ export I_MPI_STATS=ipm
$ mpirun -np 16 xhpl
```

By default, this will generate a file called stats.ipm. Listing 1-1 shows an example of the MPI statistics gathered for the well-known High Performance Linpack (HPL) benchmark.[8] (We will return to this benchmark throughout this book, by the way.)

3

Listing 1-1. MPI Statistics for the HPL Benchmark with the Most Interesting Fields Highlighted

```
Intel(R) MPI Library Version 5.0

Summary MPI Statistics
Stats format: region
Stats scope : full


########################################################################
#
# command : /home/book/hpl/./xhpl_hybrid_intel64_dynamic (completed)
# host    : esg066/x86_64_Linux          mpi_tasks : 16 on 8 nodes
# start   : 02/14/14/12:43:33            wallclock : 2502.401419 sec
# stop    : 02/14/14/13:25:16            %comm     : 8.43
# gbytes  : 0.00000e+00 total            gflop/sec : NA
#
########################################################################
# region  : *   [ntasks] = 16
#
#                       [total]      <avg>        min         max
# entries               16           1            1           1
# wallclock             40034.7      2502.17      2502.13     2502.4
# user                  446800       27925        27768.4     28192.7
# system                1971.27      123.205      102.103     145.241
# mpi                   3375.05      210.941      132.327     282.462
# %comm                              8.43032      5.28855     11.2888
# gflop/sec             NA           NA           NA          NA
# gbytes                0            0            0           0
#
#
#                       [time]       [calls]      <%mpi>      <%wall>
# MPI_Send              2737.24      1.93777e+06  81.10       6.84
# MPI_Recv              394.827      16919        11.70       0.99
# MPI_Wait              236.568      1.92085e+06  7.01        0.59
# MPI_Iprobe            3.2257       6.57506e+06  0.10        0.01
# MPI_Init_thread       1.55628      16           0.05        0.00
# MPI_Irecv             1.31957      1.92085e+06  0.04        0.00
# MPI_Type_commit       0.212124     14720        0.01        0.00
# MPI_Type_free         0.0963376    14720        0.00        0.00
# MPI_Comm_split        0.0065608    48           0.00        0.00
# MPI_Comm_free         0.000276804  48           0.00        0.00
# MPI_Wtime             9.67979e-05  48           0.00        0.00
# MPI_Comm_size         9.13143e-05  452          0.00        0.00
# MPI_Comm_rank         7.77245e-05  452          0.00        0.00
# MPI_Finalize          6.91414e-06  16           0.00        0.00
# MPI_TOTAL             3375.05      1.2402e+07   100.00      8.43
########################################################################
```

From Listing 1-1 you can deduce that MPI communication occupies between 5.3 and 11.3 percent of the total runtime, and that the MPI_Send, MPI_Recv, and MPI_Wait operations take about 81, 12, and 7 percent, respectively, of the total MPI time. With this data at hand, you can see that there are potential load imbalances between the job processes, and that you should focus on making the MPI_Send operation as fast as it can go to achieve a noticeable performance hike.

Note that if you use the full IPM package instead of the built-in statistics, you will also get data on the total communication volume and floating point performance that are not measured by the Intel MPI Library.

Optimize Process Placement

The Intel MPI Library puts adjacent MPI ranks on one cluster node as long as there are cores to occupy. Use the Intel MPI command line argument -ppn to control the process placement across the cluster nodes. For example, this command will start two processes per node:

```
$ mpirun -np 16 -ppn 2 xhpl
```

Intel MPI supports process pinning to restrict the MPI ranks to parts of the system so as to optimize process layout (for example, to avoid NUMA effects or to reduce latency to the InfiniBand adapter). Many relevant settings are described in the *Intel MPI Library Reference Manual.*[9]

Briefly, if you want to run a pure MPI program only on the physical processor cores, enter the following commands:

```
$ export I_MPI_PIN_PROCESSOR_LIST=allcores
$ mpirun -np 2 your_MPI_app
```

If you want to run a hybrid MPI/OpenMP program, don't change the default Intel MPI settings, and see the next section for the OpenMP ones.

If you want to analyze Intel MPI process layout and pinning, set the following environment variable:

```
$ export I_MPI_DEBUG=4
```

Optimize Thread Placement

If the application uses OpenMP for multithreading, you may want to control thread placement in addition to the process placement. Two possible strategies are:

```
$ export KMP_AFFINITY=granularity=thread,compact
$ export KMP_AFFINITY=granularity=thread,scatter
```

The first setting keeps threads close together to improve inter-thread communication, while the second setting distributes the threads across the system to maximize memory bandwidth.

Programs that use the OpenMP API version 4.0 can use the equivalent OpenMP affinity settings instead of the KMP_AFFINITY environment variable:

```
$ export OMP_PROC_BIND=close
$ export OMP_PROC_BIND=spread
```

If you use I_MPI_PIN_DOMAIN, MPI will confine the OpenMP threads of an MPI process on a single socket. Then you can use the following setting to avoid thread movement between the logical cores of the socket:

```
$ export KMP_AFFINITY=granularity=thread
```

Tuning Intel Composer XE

If you have access to the source code of the application, you can perform optimizations by selecting appropriate compiler switches and recompiling the source code.

Analyze Optimization and Vectorization Reports

Add compiler flags -qopt-report and/or -vec-report to see what the compiler did to your source code. This will report all the transformations applied to your code. It will also highlight those code patterns that prevented successful optimization. Address them if you have time left.

Here is a small example. Because the optimization report may be very long, Listing 1-2 only shows an excerpt from it. The example code contains several loop nests of seven loops. The compiler found an OpenMP directive to parallelize the loop nest. It also recognized that the overall loop nest was not optimal, and it automatically permuted some loops to improve the situation for vectorization. Then it vectorized all inner-most loops while leaving the outer-most loops as they are.

Listing 1-2. Example Optimization Report with the Most Interesting Fields Highlighted

```
$ ifort -O3 -qopenmp -qopt-report -qopt-report-file=stdout -c example.F90

    Report from: Interprocedural optimizations [ipo]

[...]

OpenMP Construct at example.F90(8,7)
remark #15059: OpenMP DEFINED LOOP WAS PARALLELIZED
OpenMP Construct at example.F90(25,7)
remark #15059: OpenMP DEFINED LOOP WAS PARALLELIZED

[...]
```

```
LOOP BEGIN at example.F90(9,2)
   remark #15018: loop was not vectorized: not inner loop

   LOOP BEGIN at example.F90(12,5)
      remark #25448: Loopnest Interchanged : ( 1 2 3 4 ) --> ( 1 4 2 3 )
      remark #15018: loop was not vectorized: not inner loop

   LOOP BEGIN at example.F90(12,5)
      remark #15018: loop was not vectorized: not inner loop

[...]

               LOOP BEGIN at example.F90(15,8)
                  remark #25446: blocked by 125   (pre-vector)
                  remark #25444: unrolled and jammed by 4   (pre-vector)
                  remark #15018: loop was not vectorized: not inner loop

               LOOP BEGIN at example.F90(13,6)
                  remark #25446: blocked by 125   (pre-vector)
                  remark #15018: loop was not vectorized: not inner loop

                  LOOP BEGIN at example.F90(14,7)
                     remark #25446: blocked by 128   (pre-vector)
                     remark #15003: PERMUTED LOOP WAS VECTORIZED
                  LOOP END

                  LOOP BEGIN at example.F90(14,7)
                  Remainder
                     remark #25460: Loop was not optimized
                  LOOP END
               LOOP END
            LOOP END

[...]

            LOOP END
         LOOP END
      LOOP END
   LOOP END
LOOP END

LOOP BEGIN at example.F90(26,2)
   remark #15018: loop was not vectorized: not inner loop

   LOOP BEGIN at example.F90(29,5)
      remark #25448: Loopnest Interchanged : ( 1 2 3 4 ) --> ( 1 3 2 4 )
      remark #15018: loop was not vectorized: not inner loop
```

```
              LOOP BEGIN at example.F90(29,5)
                 remark #15018: loop was not vectorized: not inner loop

                 LOOP BEGIN at example.F90(29,5)
                    remark #15018: loop was not vectorized: not inner loop

                    LOOP BEGIN at example.F90(29,5)
                       remark #15018: loop was not vectorized: not inner loop

                       LOOP BEGIN at example.F90(29,5)
                          remark #25446: blocked by 125   (pre-vector)
                          remark #25444: unrolled and jammed by 4   (pre-vector)
                          remark #15018: loop was not vectorized: not inner loop
[...]
                    LOOP END
                 LOOP END
              LOOP END
           LOOP END
      LOOP END
LOOP END
```

Listing 1-3 shows the vectorization report for the example in Listing 1-2. As you can see, the vectorization report contains the same information about vectorization as the optimization report.

Listing 1-3. Example Vectorization Report with the Most Interesting Fields Highlighted

```
$ ifort -O3 -qopenmp -vec-report=2 -qopt-report-file=stdout -c example.F90

[...]

LOOP BEGIN at example.F90(9,2)
   remark #15018: loop was not vectorized: not inner loop

   LOOP BEGIN at example.F90(12,5)
      remark #15018: loop was not vectorized: not inner loop

      LOOP BEGIN at example.F90(12,5)
         remark #15018: loop was not vectorized: not inner loop

         LOOP BEGIN at example.F90(12,5)
            remark #15018: loop was not vectorized: not inner loop

            LOOP BEGIN at example.F90(12,5)
               remark #15018: loop was not vectorized: not inner loop
```

```
          LOOP BEGIN at example.F90(12,5)
             remark #15018: loop was not vectorized: not inner loop

          LOOP BEGIN at example.F90(15,8)
             remark #15018: loop was not vectorized: not inner loop

             LOOP BEGIN at example.F90(13,6)
                remark #15018: loop was not vectorized: not inner loop

             LOOP BEGIN at example.F90(14,7)
                remark #15003: PERMUTED LOOP WAS VECTORIZED
             LOOP END
```

[...]

```
             LOOP END
          LOOP END

          LOOP BEGIN at example.F90(15,8)
          Remainder
             remark #15018: loop was not vectorized: not inner loop

             LOOP BEGIN at example.F90(13,6)
                remark #15018: loop was not vectorized: not inner loop
```

[...]

```
             LOOP BEGIN at example.F90(14,7)
                remark #15003: PERMUTED LOOP WAS VECTORIZED
             LOOP END
```

[...]

```
             LOOP END
          LOOP END
       LOOP END
```

[...]

```
          LOOP END
       LOOP END
     LOOP END
  LOOP END
LOOP END
```

[...]

Use Interprocedural Optimization

Add the compiler flag -ipo to switch on interprocedural optimization. This will give the compiler a holistic view of the program and open more optimization opportunities for the program as a whole. Note that this will also increase the overall compilation time.

Runtime profiling can also increase the chances for the compiler to generate better code. Profile-guided optimization requires a three-stage process. First, compile the application with the compiler flag -prof-gen to instrument the application with profiling code. Second, run the instrumented application with a typical dataset to produce a meaningful profile. Third, feed the compiler with the profile (-prof-use) and let it optimize the code.

Summary

Switching to Intel MPI and Intel Composer XE can help improve performance because the two strive to optimally support Intel platforms and deliver good out-of-the-box (OOB) performance. Tuning measures can further improve the situation. The next chapters will reiterate the quick and dirty examples of this chapter and show you how to push the limits.

References

1. Intel Corporation, "Intel(R) MPI Library," http://software.intel.com/en-us/intel-mpi-library.

2. Intel Corporation, "Intel(R) Composer XE Suites," http://software.intel.com/en-us/intel-composer-xe.

3. Argonne National Laboratory, "MPICH: High-Performance Portable MPI," www.mpich.org.

4. Ohio State University, "MVAPICH: MPI over InfiniBand, 10GigE/iWARP and RoCE," http://mvapich.cse.ohio-state.edu/overview/mvapich2/.

5. International Business Machines Corporation, "IBM Parallel Environment," www-03.ibm.com/systems/software/parallel/.

6. Intel Corporation, "Intel Fortran Composer XE 2013 - Documentation," http://software.intel.com/articles/intel-fortran-composer-xe-documentation/.

7. The IPM Developers, "Integrated Performance Monitoring - IPM," http://ipm-hpc.sourceforge.net/.

8. A. Petitet, R. C. Whaley, J. Dongarra, and A. Cleary, "HPL : A Portable Implementation of the High-Performance Linpack Benchmark for Distributed-Memory Computers," 10 September 2008, www.netlib.org/benchmark/hpl/.

9. Intel Corporation, "Intel MPI Library Reference Manual," http://software.intel.com/en-us/node/500285.

CHAPTER 2

■ ■ ■

Overview of Platform Architectures

In order to optimize software you need to understand hardware. In this chapter we give you a brief overview of the typical system architectures found in the high-performance computing (HPC) today. We also introduce terminology that will be used throughout the book.

Performance Metrics and Targets

The definition of *optimization* found in Merriam-Webster's *Collegiate Dictionary* reads as follows: "an act, process, or methodology of making something (as a design, system, or decision) as fully perfect, functional, or effective as possible."[1] To become practically applicable, this definition requires establishment of clear success criteria. These objective criteria need to be based on quantifiable metrics and on well-defined standards of measurement. We deal with the metrics in this chapter.

Latency, Throughput, Energy, and Power

Let us start with the most common class of metrics: those that are based on the total time required to complete an action–for example, the time it takes for a car to drive from the start to the finish on a race track, as shown in Figure 2-1. Execution (or *wall-clock*) time is one of the most common ways to measure application performance: to measure its *runtime* on a specific system and report it in seconds (or hours, or sometimes days). In this context, the time required to complete an action is a typical *latency metric*.

Figure 2-1. *Runtime: observed time interval between the start and the finish of a car on a race track*

The runtime, or the period of time from the start to the completion of an application, is important because it tells you how long you need to wait for the results. In networking, *latency* is the amount of time it takes a data packet to travel from the source to the destination; it also can be referred to as the *response time*. For measurements inside the processor, we often use the term *instruction latency* as the time it takes for a machine instruction entering the execution unit until results of that instruction are available—that is, written to the register file and ready to be used by subsequent instructions. In more general terms, *latency* can be defined as the observed time interval between the start of a process and its completion.

We can generalize this class of metrics to represent more of a general class of *consumable resources*. Time is one kind of a consumable resource, such as the time allocated for your job on a supercomputer. Another important example of a consumable resource is the amount of *electrical energy* required to complete your job, called *energy to solution*. The official unit in which energy is measured is the *joule*, while in everyday life we more often use watt-hours. One watt-hour is equal to 3600 joules.

The amount of energy consumption defines your electricity bill and is a very visible item among operating expenses of major, high-performance computing facilities. It drives demand for optimization of the energy to solution, in addition to the traditional efforts to reduce the runtime, improve parallel efficiency, and so on. Energy optimization work has different scales; going from giga-joules (GJ, or 10^9 joules) consumed at the application level, to pico-joules (pJ, or 10^{-12} joules) per instruction.

One of the specific properties of the latency metrics is that they are *additive,* so that they can be viewed as a cumulative sum of several latencies of subtasks. This means that if the application has three subtasks following one after another, and these subtasks take times T_1, T_2 and T_3, respectively, then the total application runtime is $T_{app} = T_1 + T_2 + T_3$.

Other types of metrics describe the amount of work that can be completed by the system per unit of time, or per unit of another consumable resource. One example of car performance would be its speed defined as the distance covered per unit of time; or of its fuel efficiency, defined as the distance covered per unit of fuel—, such as miles per gallon. We call these metrics *throughput metrics*. For example, the number of instructions per second (IPS) executed by the processor, or the number of floating point operations per second (FLOPS) are both throughput metrics. Other widely used metrics of this class are memory bandwidth (reaching tens and hundreds of gigabytes per second these days), and network interconnection throughput (in either bits per second or bytes per second). The unit of power (watt) is also a throughput metric that is defined as energy flow per unit of time, and is equal exactly to 1 joule per second.

You may encounter situations where throughput is described as the inverse of latency. This is correct only when both metrics describe the same process applied to the same amount of work. In particular, for an application or kernel that takes one second to complete 10^9 arithmetic operations on floating point numbers, it is correct to state that its throughput is 1 GFLOPS (gigaFLOPS, or 10^9 FLOPS).

However, very often, especially in computer networks, latency is understood as the time from the beginning of the packet shipment until the first data arrives at the destination. In this context, latency will not be equal to the inverse value of the throughput. To grasp why this happens, compare sending a very large amount of data (say, 1 terabyte (TB), which is 10^{12} bytes) using two different methods[2]:

1. Shipping with overnight express mail

2. Uploading via broadband Internet access

The overnight (24-hour) shipment of the 1TB hard drive has good throughput but lousy latency. The throughput is $(1 \times 10^{12} \times 8)$ bits / $(24 \times 60 \times 60)$ seconds = about 92 million bits per second (bps), which is comparable to modern broadband networks. The difference is that the overnight shipment bits are delayed for a day and then arrive all at once, but the bits we send over the Internet start appearing almost immediately. We would say that the network has much better latency, even though both methods have approximately the same throughput when considered over the interval of one day.

Although high throughput systems may have low latency, there is no causal link. Comparing a GDDR5 (Graphics Double Data Rate, version 5) vs. DDR3 (Double Data Rate, type 3) memory bandwidth and latency, one notices that systems with GDDR5 (such as Intel Xeon Phi coprocessors) deliver three to five times more bandwidth, while the latency to access data (measured in an idle environment) is five to six times lower than in systems with DDR3 memory.

Finally, a graph of latency versus load looks very different from a graph of throughput versus load. As we will see later in this chapter, memory access latency goes up exponentially as the load increases. Throughput will go up almost linearly at first, then levels out to become nearly flat when the physical capacity of the transport medium is saturated. Simply by looking at a graph of test results and keeping those features in mind, you can guess whether it is a latency graph or a throughput graph.

Another important concept and property of a system or process is its degree of concurrency or parallelism. *Concurrency* (or *degree of concurrency*) is defined as the number of work items that can potentially be performed simultaneously. In the example illustrated by Figure 2-2, where three cars can race simultaneously, each on its own track, we would say this system has concurrency of 3. In computation, an example of concurrency would be the simultaneous execution of multiple, structurally different application "threads" by a multicore processor. Presence of concurrency is an intrinsic property of any modern high-performance system. Processes running on different machines of a cluster form a common system that executes application code on multiple machines at the same time. This, too, is an example of concurrency in action.

Figure 2-2. *A system with the degree of concurrency equal to 3*

Cantrill and Bonwick describe three fundamental ways of using concurrency to improve application performance.[3] At the same time, these three ways represent the typical optimization targets for either latency or throughout metrics:

- *Increase throughput:* By executing multiple tasks concurrently, the general system throughput can be increased.

- *Reduce latency:* A given amount of work is completed in shorter time by dividing it into parts that can be completed concurrently.

- *Hide latency:* Multiple long-running tasks are executed in parallel by the underlying system. This is particularly effective when some tasks are blocked (for example, if they must wait upon disk or network I/O operations), while others can proceed independently.

Peak Performance as the Ultimate Limit

Every time we talk about performance of an application running on a machine, we try to compare it to the maximum attainable performance on that specific machine, or *peak performance* of that machine. The ratio between the achieved (or measured) performance and the peak performance gives the *efficiency* metric. This metric is often used to drive the performance optimization, for an increase in efficiency will also lead to an increase in performance according to the underlying metric. For example, efficiency for the wall-clock time is the fraction of time that is spent doing useful work, while efficiency for throughout is a measure of useful capacity utilization.

Consider the example of how to quantify efficiency for a network protocol. Network protocols normally require each packet to contain a header and a footer. The actual data transmitted in the packet is then the size of the packet minus the protocol overhead. Therefore, efficiency of using the network, from the application point of view, is reduced from the total utilization according to the size of the header and the footer. For Ethernet, the frame payload size equals 1536 bytes. The TCP/IP header and footer take 40 bytes extra. Hence, efficiency here is equal to 1536 / 1576 × 100, or 97.5 percent.

Understanding the limitations of maximum achievable performance is an important step in guiding the optimization process: the limits are always there! These limits are driven by physical properties of the available materials, maturity of the technology, or (trivially) the cost. Particularly, the propagation of signals along the wires is limited by the speed of light in the respective material. Thus, the latency for completing any work using electronic equipment will always be greater than zero. In the same way, it is not possible to build an infinitely wide highway, for its throughput will always be limited by the number of lanes and their individual throughputs.

Scalability and Maximum Parallel Speedup

The ability to increase performance by using more resources in parallel (for example, more processors) is called *scalability*. The basic approach in high-performance computing is to use many computational resources in parallel to solve one problem, and to add still more resources if higher performance is required. Scalability analysis indicates how efficient an application is using the increasing numbers of parallel computing elements, such as cores, vector units, memory, or network connections.

Increase in performance before and after addition of the resources is called *speedup*. When talking about throughput-related metrics, speedup is expressed as the ratio of the throughput after addition of the resources versus the original throughput. For latency metrics, speedup is the ratio between the original latency and the latency after addition of the resources. This way speedup is always greater than 1.0 if performance improves. If the ratio goes below 1.0, we call this negative speedup, or simply *slowdown*.

Amdahl's Law, also known as Amdahl's argument,[4] is used to find the maximum expected improvement for an entire application when only a part of the application is improved. This law is often used in parallel computing to predict the theoretical maximum speedup that can be achieved by adding multiple processors. In essence, Amdahl's Law says that speedup of a program using p processors in parallel is limited by the time needed for the nonparallel fraction of the program (f), according to the following formula:

$$Speedup \leq \frac{p}{1 + f \cdot (p-1)}$$

where f takes values between 0 and 1.

As an example, think about an application that needs 10 hours when running on a single processor core, where a particular portion of the program takes two hours to execute and cannot be made parallel (for instance, since it performs sequential I/O operations). If the remaining 8 hours of the runtime can be efficiently parallelized, then regardless of how many processors are devoted to the parallelized execution of this program, the minimum execution time cannot be less than those critical 2 hours. Hence, speedup is limited by at most five times (usually denoted as 5x). In reality, even this 5x speedup goal is not attainable, since infinite parallelization of code is not possible for the parallel part of the application. Figure 2-3 illustrates Amdahl's law in action. If the parallel component is made 50 times faster, then the maximum speedup with 20 percent of time taken by the serial part will be equal to 4.63x.

15

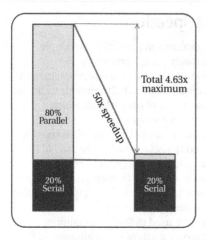

Figure 2-3. *Illustration of Amdahl's Law*

It may be depressing to realize that the maximum possible speedup will be limited by something you can't improve by adding more resources. Even so, consider the same speedup problem from another angle: what happens if the amount of work in the parallelizable part of the execution can be increased?

If the relative share of time taken by the serial portion of the application remains unchanged with the increase of the workload size, there is no inherent speedup factor available, and as illustrated in Figure 2-4 (left), Amdahl's Law still works. However, John Gustafson observed that there was significant speedup opportunity available if the serial component shrank in size relative to the parallel part as the amount of data processed by the application (and consequently the amount of computation) expanded.[5]

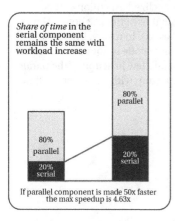
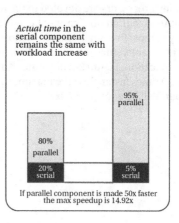

Figure 2-4. *Illustration of Gustafson's observation*

This observation leads to two kinds of scalability metrics:

- *Strong scaling*: How performance varies with the number of computing elements for a fixed *total problem size*. In strong scaling, *perfect scaling* (i.e., when performance improves linearly) is achieved when speedup is equal to the number of computing elements involved.

- *Weak scaling*: How performance varies with the number of computing elements for a fixed problem size *per processor*, and additional computing elements are used to solve a larger total problem. In the case of weak scaling, perfect scaling is achieved if the runtime remains constant while the workload is increased proportionally to the number of computing elements involved.

Bottlenecks and a Bit of Queuing Theory

Performance analysis is a process of identifying bottlenecks and removing them, with the objective of increasing overall application performance. Certain parts of the application that limit performance of the entire application are called *performance bottlenecks*. The significance of the term *bottleneck* can be illustrated with the same car metaphor that we have used before (see Figure 2-5). When there is a toll gate on the road that can process only one car at a time, the rate at which cars will pass along the highway (that is, highway throughput) is limited by the width of the toll gate, irrespective of how many more lanes are on the road before and after it. In other words, the toll gate is a bottleneck. By increasing the width of the toll gate, it is possible to increase the rate of cars on the highway.

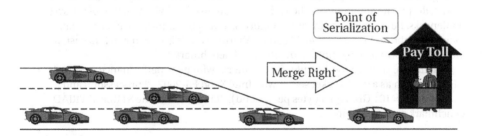

Figure 2-5. Bottlenecks on the road are commonly known as traffic jams

As shown in Figure 2-5, bottlenecks can create traffic jams on the highway. Using the terminology of queuing theory,[6] we are talking about the toll gate as a single service center. Customers (here, cars) arrive at this service center at a certain rate, called *arrival rate* or *workload intensity*. There is also certain duration of time required to collect money from each car, which is referred to as *service demand*. For specific parameter values of the workload intensity and the service demand, it is possible to analytically evaluate this model and produce performance metrics, such as *utilization* (proportion of time when the server point is busy), *residence time* (average time spent at the service center by a customer), *length of the queue* (average number of customers waiting at the service center), and *throughput* (rate at which customers depart from the service center).

This approach is widely used by *queuing network modeling*, where a computer system is represented as a network of queues—that is, a collection of service centers that represent system resources and customers who represent users or transactions. This model provides a framework for gathering, organizing, evaluating, and understanding information about the computer system, as well as for identifying possible bottlenecks and testing ideas for system improvement. Such models are widely used for quantitative analysis during computer system design and the application development process.

Roofline Model

Amdahl's law and the queuing network models both offer "bound and bottleneck analysis," and they work quite well in many cases. However, both complexity and the level of concurrency of modern high-performance systems keep increasing. Indeed, even smartphones today have complex multicore chips with pipelines, caches, superscalar instruction issue, and out-of-order execution, while the applications increasingly use tasks and threads with asynchronous communication between them. Quantitative queuing network models that simulate behavior of very complex applications on modern multicore and heterogeneous systems have become very complex. At the same time, the speed of microprocessor development has outpaced the speed of the memory evolution; and in most cases, specifically in high-performance computing, the bandwidth of the memory subsystem is often the main bottleneck.

In search of a simplified model that would relate processor performance to the off-chip memory traffic, Williams, Waterman, and Patterson observed that that "the Roofline [model] sets an upper bound on performance of a kernel depending on the kernel's operational intensity."[7] The *Roofline model* subsumes two platform specific ceilings in one single graph: floating-point performance and memory bandwidth. The model, despite its apparent simplicity, provides an insightful visualization of the system bottlenecks. Peak floating point and memory throughput performances can usually be found from the architecture specifications. Alternatively, it is possible to find sustained memory performance by running the STREAM benchmark.[8]

Figure 2-6 shows a roofline plot for a platform with peak performance $P = 518.4$ GFLOPS (such as a dual-socket server with Intel Xeon E5-2697 v2 processors) and bandwidth $B = 101$ GB/s (gigabytes per second) attainable with the STREAM TRIAD benchmark on this system.

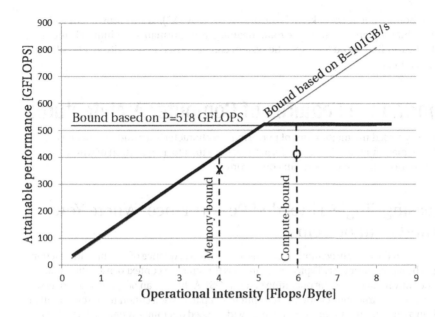

Figure 2-6. *Roofline model for dual Intel Xeon E5-2697 v2 server with DDR3-1866 memory*

The horizontal line shows peak performance of the computer. This is a hardware limit for this server. The X-axis represents amount of work (in number of floating point operations, or Flops) done for every byte of data coming from memory: Flops/byte (here, "Flops" stands for the plural of "Flop"–the number of floating point operations, rather than FLOPS, which is Flops per second). And the Y-axis represents gigaFLOPS (10^9 FLOPS), which is a throughput metric showing the number of floating point operations executed every second (Flops/second, or FLOPS). With that, taking into account that

$$bytes / second = \frac{Flops / second}{Flops / byte},$$ the memory throughput metric gigabytes/second is

represented by a line of unit slope in Figure 2-6. Thus, the slanted line shows the maximum floating point performance that the memory subsystem can support for the given operational intensity. The following formula drives the two performance limits in the graph shown in Figure 2-6:

$$Attainable\ performance[GLOPS]$$
$$= \min \left\{ \begin{array}{l} Peak\ floating\ point\ performance, \\ Peak\ memory\ bandwidth \times Operational\ intensity \end{array} \right\}$$

The horizontal and diagonal lines form a kind of roofline, and this gives the model its name. The roofline sets an upper bound on performance of a computational kernel depending on its operational intensity. Improving performance of a kernel with operational intensity of 6 Flops/byte (shown as the dotted line marked by "O" in the plot) will hit the flat part of the roof, meaning that the kernel performance is ultimately compute-bound. For another kernel (the one marked by "X"), any improvement will eventually hit the slanted part of the roof, meaning its performance is ultimately memory bound. The roofline found for a specific system can be reused repeatedly for classifying different kernels.

Performance Features of Computer Architectures

We have discussed the major types of performance characteristics and approaches to estimate maximum attainable performance. Let's turn to a discussion of where the potential performance increases can come from.

Increasing Single-Threaded Performance: Where You Can and Cannot Help

We will refer to the basic execution context as a *thread*—a sequence of machine instructions executed by a processor core. Typically, a thread is the smallest context of execution that is independently managed by the operating system (OS). A thread can be granted a processor core to execute instructions on, or it can be put to sleep to free execution resources for other threads in a queue. Under Linux OS, the most widely used operating system in HPC these days,[9] kernel threads and processes are the same entity: simply a runable task. Later, when we talk about hybrid programing, we will want to distinguish processes and threads. But for now let us leave them as a software thread or task, understanding that at any given moment each processor core executes instructions from a single task. Making these instructions run faster is the essence of application optimization.

Performance of a single thread can be defined by number of instructions executed per second (IPS) and calculated as a product of two values (IPS = CPS × IPC):

1. Number of processor clock *cycles per second* (CPS). It is more often called *processor clock frequency*, or simply frequency, and is measured in Hertz (Hz), or for most processors in gigaHertz (GHz), which is 10^9 Hertz.

2. Number of instructions executed per processor clock tick, *instructions per cycle* (IPC).

An application usually cannot do anything about the processor frequency: it is something defined at the manufacturing time and considered fixed or at least not directly changeable when an application is running. In contrast, the IPC is a function of both the processor microarchitecture and your application. The microarchitecture is an internal implementation of the processor. Very simple microarchitectures can execute a maximum of only one instruction per cycle; they are called *scalar*. More sophisticated ones can execute concurrently several instructions at every clock cycle and are known as *superscalar*.

The ability of a processor to produce results for several instructions in parallel is a very important first step toward achieving greater application performance. Since processors have reached the limit of the affordable heat dissipation (that happens around 2.5 to 3.5 GHz, depending on complexity of the chip), the frequency of modern processors does not grow as fast as required to deliver new levels of performance to demanding customers. Superscalar microarchitectures that are predominant among high-performance focused processors these days provide a much needed solution to the frequency problem. Modern x86 superscalar processors (such as the Intel Core family) can complete up to four instructions per cycle, so it would be as if the frequency was effectively increased four times in a scalar processor. This book was written using a computer with 2.5 GHz Intel Core i5 processor. If it were written on a scalar processor, such as the older Intel 486, the processor would need to run at approximately 10 GHz to be equal in peak performance.

Superscalar execution provides a great way to improve application performance. However, it is to a large extent simply a capability of the processor that needs to be exploited to yield real benefit in application performance. When we talk about microarchitecture optimization in Chapter 7, we review cases when a superscalar processor does not execute as many instructions as it could, and how to fix that. But before we go any further, it is important to note that very often during the optimization process we use a multiplicative inverse of IPC called *CPI*, or *clocks per instruction* . With some simplification we can use the relationship CPI = 1 / IPC without losing many details. Many performance profiling tools (such as Intel VTune Amplifier XE,[10] discussed in greater details in Chapters 6 and 7) use CPI instead of IPC to make it easier to correlate observed CPI metrics with table data on latencies that are traditionally provided for each instruction in processor cycles.

It is important to familiarize yourself with both metrics and be able to assess their values. For example, when a profiler tells you that the average CPI is equal to 2 (meaning it takes two cycles on average to complete every instruction), that means IPC is equal to 0.5 (or one instruction completed every two processor cycles). This level of performance would be rather bad for a modern processor that can (theoretically) reach 4 IPC (delivering results for four instructions every cycle) and the best achievable average CPI of 0.25. Luckily, such an application or piece of code under consideration provides great opportunity for optimization.

Process More Data with SIMD Parallelism

Another way to increase performance of each thread is to look at the data being processed. So far we have only discussed the limit of each processor core with respect to the instructions, but not with respect to the data each instruction works with. The next natural way to optimize an application execution is to let each instruction deal with more than one element of data at a time. Michael J. Flynn gave this approach the name SIMD, standing for Single Instruction Multiple Data single instruction, multiple data.[11] As it obviously follows from its name, in this approach a compute instruction produces results for multiple elements of data using the same instruction on those multiple elements. As illustrated in Figure 2-7, the addition symbol + simultaneously produces results for four elements of the arrays a and b. To execute this way, elements of the arrays are packed into vectors of length 4 with the operation applied to each separate element pair concurrently.

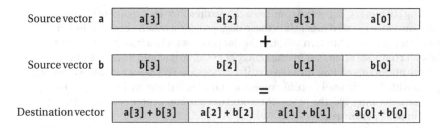

Figure 2-7. *SIMD approach: single instruction produces results for several data elements simultaneously*

Following this principle, the SIMD vector instruction sets implement not only basic arithmetic operations (such as additions, multiplications, absolute values, shifts, and divisions) but also many other useful instructions present in nonvectorized instruction sets. They also implement special operations to deal with the contents of the vector registers—for example, any-to-any permutations—and gather instructions that are useful for vectorized code that accesses nonadjacent data elements.

SIMD extensions for the x86 instruction set were first brought into the Intel architecture under the Intel MMX brand in 1996 and were used in Pentium processors. MMX had a SIMD width of 64 bits and focused on integer arithmetic. Thus, two 32-bit integers, or four 16-bit integers (as type short in C), or eight 8-bit integer numbers (C type char), could be processed simultaneously. Note also that the MMX instruction set extensions for x86 supported both signed and unsigned integers.

New SIMD instruction sets for x86 processors added support for new operations on the vectors, increased the SIMD data width, and added vector instructions to process floating point numbers much demanded in HPC. In 1999, SIMD data width was increased to 128 bits with SSE (Streaming SIMD Extensions), and each SSE register (called xmm) was able to hold two double precision floating point numbers or two 64-bit integers, four single precision floats or four 32-bit integers, eight 16-bit integers or 16 single-byte elements.

In 2008, Intel announced doubling of the vector width to 256 bits in Intel AVX (Advanced Vector eXtensions) instruction set. The extended register was called ymm. The ymm registers can hold twice as much data as the SSE's xmm registers. They support packed data types for modern x86 processor cores (for instance, in the fourth-generation Intel Core processors with microarchitecture, codenamed Haswell), as shown in Figure 2-8.

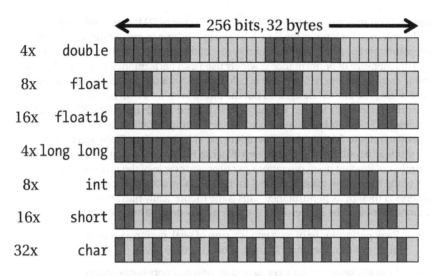

Figure 2-8. *AVX registers and supported packed data types*

The latest addition to Intel AVX, announced in 2013, includes definition of Intel Advanced Vector Extensions 512 (or AVX-512) instructions. These instructions represent a leap ahead to the 512-bit SIMD support (And guess what? The registers are now called zmm). Consequently, up to eight double precision or 16 single precision floating point numbers, or eight 64-bit integers, or 16 32-bit integers can be packed within the 512-bit vectors. Figure 2-9 shows the relative sizes of SSE, AVX, and AXV-512 SIMD registers with highlighted packed 64-bit data types (for instance, double precision floats).

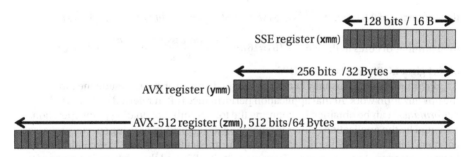

Figure 2-9. *SSE, AVX, and AVX-512 vector registers with packed 64-bit numbers*

Now that you're familiar with the important concepts of SIMD processing and superscalar microarchitectures, the time has come to discuss in greater detail the FLOPS (floating point operations per second) metric, one of the most cited HPC performance metrics. This measure of performance is widely used as a performance metric in the field of scientific computing where heavy use of calculations with the floating point numbers is very common. The last "S" designates not the plural form for FLOP but a ratio "per second" and is historically written without a slash (/) and avoiding double "S" (i.e., FLOPS instead of Flops/S). In our book we will stick to the common practice. In some situations, we will need to refer to floating point operations, so abbreviate it as Flops and produce required ratios as needed. For example, we will write Flops/cycle when there is a need to count number of floating point operations per processor cycle of the processor core.

One of the most often quoted metrics for individual processors or complete HPC systems is their peak performance. This is the theoretically maximum possible performance that could be delivered by the system. It is defined as follows:

- Peak performance of a system is a sum of peak performances of all computing elements (namely, cores) in the system.

- Peak performance for a vectorized superscalar core is calculated as the number of independent floating point arithmetic operations that the core can execute in parallel, multiplied by the number of vector elements that are processed in parallel by these operations.

As an example, if you have a cluster of 16 nodes, each with a single Intel Xeon E3-1285 v3 processor that has four cores with Haswell microarchitecture running at 3.6 GHz, it will have peak performance of 3686.4 gigaFLOPS (or 10^9 FLOPS). Using the FMA (fused multiply add, which is $b = a \times b + c$) instruction, a Haswell core can generate four Flops/cycle (via execution of two FMAs per cycle) with a SIMD vector putting out four results per cycle, thus delivering peak performance of 57.6 gigaFLOPS at the frequency of 3.6 GHz: $4 \dfrac{Flops}{cycle} \times 4 SIMD \times 3.6 GHz = 57.6 GFLOPS$. Multiplying this by total number of cores in the cluster $(64 = 16 nodes \times 1 \dfrac{processor}{node} \times 4 \dfrac{cores}{processor})$ gives 3686.4 gigaFLOPS, or 3.68 teraFLOPS.

Peak performance usually cannot be reached, but it serves as a guideline for the optimization work. Actual application performance (often referred as *sustained performance*) can be obtained by counting the total number of floating point operations executed by the application (either by analyzing the algorithm or using special processor counters), and then dividing this number by the application runtime in seconds. The ratio between measured application performance (in FLOPS) and the peak performance of the system it was run on, multiplied by 100 percent, is often referred to as *computational efficiency*, which demonstrates what share of theoretically possible performance of the system was actually used by the application. The best efficiencies close to 95 percent are usually obtained by highly tuned computational kernels, such as BLAS (Basic Linear Algebra Subprograms), while mainstream HPC applications often achieve efficiencies of 10 percent and lower.

Distributed and Shared Memory Systems

So far we have discussed how application performance can be improved by increasing the amount of work done in parallel inside a processor core: by allowing more instructions to execute in parallel in superscalar microarchitectures, and by making each instruction process more data using the SIMD paradigm. As the next step we discuss two types of parallelism that can be employed to further enhance application performance. The main difference visible to you as a software developer is how the memory is shared and accessed by the processors. In the *shared memory* approach, multiple application threads can access all the memory simultaneously in a transparent. In the *distributed memory* approach, there is local and remote memory, and in order to work on any piece of data, that data has to be first copied into the local memory of the thread or process.

Use More Independent Threads on the Same Node

The first approach we will discuss harnesses several threads belonging to one program that can simultaneously access the same memory locations. Application threads can communicate through this *shared memory* with each other and avoid redundant copies of data. Shared memory is an efficient means of passing data between program threads. To connect multiple processors (each with multiple cores), the underlying system needs to have robust hardware to support arbitration and ordering of the memory requests.

In a shared memory system, the memory is presented to the application as a uniform, contiguous address range, while in fact the cost of accessing different parts of the memory by different processors may not be the same. Since most modern high-performance processors contain integrated memory controllers, there is some memory attached to each processor that is called *local memory* of that processor. Memory attached to other processors in the same system then needs to be accessed through an internal interconnect, such as Intel QuickPath Interconnect (QPI), that provides hardware mechanisms for all memory in the system to appear as one contiguous address space. There may be additional latency associated with accessing this *remote memory* over the latency for accessing the local memory. Shared memory systems that have this extra latency are called Non-Uniform Memory Access (NUMA) systems.

Impact from NUMA can be characterized by the ratio between the latencies for remote and local memory access. This ratio is called the *NUMA factor*. For example, in a dual-processor server with Intel Xeon E5-2697 v2 processors, local memory access latency (measured in the idle case) is around 50-70 ns (nanoseconds, or 10^{-9} second), while for remote memory access latency is equal to 90-110 ns, which leads to the NUMA factor for this system of approximately 1.5. The larger the shared memory system is, the larger the NUMA factor normally becomes. In fact, you may even find several different NUMA factors within larger systems. As a result, it is more difficult to optimize applications for these systems.

A generic diagram of a shared memory system in Figure 2-10 shows four processors, P0...P3, accessing shared memory divided into two NUMA regions, where memory local to P0 and P1 will be remote for P2 and P3, and vice versa.

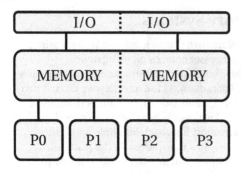

Figure 2-10. *Shared memory system diagram*

To get details on the NUMA topology of your system, use the numactl tool that is available for all major Linux distributions. On our workstation, the execution of numactl tool with the --hardware argument displays the following information (see Listing 2-1):

Listing 2-1. Output of the numactl --hardware Command

```
available: 2 nodes (0-1)
node 0 cpus: 0 1 2 3 4 5 6 7 8 9 10 11 24 25 26 27 28 29 30 31 32 33 34 35
node 0 size: 65457 MB
node 0 free: 57337 MB
node 1 cpus: 12 13 14 15 16 17 18 19 20 21 22 23 36 37 38 39 40 41 42 43 44
             45 46 47
node 1 size: 65536 MB
node 1 free: 59594 MB
node distances:
node   0   1
  0:  10  21
  1:  21  10
```

The output of the numactl tool shows two NUMA nodes, each with 24 processors (and just a hint-these are twelve physically independent cores with two threads each), and 64 GB of RAM per NUMA node, or 128 GB in the server in total.

In a similar manner to physical memory, the Input/Output subsystem and the I/O controllers are shared inside the multiprocessor systems, so that any processor can access any I/O device. Similarly to memory controllers, the I/O controllers are often integrated into the processors, and latency to access local and remote devices may differ. However, since latency associated with getting data from or to external I/O devices is significantly higher than the latency added by crossing the inter-processor network (such as QPI), this additional inter-processor network latency can be ignored in most cases. We will discuss specific I/O related issues in greater detail in Chapter 4.

Don't Limit Yourself to a Single Server

Unfortunately, there are practical limits to the size of a single system with shared memory, mostly driven by cost of building the hardware, as well as by overheads associated with the memory arbitration logic.

To achieve higher performance than a single shared memory system could offer, it is more beneficial to put together several smaller shared memory systems, and interconnect those with a fast network. Such interconnection does not make the memory from different boxes look like a single address space. This leads to the need for software to take care of copying data from one server to another implicitly or explicitly. Figure 2-11 shows an example system.

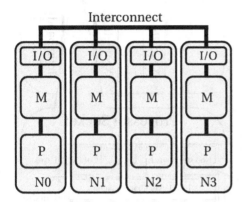

Figure 2-11. *Diagram of a distributed memory system*

Figure 2-11 shows a computer with four nodes, N0–N3, interconnected by a network, also called *interconnect* or *fabric*. Processors in each node have their own dedicated private memory and their own private I/O. In fact, these nodes are likely to be shared memory systems like those we have reviewed earlier. Before any processor can access data residing in another node's private memory, that data should be copied to the private memory of the node that is requesting the data. This hardware approach to building a parallel machine is called *distributed memory*. The additional data copy step, of course, has additional penalty associated with it, and the performance impact greatly depends on characteristics of the interconnect between the nodes and on the way it is programmed.

HPC Hardware Architecture Overview

Modern HPC hardware is quite complex, following several levels of integration, as presented in Figure 2-12. Each processor core contains several execution units, driven by out-of-order execution pipelines. Several cores in each processor may run at different frequencies to optimize the total system power consumption and keep it in balance with the application throughput. Complexity is further increased by the hierarchical cache subsystems and nonuniform memory access at the system level. One level up, several shared memory servers are assembled into a distributed memory cluster, using one or more dedicated interconnection networks.

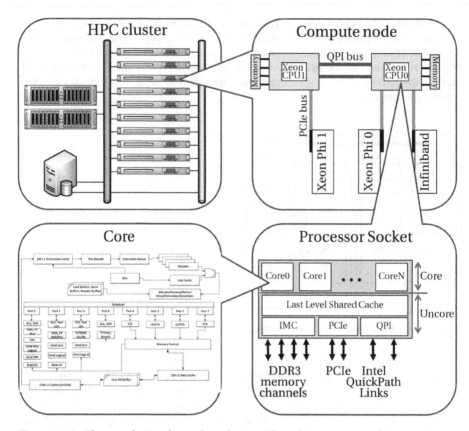

Figure 2-12. *The complexity of a modern cluster with multi-processor, multicore systems*

A Multicore Workstation or a Server Compute Node

Let us start with an overview of a simple workstation or a desktop computer. It has at least one processor and that processor very likely has multiple cores.

A *core* is an independent piece of hardware that does not share any hardware resources with other cores inside the processor. The core executes instructions of a computer program by performing requested arithmetical, logical, input/output, and other operations. Supported instructions are usually hardwired into the cores. They are called the *instruction set*. This is the language that the processor speaks, and it won't understand a different one. All instructions for mainstream Intel processors are based on the x86 instruction set, with multiple extensions, known as MMX, SSE, AES-NI, AVX, etc. The supported instruction set and the architecture state (including all the registers visible to the instructions, flags, etc.) define a *core architecture*.

The internal implementation that defines how exactly the instructions are handled to produce expected results may, and in fact does, vary from one processor to another. As an example, an Intel Atom processor and an Intel Xeon processor share the same instruction set architecture, meaning that you can run exactly the same operating system and application software on these two. However, internal implementations of these two processor cores are very different.

We refer to the internal implementations as *microarchitecture*. Thus, the Haswell microarchitecture that is the basis for Intel Xeon E3-1200 v3 processors is very different from the Silvermont microarchitecture used to build cores for Intel Atom C2000 processors. Detailed microarchitecture differences and specific optimization techniques are described in the *Intel 64 and IA-32 Architectures Optimization Reference Manual*.[12] This 600-page document describes a large number of Intel x86 cores and explains how to optimize software for IA-32 and Intel 64 architecture processors.

The addendum to the aforementioned *Intel 64 and IA-32 Architectures Optimization Reference Manual* contains data useful for quantitative analysis of the typical latencies and throughputs of the individual processor instructions. The primary objective of this information is to help the programmer with the selection of the instruction sequences (to minimize chain latency) and in the arrangement of the instructions (to assist in hardware processing).

However, this information also provides an understanding of the scale of performance impact from various instruction choices. For instance, typical arithmetic instruction latencies (reported in the number of clock cycles that are required for the execution core to complete the execution of the instruction) are one to five cycles (or 0.4-2 ns when running at 2.5 GHz) for simple instructions such as addition, multiplication, taking maximum or minimum value. Latency can reach up to 45 cycles (or 18 ns at 2.5 GHz) for division of double precision floating point numbers.

Instruction throughput is reported as the number of clock cycles that need to pass before the issue ports can accept the same instruction again. This helps to estimate the time it would take, for example, for a loop iteration to complete in presence of a cross-loop dependency. For many instructions, throughput of an instruction can be significantly smaller than its latency. Sometimes latency is given as just one half of the clock cycle. This occurs only for the double-speed execution units found in some microprocessors.

The same manual provides estimates for the best-case latencies and throughput of the dedicated caches: the first (L1) and the second (L2) level caches, as well as the translation lookaside buffers (TLBs). Particularly, on the latest Haswell cores, the load latency from L1 data cache may vary from four to seven cycles (or 1.6-2.8 ns at 2.5 GHz), and the peak bandwidth for data is equal to 64 (Load) + 32 (Store) bytes per cycle, or up to 240 GB/s aggregate bandwidth (160 GB/s to load data and 80 GB/s to store the data).

The architecture of modern Intel processors supports flexible integration of multiple processor cores with a shared *uncore* subsystem. Uncores usually contain integrated DRAM (Dynamic Random Access Memory) controllers, PCI Express I/O, Quick Path Interconnect (QPI) links, and the integrated graphics processing units (GPUs) in some models, as well as a shared cache (L2 or L3, depending on the processor, which is often called the Last Level Cache, or LLC). An example of the system integration view of four cores with uncore components is shown in Figure 2-13.

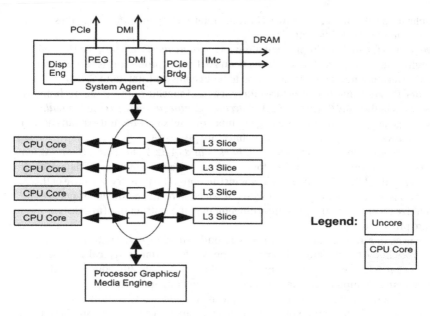

Figure 2-13. *Four-core processor integration of Intel microarchitecture, codenamed Haswell*

Uncore resources typically reside farther away from the cores on the processor die, so that typical latencies to access uncore resources (such as LLC) are normally higher than that for a core's own resources (such as L1 and L2 caches). Also, since the uncore resources are shared, the cores compete for uncore bandwidth. The latency of accessing uncore resources is not as deterministic as the latency inside the core. For example, the latency of loading data from LLC may vary from 26 to 60 cycles (or from 10.4 to 24 ns for a 2.5 GHz processor), comparing to the typical best case of 12 cycles (or 4.8 ns) load latency for the L2 cache.

Cache bandwidth improvements in the Haswell microarchitecture over the older Sandy Bridge/Ivy Bridge microarchitectures doubled the number of bytes loaded and stored per clock cycle from 32 and 16 to 64 and 32, respectively. Last Level Cache bandwidth also jumped from 32 bytes per cycle to 64 bytes. At the same time, typical access latencies stayed unchanged between the microarchitecture generations. This confirms the earlier observation related to the bandwidth vs. latency development.

As for the next level in the memory hierarchy, the computer main memory, its latency further increases and its bandwidth drops. Figure 2-14 shows schematically the relative latency and bandwidth capabilities in the memory hierarchy of a quad-core Haswell-based Intel Xeon Processor E3-1265L v3 processor.

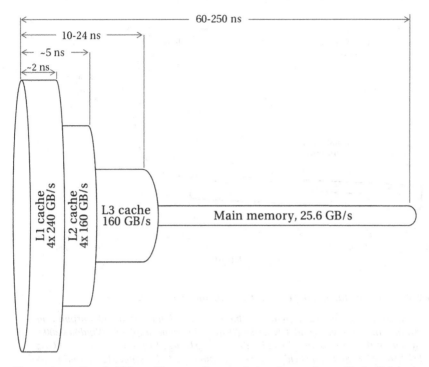

Figure 2-14. *Bandwidth and latency characteristics of a quad-core Haswell-based processor*

Another important aspect of the memory latency is that the effective time to load or store data goes up with higher utilization of the memory busses. Figure 2-15 shows the results of the latency measurement performed as a function of intensity of the memory traffic for a dual-socket server. Here, two generations of server processors are compared, with cores based on the Sandy Bridge and Ivy Bridge. The newer Ivy Bridge-based processors (specifically Intel Xeon E5-2697 v2) support faster memory running at 1866 MHz and contain improvements in the efficiency of the memory controller implementation over the previous generation, Intel Xeon E5-2690 processor built with eight Sandy Bridge cores and memory running at 1600 MHz. Despite the increase of the core count and faster DRAM speed, latency is about the same in both cases when the concurrency of memory requests is low (and thus the consumed memory bandwidth is far below the physical limits).

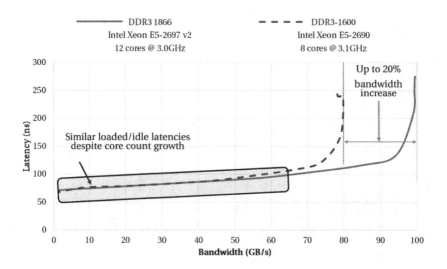

Figure 2-15. *Memory latency dependency from memory bus load**

*Based on measurements done using a latency/bandwidth tool internal to Intel Corporation. Memory traffic mix: 66% Reads and 33% writes (Request for ownership). OS: Windows 2008 R2 SP1, System configurations: Intel Xeon E5 2697 v2 (Ivy Bridge-EP): 12C, nominal 2.7 GHz [July 2013], Xeon E5 2690 (Sandy Bridge-EP): 8C, nominal 2.9 GHz [Sept 2011], 1 dual-ranked RDIMM per channel, 4 channels, varied DDR frequencies, pre-production BIOS

In this case, latency is determined by the internal organization of the memory hierarchy rather than by the DRAM speed and technology. Only when concurrency increases, generating more load/store requests, and the consumed memory bandwidth reaches the wire speed limit, the latency difference becomes noticeable. Another outcome from this measurement is that memory latency does vary significantly, depending on the load of the memory bus: from 60 to 70 ns in idle case (that will be 160-170 processor core cycles at 2.5 GHz), up to around 250 ns for the loaded case (over 600 cycles).

Coprocessor for Highly Parallel Applications

Recent years have seen the rise of accelerators and coprocessor targeting highly parallel applications. One example would be Intel's Xeon Phi family of coprocessors that feature a highly parallel microprocessor with up to 61 cores running at up to 1.2 GHz, with 16 GB of GDDR5 memory clocked at up to 5.5 GHz, and an integrated system management controller. The coprocessor runs Linux OS. It can even be seen as a standalone computational node, although the presence of a host processor is still required to boot and initialize the coprocessor.

The coprocessors found in HPC these days focus on delivering higher throughput. They can achieve over 1 TFLOPS of peak floating point performance with peak memory bandwidth reaching 350 GB/s. However, great throughput comes at the expense of latency: the coprocessors usually run at frequencies around 1 GHz (2.5-3x slower than standalone processors), and GDDR5 access latency is at least a factor of two times higher versus DDR3 in a standard server. However, for a subset of applications, where higher latency can be hidden by much higher concurrency, noticeable performance benefit comes from the significantly higher throughput in hardware.

One important performance and programmability aspect of coprocessor is that they are attached to the main processor(s) over the PCI Express (PCIe) bus. Often they have to involve the host processor to execute I/O operations or perform other tasks. The second-generation PCIe bus that is used in Intel Xeon Phi coprocessors can deliver up to 80 Gbps (gigabits per second) of peak wire bandwidth in every direction via a x16 connector. This translates into approximately 7 GB/s of sustained bandwidth, for the overhead includes 8/10 encoding scheme used to increase reliability of data transfers over the bus. This also adds latency between the host processor and the coprocessor, on the order of 200-300 ns, or more if the bus is heavily loaded. In heterogeneous applications that use both the central processors and the coprocessors in a system, it is important to hide this added latency of communications over the PCIe bus.

Group of Similar Nodes Form an HPC Cluster

When a single server is not enough to solve a scientific or technology problem in a sufficiently short time, people put together several nodes and wire them with a dedicated communication network to form a distributed memory system, called a *cluster*. For this approach to work, every node adds a special adapter for a fast network, such as 10 gigabit Ethernet or InfiniBand. The software stack needs to support message passing between the nodes, so that it becomes more sophisticated. Two dual-processor servers with two Intel Xeon Phi coprocessors each clustered together with InfiniBand interconnect are shown in Figure 2-16.

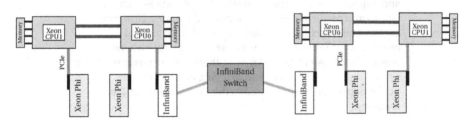

Figure 2-16. *Cluster of two nodes*

All of the most popular interconnects use the PCIe bus to connect to the processors in the system, and thus they inherit all the latency and bandwidth limitations specific to PCIe. On top of this, since both Ethernet and InfiniBand are designed to scale to a much larger number of communicating agents in the network (at least tens of thousands) than PCIe, their protocol overheads and cost of packet routing are significantly higher compared to the PCIe bus used inside the server.

Typical latencies of modern, widely used interconnects are around 1.5 to 15 microseconds (which is 1,500-15,000 ns, or thousands and tens of thousands of processor cycles) for point-to-point communication between two application processes, including the overheads associated with the utilized message passing protocol and its software implementation. However, bandwidth of these fast interconnects is closer to what can be found inside the server. For instance, the fastest InfiniBand peak data rate is 56 Gbps. This results in approximately 6.5 GB/s attainable bandwidth between two nodes in one direction. Latency is often a higher limiting factor, unless it is hidden by the applications via overlapping communications and computations, and using optimized algorithms for collective communication between large numbers of nodes.

Another important factor that influences performance of a parallel application in a cluster environment, especially with a very large number of nodes, is the interconnect topology. The PCIe bus used inside each node usually provides a very simple point-to-point or star topology. More complex, though scalable, topologies are used in the HPC cluster interconnects. The Fat Tree topology is probably the most popular one, despite a cost that grows with the size of the cluster. The InfiniBand network supports several multiple topology choices, including All-to-All, Fat Tree, Torus, and Hypercube topologies, as shown in Figure 2-17. There is no single, best topology; its choice and suitability are determined by the needs of the application and by the target metrics and cost implications. Here is a brief outline of the advantages and drawbacks of several interconnect topologies:

- *All-to-All topologies* are ideal for applications that are highly sensitive to communication latency, since the All-to-All topology requires the minimum number of hops between the communicating agents. Even though an asynchronous fabric with high bisection bandwidth can be built using the All-to-All topology, it is restricted to relatively small clusters due to the limited switch port counts.

- *Fat Tree* topologies are well suited for the majority of clusters and applications. Fat Tree topologies can provide asynchronous fabrics and predictable latency between the nodes. However, cabling and switching become increasingly difficult and expensive as the cluster size grows, with very large switches required for larger clusters. Anyway, there are clusters comprising several thousands of nodes and reaching PetaFLOPS of performance that are organized in the nonblocking Fat Tree topology.

- *Hypercube, Torus,* and other topologies are best suited for very large node counts. They provide rich bandwidth capabilities, and they scale easily from small to extremely large clusters. These topologies are usually much harder to design and implement. They can present additional scalability challenges and introduce variable hop count and latency with the increasing cluster size. Inconsistent hop counts can result in unpredictable application behavior owing to unequal latency between the nodes.

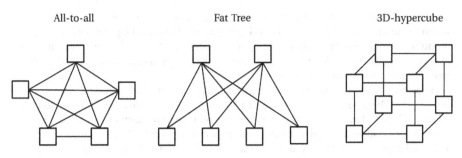

Figure 2-17. *Typical interconnection topologies found in HPC*

Other Important Components of HPC Systems

In reality, to get the most out of an HPC system, it is not enough to just rely on the best components in servers, packed together in a balanced way for your applications. Several other elements are important from the point of view of overall cluster performance and efficiency.

Specifically, HPC systems are used for applications that require a lot of memory, so that multiple nodes are used simultaneously in a scale-out fashion to provide the required amount of memory. Quite often, such applications either get a lot of data as their input (so-called Big Data applications) or produce huge amounts of output (typical scientific simulations). Handling huge amounts of data requires good storage arrangements. Development of scalable parallel storage and file systems to meet specific demands of HPC or Big Data applications can be viewed as a special art.

A single storage server along with a large compute cluster is likely not the best possible setup. Although it will work, a single network link, a single RAID adapter, or, in the worst case, a single disk will likely become a bottleneck, serializing all your cluster nodes around the single storage node. A better approach widely used in HPC today is to parallelize the storage or cluster it. Following the approach similar to the computing capacity, you can use several storage nodes to provide throughput and increase the level of concurrency of disk operations to sustain the high number of I/O requests issued by the computing cluster nodes. On top of clustered hardware, use of parallel I/O operations is usually implemented in the application or system software.

However, latency of single I/O operations is usually quite high. Here we see the milliseconds of time (as visible by the user application) that small I/O transactions can take. If your application does a lot of small-size reads/writes at random locations or from/to many different files, solid state drives attached to PCIe bus on the storage nodes promise significant increase in performance for small I/O operations. With an optimized file system and network stack, latencies of single I/O operations with small payloads drop down to a few hundred or even tens of microseconds.

Another really important component of an HPC system is a job scheduler. This is a software component, but it influences hardware utilization and overall cluster utilization efficiency. Its main purposes are planning the execution of user batch jobs, scheduling them for execution, deploying the user run script and executable file(s) to the allocated cluster nodes, organizing input and gathering output, terminating the application, and collecting accounting information. There are multiple open-source and commercial schedulers available to choose from.

It is worth noting that job schedulers take their portion of time for every job execution, and this time can reach seconds per job submission. The good news is that scheduling takes place only before the application starts and may add some time after the job ends (for the clean-up). So, if your job takes several days to run on a cluster, these few seconds have a small relative impact.

However, sometimes people need to run a large number of smaller jobs. For example, if each job takes a couple of minutes to run, but there are many jobs (up to tens of thousands have been observed in real life), the relative time taken by the job scheduler becomes very visible. Most job schedules offer special support for large number of smaller jobs with identical parameters via so-called job arrays. If your application is of that kind, please take some time to study how to make effective use of your cluster's scheduling software.

Summary

This chapter briefly overviewed the main terms and concepts pertaining to the performance analysis and gave an overview of the modern high-performance computing platforms. Certainly, this is the minimum information needed to help you get started on the subject or to refresh your existing knowledge.

If you are interested in computer architecture, you may enjoy the book *Computer Architecture: A Quantitative Approach*.[13] In the fourth edition of this book, the authors increase their coverage of multiprocessors and explore the most effective ways of achieving parallelism as the key to unlocking the power of modern architectures.

We also found an easy-to-read guide in the book *Introduction to High Performance Computing for Scientists and Engineers*, written by Georg Hager and Gerhard Wellein.[14] It contains a great overview of platforms architectures, as well as recommendations for application optimization specific to the serial, multi-threaded, and clustered execution.

In his article *Latency Lags Bandwidth*, David Patterson presents an interesting study that illustrates a chronic imbalance between bandwidth and latency.[15] He lists half a dozen performance milestones to document this observation, highlights many reasons why this happens, and proposes a few ways to cope with the problem, as well as gives a rule of thumb to quantify it, plus an example of how to design systems based on this observation.

For readers interested in the queuing network modeling, we recommend the book *Quantitative System Performance: Computer System Analysis Using Queuing Network Models*.[16] It contains an in-depth description of the methodology and a practical guide to and case studies of system performance analysis. It also provides great insight into the major factors affecting the performance of computer systems and quantifies the influence of the system bottlenecks.

The fundamentals and practical methods of the queuing theory are described in the book *Queueing Systems: Theory*.[17] Step-by-step derivations with detailed explanation and lists of the most important results make this treatise useful as a handbook.

References

1. *Merriam-Webster Collegiate Dictionary*, 11th ed. (Springfield, MA: Merriam-Webster, 2003).
2. A. S. Tanenbaum, *Computer Networks* (Englewood Cliffs, NJ: Prentice-Hall, 2003).
3. B. Cantrill and J. Bonwick, "Real-World Concurrency," *ACM Queue* 6, no. 5 (September 2008): 16–25.
4. G. M. Amdahl, "Validity of the Single Processor Approach to Achieving Large-Scale Computing Capabilities," AFIPS '67 (Spring) Proceedings of the 18–20 April 1967, spring joint computer conference, 483–85.
5. J. L. Gustafson, "Reevaluating Amdahl's law," *Communications of the ACM* 31, no. 5 (May 1988): 532–33.
6. "Queueing theory," Wikipedia, http://en.wikipedia.org/wiki/Queueing_theory.
7. S. Williams, A. Waterman, and D. Patterson, "Roofline: An Insightful Visual Performance Model for Multicore Architectures," *Communications of the ACM - A Direct Path to Dependable Software* 52, no. 4 (April 2009): 65–76.
8. J. McCalpin, "Memory Bandwidth and Machine Balance in Current High Performance Computers," *IEEE Computer Society Technical Committee on Computer Architecture (TCCA) Newsletter*, December 1995.
9. IDC (International Data Corporation), "HPC Market Update: 2012," September 2012, www.hpcuserforum.com/presentations/dearborn2012/IDCmarketslidesChirag-Steve.pdf.
10. Intel Corporation, "Intel VTune Amplifier XE 2013," http://software.intel.com/en-us/intel-vtune-amplifier-xe.
11. M. J. Flynn, "Very High-speed Computing Systems," *Proceedings of IEEE* 54 (1966): 1901–909.
12. Intel Corporation, *Intel 64 and IA-32 Architectures Optimization Reference Manual*, www.intel.com/content/www/us/en/architecture-and-technology/64-ia-32-architectures-optimization-manual.html.
13. J. L. Hennessy and D. A. Patterson, *Computer Architecture: A Quantitative Approach*, 4th ed. (Burlington, MA: Morgan Kaufmann, 2006).
14. G. Hager and G. Wellein, *Introduction to High Performance Computing for Scientists and Engineers* (Boca Raton, FL: CRC Press, 2010).
15. D. A. Patterson, "Latency Lags Bandwith," *Communications of the ACM - Voting Systems*, January 2004, pp. 71–75.
16. E. D. Lazowska, J. Zahorjan, G. S. Graham, and K. C. Sevcik, *Quantitative System Performance: Computer System Analysis Using Queueing Network Models* (Upper Saddle River, NJ: Prentice-Hall, 1984).
17. L. Kleinrock, *Queueing Systems: Theory*, vol. 1 (Hoboken, NJ: John Wiley, 1976).

CHAPTER 3

■ ■ ■

Top-Down Software Optimization

The tuning of a previously unoptimized hardware/software combination is a difficult task, one that even experts struggle with. Anything can go wrong here, from the proper setup to the compilation and execution of individual machine instructions. It is, therefore, of paramount importance to follow a logical and systematic approach to improve performance incrementally, continuously exposing the next bottleneck to be fixed.

This chapter provides such a framework. We will talk very little here about what and how to tune but, rather, leave that to subsequent chapters to consider in detail. We will instead specify the necessary requirements for the workload, application, and benchmarking; and we will provide a systematic staged tuning process, the so-called *top-down approach*. In this process, the performance tuning is considered at three different levels: system, application, and microarchitecture. Each level will be tuned iteratively to convergence, possibly exposing further bottlenecks at other levels.

The Three Levels and Their Impact on Performance

Most people think about performance tuning of HPC applications as the process of tuning the actual source code, but as we shall see, this is only part of the story.

We discussed latency and throughput in Chapter 2. Let us have a look at the typical access latency and throughput for different components in an HPC system that was discussed there. This information is summarized in Table 3-1, with a few numbers deliberately rounded to the nearest order of magnitude.

Table 3-1 shows a trend of diminishing latency and increasing throughput as we move closer and closer to the execution of instructions. Indeed, the whole process might be thought of as a pipeline provisioning data to the processor core, delivering it through the cache hierarchy from the operating system memory, or even farther away from the external node's memory or a hard disk.

Performance follows the weakest-link paradigm: if one stage of the pipeline does not work according to expectations, the rest of the pipeline will starve. While optimizing this pipeline, we should start with the biggest potential bottlenecks first—at the top of this list, working our way down, as shown in Figure 3-1. Indeed, it makes little sense to start working on the branch misprediction impact while the application spends most of its time in the network communication or cache misses. Once we have made sure data is available in the cache, a continuously occurring branch misprediction does have a huge relative impact.

Table 3-1. *Memory Technologies and Their Latency and Throughput (to the Order of Magnitude)*

Component	Typical Latency	Typical Throughput
Local SATA HDD	~1 ms	100 MB/s
Local SATA SSD	~1 ms	500 MB/s
1GB Ethernet	~15 us	100 MB/s
10GB Ethernet	~4 us	1 GB/s
Infiniband FDR	1.5 us	~6.5 GB/s
Local memory (loaded)	~250 ns	~100 GB/s
Local memory (idle)	~60 ns	0 GB/s
Remote memory (idle)	~100 ns	0 GB/s
QPI (intersocket)	~100 ns*	~64 GB/s
L3 cache access	10-25 ns	~160 GB/s
L2 cache access	~5 ns	~160 GB/s
L1 cache access	2-3 ns	~240 GB/s
XOR instruction	~6 ns	~2.5 Ginstruction/s
Branch misprediction	~7 ns	-
SIMD Division instruction	~16 ns	~1 Ginstruction/s

*QPI remote connection latency is hardly observable on the backdrop of the remote memory latency mentioned above.

Considering Table 3-1, the tuning of a system/software combination may be intuitively broken down into three stages, which are roughly ordered according to the data flow and their *impact time*—that is, the time impact that an inefficiently working part could make on the execution:

- *System*: This is the computer hardware and system software as such and all that brings it to life: the hard disk, the network interfaces, the memory, the BIOS, the operating system, the job manager, the cooling system, and the processor. All of these components require proper setup and configuration for the considered application workload to deliver the expected performance.

- *Application*: This is the part that the user is most exposed to, since this is what he writes or modifies as source code. The application level comprises the algorithmic implementation, the use of external application programming interfaces (APIs), locks, heap, stack, and so on. One central point of the application level is the proper management of data and the access thereto. In particular, this includes the parallelization in two flavors: the shared and distributed memory programming.

- *Microarchitecture*: For most people this is the most obscure level. It is concerned with the efficient use of the processor-internal resources by the application. For example, how efficient is the processor interpreting the strange hex numbers in your binary? How many instructions does the processor complete per cycle? Does an instruction wait most of the time for another one to complete? Is the processor able to predict the conditional branches in your code? Generally, one does not want to know about all of this, but this is where the battle is decided at the last stage of the optimization process.

It is important to understand that bottlenecks in the higher levels may hide bottlenecks in the lower ones. On the other hand, improvements in the lower levels can create bottlenecks at the higher levels. Figure 3-1 shows an overview of the individual levels.

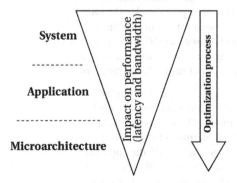

Figure 3-1. Bottleneck levels and their impact on performance of applications

System Level

Before worrying about the code of your application, the most important and impactful tuning can be achieved looking at the system components of the compute node, interconnect, and storage. No matter how advanced and skillfully implemented an algorithm is, a wrongly configured network, a forgotten file I/O, or a misplaced memory module in a NUMA system can undo all the effort you put into careful programming.

In many cases, you will be using a system that is in good shape. Particularly if you are a user of an HPC compute center, your system administrators will have taken care in choosing the components and their sound setup. Still, not even the most adept system administrator is immune to a hard disk failure, the cooling deficits of an open rack door, or a bug in a freshly installed network driver. No matter how well your system seems to be maintained, you want to make sure it really does perform to its specification.

You'll find a detailed description of the system tuning in Chapter 4, but here we give an overview of the components and tools. For an HPC system, the hardware components affecting performance at a system level are mostly as follows:

- *Storage and file systems*: As the most of HPC problems deal with large amounts of data, an effective scaling storage hierarchy is critical for application performance and scaling. If storage is inadequate in terms of bandwidth or access latency, it may introduce serialization into the entire application. Taking into account Amdahl's Law (discussed in Chapter 2), this should be considered as the first optimization opportunity.

- *Cluster interconnection hardware and software*: HPC applications do not only demand high bandwidth and low latency for point-to-point exchanges. They also demand advanced capabilities to support collective communications between very large numbers of nodes. A single parameter set wrongly here may completely change the relevant performance characteristics of the network.

- *Random access memory (RAM)*: The RAM attached to the integrated memory controller of a CPU comes in packages called dual-Inline memory modules (DIMMs). The memory controller supports a number of channels that can be populated with several DIMMs. At the same time, different specifications of DIMMs may be supported by the memory controller, such as DIMMs of different sizes in the same channel. Asymmetry in either size or placement of the DIMMs may result in substantial performance degradation.

- *Platform compute/memory balance*: As discussed in Chapter 2, each system has its compute/memory performance balance that can be visualized by the Roofline model. Depending on the specific platform configuration (including the number of cores, their speed and capabilities, and the memory type and speed), the application may end up being memory or compute bound, and these specific platform characteristics will define the application performance.

- *Basic input-output system (BIOS)*: The BIOS is used to bootstrap the system (that is, starting the OS without having full knowledge of the components used), but more importantly, it is also used to configure certain hardware features that can only be set at the boot time. Examples for such features are:

  - *NUMA mode*: Does the BIOS present the system memory as local to a socket or as one homogeneous memory region? Inefficient memory initialization may introduce significant system-level bottlenecks for particular applications.

  - *Processor and RAM frequencies*: The central processor unit (CPU) and RAM can operate under different frequency policies. The CPU, for instance, will try to assume a low-frequency state if no activity is detected, so as to save energy. Latest CPU and RAM specifications need to be supported by the BIOS in order to give the best performance. At the same time, CPU frequency variations driven by desire of saving power may lead to unpleasant load-imbalance issues.

- *Operating system (OS)*: The OS seems somewhat misplaced in the hardware category, since it is indeed software. But once you access the memory, you are actually interacting with the OS, since it will abstract the true memory away from you. So, to some degree, the OS is a proxy to hardware and should be treated in the same category. The OS should be kept up to date, and the version installed should support the features of the CPU and the rest of the system that are essential for performance. For instance, the use of the advanced vector extensions (AVX) and NUMA must be supported by the OS. Apart from this, the most critical point from the OS perspective is the drivers that allow hardware components to be operated from the user space. Examples of this are InfiniBand network cards, hard disk interfaces, and so forth.

All of these components need to be tested and benchmarked. A detailed guide on how to identify, find root causes for, and fix system level bottlenecks is provided in Chapter 4.

■ **Note**   System-level performance impact 2x–10x.

Application Level

After the bottlenecks at the system level are successfully cleared, the next category we enter is the application level: we are actually getting our hands on the code here! Application-level tuning is more complicated than system level because it requires a certain degree of understanding of algorithmic details. At the system level, we dealt with standard components—CPUs, OS, network cards, and so on. We rarely can change anything about them, but they need to be carefully chosen and correctly set up. At the application level, things change. Software is seldom made from standard components: most of its functionality is different from all other software. The essential part causing this differentiation is the algorithm(s) used and the implementation thereof.

Note that optimization should not mean a major rewrite. You don't want to change the general algorithm as such. A finite difference program should remain that way, even if finite elements might be more suitable. We are, rather, talking about optimizing the algorithm at hand and the plethora of smaller algorithms that it is built from.

Working Against the Memory Wall

As explained in Chapter 2, performance of modern HPC systems comes from two main sources: SIMD vectorization and parallelization. Both need to be considered at the application level. One central problem still needs to be addressed, however: the divergence of processor and memory performance. Moore's Law promises doubling of the number of transistors on a fixed silicon area roughly every two years.[1] This implies to some degree a doubling of performance as well, because when you talk about doubling the number of processing cores on a chip, you have twice the available space. Even if the number of cores doesn't double, there might be other uses for these additional transistors, such as the AVX1 and AVX2 instruction sets, each of which doubles the floating point operations that can be processed per cycle. Note also that the ever-faster, ever-bigger, and increasingly more efficient caches are part of this development.

When you leave the boundaries of the processor, though, there is no such rapid development. Dynamic RAM (DRAM) performance grows at 1.2x in the same time as the CPU performance grows 2x. The observation that this would lead to a starving CPU was first put forward by W. A. Wulf and S. A. McKee in 1994.[2] It did not come out quite as bad as predicted—more cache levels, larger cache sizes, integrated memory controllers, and more memory channels in combination with the CPU hardware prefetchers mitigated this predicted trend to some degree. Still, there is increasing pressure on the memory subsystem, and so application tuning should focus there. Chapter 8 deals with the respective optimization techniques in detail.

The impact of proper data management may be estimated to be in the order of the cache latency at different levels compared to the latency of RAM access:

$$S = \frac{L_{RAM}}{L_{cache_n}}$$

$$S = \frac{L_{RAM}}{L_{cache_n}}$$

This ratio ranges between 2x and 5x.

■ **Note**   Data layout and access performance impact: 2–5x.

The Magic of Vectors

Once data is readily available in the cache, computation itself might become the bottleneck. Now, SIMD vectors come into play. As described in Chapter 2, a SIMD instruction can execute the same arithmetic operation on different elements of a SIMD vector at the same time, as shown in Figure 3-2. Usually, the compiler does a decent job vectorizing code even in a very complex environment, but there are reasons it might not be able to vectorize your code. The Intel Compiler has some very useful reporting that will tell you exactly why the compiler cannot vectorize a particular loop. In the figure, vmulpd two SIMD AVX vectors containing four double elements each or one SIMD vector and a memory reference. The assembly code shows that the compiler already unrolls the loop by 4.

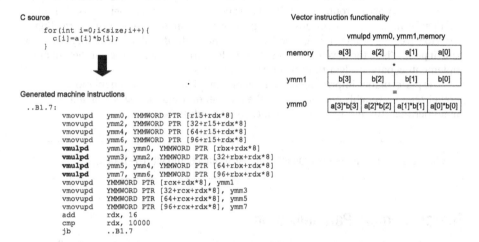

Figure 3-2. *Example for an automatic vectorization by the compiler in C source code, and the resulting assembly instructions*

The impact of vectorization on performance may be estimated by the number of vector elements of a given type that can be processed in parallel. For double precision/AVX, the possible speedup is four times; for single precision, it's eight times.

■ **Note**   Vectorization performance impact (double precision): 4x.

Distributed Memory Parallelization

The most important parallelization technique in HPC is *distributed memory parallelization* that enables communication between processes that may not share a common address space (although they can, of course). The benefit of this is immediately clear: you can communicate across physically different computers and gain access to the full power of the massively parallel HPC clusters.

As in the shared-memory approach (discussed in the next section), there is need for a robust library that would abstract all the low-level details and hide from the user the differences between various interconnects available on the market. So, back in the early 1990s, a group of researchers designed and standardized the Message Passing Interface (MPI).[3] The MPI standard defines a language-independent communications protocol as well as syntax and semantics of the routines required for writing portable message-passing programs in Fortran or C/C++; nonstandard bindings are available for many other languages, including C++, Perl, Python, R, and Ruby. The MPI standard is managed by the MPI Forum[4] and is implemented by many commercial and open-source libraries.

The MPI standard was widely used as a programming model for distributed memory systems that were becoming increasingly popular in the early 1990s. As the shared memory architecture of individual systems became more popular, the MPI library evolved as well. The latest MPI-3 standard was issued in September 2012. It added fast remote memory access routines, nonblocking and sparse collective operations, and some other performance-relevant extensions, especially in the shared memory and threading area. However, the programming model clearly remains the distributed memory one with explicit parallelism: the developer is responsible for correctly identifying parallelism and implementing parallel algorithms using MPI primitives.

The performance improvement that can be gained from distributed memory parallelization is roughly proportional to the number of compute nodes available, which ranges between 10x and 1000x for the usual compute clusters.

■ **Note**   Distributed memory parallelization performance impact: 10–1000x.

Shared Memory Parallelization

The next level to look at is the *shared memory parallelization*. In contrast to the distributed memory programming, where the parallelization unit is normally a process with its own, unique address, space, shared memory programming deals with parallel execution flow in a common address space. Generally, the execution needs to take place on the same physical system. Although processes can also participate in shared memory communication, we generally think about *threads* here.

How do you make a program utilize all processors in a shared memory system? There are multiple libraries providing application program interfaces, or APIs, such as POSIX Threads,[5] that help create and manage multiple application threads. Unfortunately, a lot of threading APIs are either operating system specific (and thus not portable to other OS), or use unique features of the underlying hardware, or are simply too low-level. This is why the HPC community has been building open, portable, and hardware-agnostic programming interfaces to implement threading support in the most popular programming languages: C, C++, and Fortran. The demand from developers for a cross-platform, easy-to-use, threading API helped OpenMP[6] to become the most popular threading API by far. OpenMP consists of a set of compiler directives, as well as library routines and environment variables, that influence the program runtime behavior.

The most recent development of the OpenMP moved the OpenMP API beyond traditional management of pools of threads. In the OpenMP specification version 4.0, released in July 2013, you find support for SIMD optimizations, as well as support for accelerators and coprocessors that architecturally better fit into the distributed memory system type discussed earlier in this chapter. Chapter 5 discusses OpenMP and other threading-related optimization topics, including how to deal with the application-level bottlenecks specific to the shared memory systems programming.

The performance improvement for shared memory parallelization is roughly proportional to the number of cores available per compute node, which is from 10x to 20x in modern server architectures.

■ **Note** Shared memory parallelization performance impact: 10x–20x.

Other Existing Approaches and Methods

So far we have discussed the most popular and widely used parallel programming models for the shared and distributed memory architectures—namely, MPI and OpenMP. However, there are a couple of other methods worth mentioning.

Partitioned Global Address Space (PGAS) is a model that assumes a global memory address space that is logically partitioned, with each portion being local to each process or thread. The PGAS approach attempts to combine the advantages of the MPI programming style for distributed memory systems with the data referencing semantics used in programming shared-memory systems. The PGAS model is the basis for Unified Parallel C,[7] Coarray Fortran[8] (now a part of the Fortran standard), as well as more experimental interfaces and languages.

The SHMEM (Shared Memory) library provides a set of functions similar to MPI.[9] It is available for C and Fortran programming languages. SHMEM routines support remote data transfer, work-shared broadcast and reduction, barrier synchronization, and atomic memory operations.

Intel Thread Building Blocks (TBB)[10] and Intel Cilk Plus[11] aim at making threading and SIMD kind of parallelism easier to use. They represent a new wave of the programming interfaces being developed to address the increased need for parallelization that has reached the mainstream.

Another emerging programming model, applicable for processing large data sets in the so-called Big Data applications, using a parallel, distributed algorithm on a cluster, is MapReduce.[12] A MapReduce program consists of a Map() procedure that usually performs filtering and sorting of large arrays of data, and a Reduce() procedure that performs a summary or other reduction operation on the results of the Map() operation. The MapReduce system middleware—for example, open-source Apache Hadoop[13]— orchestrates the distributed memory servers, runs various tasks in parallel, manages all communication and data transfers between the parts of the system, and provides transparent redundancy and fault tolerance.

One thing to keep in mind when working at the algorithm level is that *you do not need to reinvent the wheel*. If there is a library available that supports the features of the system under consideration, you should use it. A good example is the standard linear algebra operations. Nobody should program a matrix-matrix multiplication or an eigenvalue solver if it is not absolutely necessary and known to deliver a great benefit. The vector-vector, matrix-vector, and matrix-matrix operations are standardized in the so-called Basic Linear Algebra System (BLAS),[14] while the solvers can be addressed via the Linear Algebra Package (LAPACK)[15] interfaces, for which many implementations are available. One of them is Intel Math Kernel Library (Intel MKL), which is, of course, fully vectorized for all available Intel architectures and additionally offers shared memory parallelization.[16]

Microarchitecture Level

Having optimized the system and the algorithmic levels, let's turn now to the problem of how the actual machine instructions are executed by the CPU. According to Table 3-1, microarchitectural changes have the least individual impact in absolute numbers, but when they are accumulated, their impact on performance may be large. Microarchitectural tuning requires a certain understanding of the operation of the individual components of a CPU (discussed in detail in Chapter 7). Here, we restrict ourselves to a very limited overview.

Addressing Pipelines and Execution

The most important features of a modern CPU that need to be addressed at the microarchitectural level are as follows:

- *Pipelining*: The concept of pipelines is addressed at various points in this book, but they play a special role in the design of a CPU. Pipelines are probably the most impactful design pattern in modern computer architecture. The idea is based on the principle of an assembly line: one stage of the pipeline provides input to the following stages. Each stage is specialized in a particular task, which reduces complexity and increases performance. However, a stall at a particular stage may easily spread across the pipeline, both up (for lack of resources) and down (for lack of tasks to address).

- *Out-of-order (OOO) execution*: This is the ability of the CPU to reorder the instructions of a program according to the readiness of the required resources. If *instruction1* depends on the input parameters that are not yet available, the CPU scheduler might schedule execution of the following *instruction2* that meets all dependency requirements.

- *Superscalarity*: Superscalarity describes the implementation of instruction-level parallelism within the CPU. A superscalar CPU features multiple independent pipelines of the same or different capabilities. The scheduler routes instructions to these pipelines depending on what type the instructions are, and tries to execute them in parallel. In the current Intel architecture codenamed Haswell, for example, the CPU can execute two FMA operations at the same time, reaching throughput of 0.5 cycles/FMA. The total number of instructions that can be executed in parallel is 4/cycle.

- *Branch prediction*: A real problem in pipelined processors is conditional branches, which are jumps to a different part of the instruction flow based on the decision computed at runtime. In this case, the pipeline has to stop issuing instructions until the decision criterion is available. In order to circumvent this problem, a special unit in the CPU predicts the criterion based on the earlier decisions. A special cache is available to store these decisions. In this way, the CPU pipeline can continue operating speculatively, assuming continuation of the instruction flow at the predicted position. If the prediction was wrong, all instructions following the wrongly predicted branch are invalid and the complete pipeline has to be flushed for the execution flow to continue with the correct instruction.

Microarchitectural performance tuning is made more difficult because the actual implementation of the technologies just described can and will change with every processor generation, and might differ considerably across different vendors. Intel's CPUs offer particular hardware functionality to access the information necessary to perform microarchitectural tuning, the so-called performance monitoring unit (PMU). The PMU offers measures that keep track of what exactly happens in the chip—for instance, how many branch predictions have been done and how many have failed. Although you can access the PMU explicitly, it is much more convenient to use a tool that does the PMU programming for you, such as Intel VTune Amplifier XE,[17] Likwid,[18] or the Perf[19] command accessing the PMU via the Linux kernel.

The impact of the microarchitectural optimization can be estimated by the product of the depth of the pipelines and the number of pipelines in the modern processor, ranging in the 10x to 20x area.

■ **Note**   The performance impact of microarchitectural tuning can be up to 10x–20x.

Closed-Loop Methodology

One of the most critical factors in the tuning process is the way you load the system. There is some ambivalence in the use of the terms *workload* and *application*. Very often, they are used interchangeably. In general, *application* means the actual code that is executed, whereas *workload* is the task and data that you give to the application. For instance, the application might be sort.exe, and the workload might be some data file that contains the names of persons.

Workload, Application, and Baseline

In the current context, we would like to take a simpler view, considering both application and workload in combination simply as the workload. This combination needs to fulfill a number of criteria to be suitable for our purposes:

1. The workload should be *measurable*—that is, there should be quantifiable metric that represents performance of the application. Such a metric can be obvious ones, like execution time or GFLOPS, or more specialized, like simulated nanoseconds/day or transactions/s.

2. Measurement of the performance metric must be *reproducible*. Upon repetitive runs of the application, the resulting numbers need to be consistent. Also, the stress exerted by the application on the system needs to be reproducible.

3. The workload should be *static*—that is, it must not vary over time, and it needs to result in the same performance, regardless of when the workload is executed. In practical terms, performance observed should not vary beyond 1 to 2 percent.

4. The workload must be *representative* of the load imposed upon the system under normal operating conditions. In other words, it should stress those parts of the system that are loaded under normal operation.

In most cases, a real application (or part thereof) and a real compute task will be used for benchmarking. This need not be the case, however, as generating representative stress might be too time-consuming and the application itself might not be designed for benchmarking. Instead, you can consider an artificial benchmark that represents the real situation but gives more detailed information about the performance of individual fractions of the code and executes much faster. A good example is CERN's HEP-SPEC benchmark,[20] a subset of SPEC that mimics the system stress exerted on the CERN computing center.

One thing that must not be forgotten is to establish a *baseline* performance of the workload before you start tuning. Without the baseline, there is no objective starting point against which to compare any consequent potential improvement.

Iterating the Optimization Process

The top-down approach provides structured prioritization of the tuning tasks at hand. We now come to the second important part of this methodology: the *closed-loop* concept. While working at one level, we execute the following scheme:

1. *Gather performance data*: Collect performance data in the metric(s) agreed.

2. *Analyze the data and identify issues*: Focus on the most time-consuming part(s). Begin by looking for unexpected results or numbers that are out of tolerance. Try to fully understand the issue by using appropriate tools. Make sure the analysis does not affect the results.

3. *Generate alternatives to resolve the issue*: Remove the identified bottlenecks. Try to keep focused on one step at a time. Rate the solutions on how difficult they are to be implemented and on their potential payback.

4. *Implement the enhancement*: Change only one thing at a time in order to estimate the magnitude of the individual improvement. Make sure none of the changes causes a slowdown and negated other improvements. Keep track of the changes so you can roll them back, if necessary.

5. *Test the results*: Check whether performance improvements are up to your expectations and that they remove the identified bottleneck.

After the last step, you restart the cycle to identify the next bottleneck (see Figure 3-3). Clearly, this loop is normally infinite, for the time to stop is determined by the amount of time left to do the job.

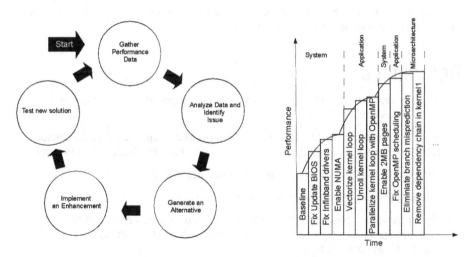

Figure 3-3. *Left: The closed-loop iterative performance optimization cycle. Right: Example performance gains by tuning through various levels*

The right graph in Figure 3-3 shows an artificial performance optimization across different levels. Note that at each level the performance saturates to some degree and that we switch levels when other bottlenecks become dominant. This can also mean going up a level again, since successful tuning of the application level might expose a bottleneck at the system level.

For example, consider an improvement in the OpenMP threading that suddenly causes the memory bandwidth to be boosted. This might very well expose a previously undiscovered bottleneck in the systems memory setup, such as DIMMs in the channels of the memory controllers having different sizes, with the resulting decreased memory bandwidth.

Summary

The methodology presented in this chapter provides a solid process to tune a system consistently with the top-down/closed-loop approach. The main things to remember are to investigate and tune your system through the following different levels:

1. System level (see Chapter 4)

2. Application level, including distributed and shared memory parallelization (see Chapters 5 and 6)

3. Microarchitecture level (see Chapter 7)

Keep iterating at each level until convergence, and proceed to the next level with the biggest impact as long as there is time left.

References

1. G. E. Moore, "Cramming More Components onto Integrated Circuits" *Electronics* 38, no. 8 (19 April 1965): 114–17.

2. W. A. Wulf, and S. A. McKee, "Hitting the Memory Wall: Implications of the Obvious," 1994, www.eecs.ucf.edu/~lboloni/Teaching/EEL5708_2006/slides/wulf94.pdf.

3. MPI Forum, "MPI Documents," www.mpi-forum.org/docs/docs.html.

4. "Message Passing Interface Forum," www.mpi-forum.org.

5. The Open Group, "Single UNIX Specification, Version 4, 2013 Edition," 2013, www2.opengroup.org/ogsys/jsp/publications/PublicationDetails.jsp?publicationid=12310.

6. OpenMP.Org, "OpenMP," http://openmp.org/wp.

7. UPC-Lang.Org., "Unified Parallel C," http://upc-lang.org.

8. Co-Array.Org, "Co-Array Fortran," www.co-array.org.

9. "SHMEM," Wikipedia, the free encyclopedia, http://en.wikipedia.org/wiki/SHMEM.

10. Intel Corporation, "Intel Threading Building Blocks (Intel TBB)," http://software.intel.com/en-us/intel-tbb.

11. Intel Corporation, "Intel Cilk Plus," http://software.intel.com/en-us/intel-cilk-plus.

12. G. Dean and S. Ghemawat, "MapReduce: Simplified Data Processing on Large Clusters," *OSDI'04: Sixth Symposium on Operating System Design and Implementation*, San Francisco, December 2004.

13. "Welcome to Apache Hadoop!," http://hadoop.apache.org.

14. NetLib.Org, "BLAS (Basic Linear Algebra Subprograms)," www.netlib.org/blas/.

15. NetLib.Org, "LAPACK — Linear Algebra PACKage," www.netlib.org/lapack/.

16. Intel Corporation, "Intel Math Kernel Library," http://software.intel.com/en-us/intel-mkl.

17. Intel Corporation, "Intel VTune Amplifier XE 2013," http://software.intel.com/en-us/intel-vtune-amplifier-xe.

18. "Likwid - Lightweight performance tools," http://code.google.com/p/likwid/.

19. "perf (Linux)" Wikipedia, the free encyclopedia, http://en.wikipedia.org/wiki/Perf_(Linux).

20. HEPiX Benchmarking Working Group, "HEP-SPEC06 Benchmark," https://w3.hepix.org/benchmarks/doku.php.

CHAPTER 4

■ ■ ■

Addressing System Bottlenecks

We start with a bold statement: every application has a bottleneck. By that, we mean that there is always something that limits performance of a given application in a system. Even if the application is well optimized and it may seem that no additional improvements are possible by tuning it on the other levels, it still has a bottleneck, and that bottleneck is in the system the program runs on. The tuning starts and ends at the system level.

When you improve your application performance to take advantage of all the features provided in the hardware, you use all available concurrency, and the application's execution approaches peak performance, but that peak performance will limit how fast the program can run. A trivial solution to improve performance in such cases is to buy a new and better piece of hardware. But to make an informed selection of new hardware, you would need to find a specific system-level bottleneck that restricts the application performance.

This chapter starts with discussion of the typical system-level tweaks and checks that one can implement before considering purchasing new hardware. These need to be seen as sanity checks of the available hardware before you invest in tuning of your applications on the other levels. The following chapters describe the tools and techniques for application optimization, yet the optimization work in the application must rely on a clean and sane system. This chapter covers what can be wrong with the system and how to find out if that specific system limitation is impacting your application performance.

Classifying System-Level Bottlenecks

System-level bottlenecks, or issues that do not allow reaching hardware peak performance, arise from limitations in either hardware or software components that are generally outside user and application control. The reality is that any computer system has hardware performance limitations. In most cases, the difference between a "good" and a "bad" system is only one thing: whether its limitations cause your application to be slow. The application developer can avoid some performance impact brought about by system bottlenecks, but generally it requires a system administrator to debug and reconfigure the system. But before an application developer or a user can produce claims to the system administrator, the bottleneck has to be identified and its impact characterized and quantified.

The root causes of system bottlenecks can be split into two major categories, depending on their origin:

1. *Condition* and the run-time environment

2. *Configuration* of hardware, firmware, or software

The first may be present temporarily, appear from time to time, and may go away and come back unless the issues are identified and fixed. The second includes issues that are really static in time unless the system is reconfigured, and they are caused by limitations in how the system was built (for instance, component selection, their assembly, and their configuration).

Identifying Issues Related to System Condition

Performance problems caused by the system condition or the environment where it operates are probably the hardest to diagnose, so let's start with them. The main cause of these system bottlenecks are the conditions under which the application executes or makes the transient changes to its runtime environment. Some specific examples include the following:

- *Shared resource conflicts*: A program running on a shared cluster may get fewer resources, depending on other applications executed on other nodes of the cluster at the same time. Two major shared resources in an HPC cluster are the *shared parallel file system* and the *interconnect between the cluster nodes*. Sometimes there can be memory-related bottlenecks when some cluster nodes are shared by different jobs, which may cause conflicts between these jobs depending on the specific scheduling.

- *Throttling*: Processors and memory modules in the cluster nodes may experience performance throttling caused by overheating or power delivery limitations. This is usually a data center–level issue, and there is really nothing an application developer can do: the system administrators and the vendor of the cluster have to revise their cooling or power delivery subsystem configurations.

- *Faults*: It may be a rather rare case, but if something in the hardware or software starts failing, it may temporally impact performance. A fault does not necessarily lead to system or application crash. Modern hardware has very sophisticated resiliency and error-correction mechanisms, and it is often able to recover from many types of errors, such as a single-bit data corruption in the memory or loss of a packet in transit. While these recovery mechanisms enable programs to continue running despite the faults occurring, they do take time for their work and may produce significant performance overhead for the user application running on the system.

Usually, detection and repair of the system-level issues is a responsibility of system administrators and the system provider. We do recommend that administrators ask vendors about Intel Cluster Ready certification for their systems. The certified cluster comes with a software tool from Intel, called the *Intel Cluster Checker*, and it's a key element of the Intel Cluster Ready validation process. The tool helps verify that cluster components are working when the cluster is being deployed and also that the components continue working together as expected throughout the cluster lifecycle. However, sometimes users need to raise awareness of observed performance problems before the issue is investigated.

There are several things you can do during development of an application or while setting up a job scripts that can help debug condition-related problems:

1. *Check shared resource conflicts by timing your code*: Insert a collection of timings into your application to gather execution time for the known long-lasting activities that depend on shared resources.

   a. For instance, if your application reads from or writes to a shared parallel file system, it may be beneficial to determine the time spent on the input/output (I/O) operations and report this time in the program output.

   b. For MPI applications, you may measure the time when there are known large message-passing operations, or routinely gather MPI time statistics produced by Intel MPI library (as discussed in Chapter 5). If in certain application runs the I/O or MPI take more time than usual, it may indicate a conflict over these shared resources or a fault in the file system (for instance, a failing disk, which may cause RAID rebuild with subsequent slowdown of I/O operations) or in the network fabric (for example, a broken cable, which may cause sporadic packet loss resulting in multiple attempts to deliver the respective messages).

2. *Count thermal and power throttling events.* Unfortunately, quite often an observed class of system-level issues is caused by throttling problems. But it is very easy to check if any thermal or power throttling occurred on any server, even if you do not have the administrative privileges. The Linux operating system kernel provides relevant counters for events such as the processor overheating or excessive power use. The script presented in Listing 4-1, here named check_throttle.sh (works for Bash compatible shells on Linux), will let you know how many throttling events have occurred since the last booting of the operating system.

Listing 4-1. Contents of check_throttle.sh Script to Count Throttling Events

```
#!/bin/sh
let CPU_power_limit_count=0
let CPU_throttle_count=0
for cpu in $(ls -d /sys/devices/system/cpu/cpu[0-9]*); do
  if [ -f $cpu/thermal_throttle/package_power_limit_count ]; then
    let CPU_power_limit_count+=$(cat $cpu/thermal_throttle/
    package_power_limit_count)
  fi
  if [ -f $cpu/thermal_throttle/package_throttle_count ]; then
    let CPU_throttle_count+=$(cat $cpu/thermal_throttle/package_
    throttle_count)
  fi
done
echo CPU power limit events: $CPU_power_limit_count
echo CPU thermal throlling events: $CPU_throttle_count
```

The expected good values for both printed lines should be *zero*, as shown in Listing 4-2.

Listing 4-2. Example of check_throttle.sh Script Run and Output

```
$ ./check_throttle.sh
CPU power limit events: 0
CPU thermal throlling events: 0
```

Anything other than zero indicates the presence of throttling events, which usually impacts performance significantly. During the throttling events, the clock frequency of the processors is reduced to save power, relying on the fact that the active power has a cubic dependency upon the voltage/frequency. Another technology to mitigate overheating of the chip is to insert duty cycles (when the processor clock is not running). This helps in reducing the processor temperature if a critical temperature is reached, but it significantly hurts performance of the applications.

3.   *Check for failure events.* Some of the more advanced techniques for detecting system-level issues may require root privileges, and thus can only be used by the system administrators. Programs such as mcelog[1] for Linux decode machine check events on modern Intel Architecture machines running a Linux OS with 64-bit kernel. Machine checks can indicate failing hardware, system overheats, bad memory modules, or other problems. If the tool is run regularly, it is useful for predicting server hardware failures before an actual server crash or there's appearance of visible performance impact on user applications.

4. *Ensure interconnect fabrics and storage are clean.* Additional areas of responsibility for the system administrators and vendors are to ensure the interconnect fabric is clean and the storage is built properly. This means that there are no bad cables, no bad ports, and no bad connectivity in the interconnection network, and that the storage arrays are complete, and are built and operated correctly.

Characterizing Problems Caused by System Configuration

The other class of issues listed above can be caused by the configuration of hardware or software that the application is run on. This is also generally outside system user control, and administrative privileges are required to alter the system settings. However, the user can check some of these settings, and may alert system administrators if any important misconfigurations are observed. For instance:

1. *Check that the system software and the operating system (OS) versions are the latest.* The OS has to be relatively new to support all important hardware features, specifically in the platforms and in the processors. As a rule of thumb (applied largely to Linux distributions), if the OS was released more than a year before the processor of the server, it likely should be updated or at least a newer kernel and major system libraries should be installed. The new processor and platform generations bring new features that almost always need proper support by the OS. Some of these features are the instruction set extensions brought out by Intel almost every year, and the changes in the mainstream server platform technologies instituted about every two years. Lack of support for the new features will not make the old OS dysfunctional; backwards compatibility normally allows old operating systems to boot and work, although inefficiencies will likely be observed.

2. *Review OS configuration.* A good OS for HPC systems has to be nondisturbing to the applications. In the HPC world (unlike some enterprise computing areas), a single user application usually exclusively owns the execution resources of several computational nodes, so the presence of any other activity on these nodes is undesirable, for this generates random interruptions of computations that may negatively impact a parallel application's performance. And it is here that most of the OS configuration issues are observed nowadays. Unfortunately, no universal checklists exist for all possible disturbing factors because there is a wide variety

of Linux distributions and site-specific packages that are still necessary on cluster compute nodes. However, there is one tool we recommend to the system administrators for analysis of the OS disturbance: PowerTOP.[2] It was originally developed by the Intel Open Source Technology Center to help identify power-hungry applications causing OS wakeups in mobile and embedded platforms. At the same time it is a great tool for reducing OS wakeups and to experiment with the various power management settings for cases where the Linux distribution has not enabled these settings by default. The interactive mode of PowerTOP helps to quickly reveal disturbing activities without expending great effort. We can run PowerTOP on our development workstation with CentOS 6.5, like this:

```
$ sudo powertop
```

■ **Note**   Here, prior to running the `powertop` command, we used another command: `sudo`. This addition instructs the operating system to use administrator or superuser privileges to execute the following command, while not asking for the super user password. In order to be able to use `sudo`, the system administrator has to delegate the appropriate permission to you—usually by means of including you in a specific group (such as `wheel` or `adm`) and editing system configuration file `/etc/sudoers`. Depending on the configuration, you may be asked to enter your password.

The output of running PowerTOP presented in Figure 4-1 shows that the OS wakeups disturbing other applications happen over 50 times per second and that the two most disturbing residents in the OS are the `kipmi0` kernel process and the `alsa` device driver for the sound system. Impact from `kipmi0` is rather large: the processing time takes 998 milliseconds every second—less than 2 milliseconds short of an entire second—thus taking away one complete core from the user applications.

```
PowerTOP 2.5      Overview    Idle stats   Frequency stats   Device stats   Tunables

Summary: 53.6 wakeups/second,  0.0 GPU ops/seconds, 0.0 VFS ops/sec and 100.9% CPU use

             Usage       Events/s    Category      Description
             998.2 ms/s     0.00      Process       [kipmi0]
             100.0%                   Device        alsa:hwC0D0
             347.0 us/s    13.4       Timer         tick_sched_timer
              27.2 us/s     8.5       Interrupt     [3] net_rx(softirq)
             273.6 us/s     3.7       Interrupt     [7] sched(softirq)
               8.3 ms/s     0.15      Process       ./src/powertop
               4.8 us/s     0.9       Process       [events/24]
              19.8 us/s     0.6       Process       [events/13]
              17.3 us/s     0.6       Process       [events/12]
              15.4 us/s     0.6       Process       [events/37]
               5.5 us/s     0.6       Process       [events/11]
              22.3 us/s     0.5       Process       [events/47]
              12.5 us/s     0.5       Process       [events/39]
              12.3 us/s     0.5       Process       [events/42]
              12.3 us/s     0.5       Process       [events/15]
              12.2 us/s     0.5       Process       [events/14]
              12.1 us/s     0.5       Process       [events/18]
              12.0 us/s     0.5       Process       [events/43]
              11.9 us/s     0.5       Process       [events/38]
              11.8 us/s     0.5       Process       [events/46]
               5.8 us/s     0.5       Process       [events/30]
               5.0 us/s     0.5       Process       [events/35]
               4.8 us/s     0.5       Process       [events/10]
               4.8 us/s     0.5       Process       [events/2]
               4.5 us/s     0.5       Process       [events/34]
               4.5 us/s     0.5       Process       [events/6]
               4.3 us/s     0.5       Process       [events/31]
               4.3 us/s     0.5       Process       [events/26]
               4.3 us/s     0.5       Process       [events/3]

<ESC> Exit
```

Figure 4-1. PowerTOP run in interactive mode

The alsa driver is the one for the sound system, which is not usually used in HPC systems and can safely be removed. In general, it is good practice to remove all unused software that by default may be installed with your favorite OS distribution (for instance, the mail servers, such as sendmail, or the Bluetooth subsystem that are not generally needed in HPC cluster compute nodes), and thus should either be uninstalled from the OS or be disabled from the startup process.

The kipmi0 is part of the OS kernel that is responsible for the work of the intelligent platform management interface (IPMI) subsystem,[3] which is often used to monitor various platform sensors, such as those for the CPU temperature and voltage. This may be required by the in-band monitoring agents of the monitoring tools like lm_sensors,[4] Ganglia,[5] or Nagios.[6] Although kipmid is supposed to use only the idle cycles, it does wake up the system and can affect application performance. The good news is that it is possible to limit the time taken by this kernel module by either adding the line `options ipmi_si kipmid_max_busy_us=1` to the `ipmi.conf` file under `/etc/modprobe.d/`, or by executing the following command:

```
$ sudo bash -c \
'echo 1 > /sys/module/ipmi_si/parameters/kipmid_max_busy_us'
```

This will limit the `kipmid` CPU time and the number of times it wakes up the OS.

After these two changes to the OS configuration, the number of wakeups per second on our test system was reduced and, more important, CPU usage went down. The CPU usage in the OS's idle state is around 1.5 percent (where at least 1 percent is taken by the PowerTOP itself), and the processor usage by the `kipmi0` is reduced to around 1 ms per second. The next biggest cause of OS wakeups is the timer process that takes only a third of a millisecond every second.

Other configurations or versions of operating systems may have a very different set of hardware and software components, but using tools like Linux `top` and the PowerTOP will help you identify the time-consumers and serve as a guide to improving system idle-state overhead.

3. *Check BIOS settings*: As the next step after OS improvement, it is worth checking important parameters of the *basic input/output system (BIOS)*. Unlike BIOS setups in client platforms, BIOS in a server provides a lot more options to tune the system characteristics for different application workloads. While the available choice of settings is a very good way to support multiple different usages of the server platforms, it may also lead to inefficient settings for your specific applications. And although the OEMs delivering high-performance computing solutions try to configure their servers in a proper way, it may still be good to follow some basic recommendations for several important BIOS settings.

    The BIOS provides a summary of detected hardware: processor type and speed, memory capacity, and frequency. For instance, if there is a memory module failure, it will not be detected and presented by the BIOS to the operating system, and the server will boot. And if the memory module failure is not noticed, the system will continue working, but the memory capacity and performance will be lower than expected.

a. As the HPC applications performance is very often dependent on the memory subsystem performance, the settings affecting the main memory are among the most important to study. One of these settings is the "NUMA mode" selection. In multi-socket platforms with the memory controllers integrated into the processor running a modern OS, enabling the NUMA support presents the physical memory of the system as a split between the local and remote to each socket (as shown in Listing 2-1 in Chapter 2). Efficient use of NUMA requires software optimizations that we discuss in greater detail in Chapter 6.

b. The status of power management technologies and power/performance settings (such as Intel Enhanced SpeedStep Technology, EIST, and Intel Turbo Mode) are available in the BIOS setup to shift the balance between energy draw and performance: reducing the power draw may negatively affect the application's speed.

c. Another source of configuration issues may lay in excessive use of the resiliency technologies built into the memory subsystem. In order to increase server uptime and prevent crashes from memory failures, it is possible to configure so-called memory mirroring, sparing, or lockstep operations. These technologies help increase server availability, but they come at a cost to memory capacity and performance, sometimes impacting memory bandwidth by a factor of 2.

■ **Note**   For the best possible performance, check that the memory is configured in the *channel interleave* or the *independent mode* the BIOS.

Understanding System-Level Performance Limits

Practically, the best way to identify system-level issues is to check the major system parameters with simple yet powerful kernel tests. These tests usually do not take a lot of time to set up and run, and they are an essential part of the acceptance process when a supercomputer is handed over from the vendor to the customer. Moreover, periodic runs of these tests may reveal system health issues during its day-to-day operation. As the HPC software paradigm to a large extent relies on a high-performing cluster of uniform (in configuration and performance) computational nodes, running these tests on every node of the cluster will help to ensure performance uniformity across all similarly configured components in the HPC system.

We distinguish several important subsystems that the kernel benchmarks should focus on:

1. *Compute subsystem*: The main processors and coprocessors that can be installed in every cluster node.

2. *Main memory subsystem*: Test the main memory performance characteristics. When Intel Xeon Phi coprocessors are installed, the GDDR5 memory of the coprocessor card needs to be tested in similar way as the main memory.

3. *Cluster interconnect network*: Used to wire the computational nodes together and to access the high-performance storage subsystem.

Each subsystem can be tested separately, and the performance results can be compared to expected good values from the vendor datasheets, as well as between different cluster nodes. There are large numbers of application kernels that can be designed to check the efficiency of different subsystems. Here we review those that have proved to be useful in practice.

Checking General Compute Subsystem Performance

One of the widely used stress tests in HPC is the *High Performance Linpack* (HPL) benchmark. It is the benchmark used to rank supercomputers in the TOP500 list published at www.top500.org twice a year. Despite this, the relevance of the HPL to real HPC applications is debated. However, it can certainly be used to validate the system performance and stability. There are many reference results for different architectures found on the TOP500 list, which gives a baseline for comparison with your results. (In the following chapters we will also use HPL a couple of times for demonstration purposes.)

The main disadvantage of the HPL benchmark is that it may be hard to set up and find optimal parameters, so bad performance may be not an indication of a slow node or cluster but, rather, be the result of poor benchmark configuration. Also with HPL, it would be hard to identify a slow node in a cluster—in case one exists. This is why Intel engineers not only ship an optimized version of the HPL benchmark along with the Intel Math Kernel Library (MKL) but also provide a small program to test compute nodes performance called nodeperf.c. This is a simple MPI program that runs a highly optimized version of a double precision general matrix multiply (DGEMM) library routine from the MKL. This routine is also the core of the HPL test. As the MKL provides optimized versions of DGEMM and many other widely used routines, you can be sure that the test will be optimized for the latest Intel microprocessors.

Let's see how to check the uniformity and performance of an eight-node cluster using the nodeperf tool. First, you may need to load the environment variables for the Intel software tools to be used shortly. The first line will load the compiler environment settings into the Bash shell, and the second will set up variables for the Intel MPI library:

```
$ source /opt/intel/composerxe/bin/compilervars.sh intel64
$ source /opt/intel/impi_latest/intel64/bin/mpivars.sh
```

You will find the scripts for the C-shell under the same folder as the scripts for the Bash-compatible shells. The source code of the nodeperf application can be found in the source folder of the HPL benchmark that comes with the Intel MKL. If Intel Parallel Studio XE 2015 Cluster Edition is installed into its default folder, you can copy the nodeperf.c source file to your current directory, where the benchmark will be compiled and later executed (it is expected that this directory is shared among all cluster nodes):

```
$ cp $MKLROOT/benchmarks/mp_linpack/nodeperf.c ./
```

Compile the nodeperf program using the Intel MPI compile wrapper script for Intel compiler with the optimizations enabled to at least -O2 level, tuning for the instruction set supported on the build machine (either by using the -xHost or by directly specifying another instruction set target as described in Table 1-1), enabling OpenMP support (-qopenmp), and linking with the MKL library for the optimized version of the DGEMM routine (-mkl):

```
$ mpiicc -O2 -xHost -qopenmp -mkl nodeperf.c -o nodeperf
```

Successful completion of the command should produce an executable binary nodeperf in the current working directory. It is ready to run. Just before the run, however, you need to set a few important environment variables that control the number of OpenMP threads and their placement on the system:

```
$ export OMP_NUM_THREADS=24
$ export OMP_PLACES=cores
```

The first command requests 24 OpenMP threads. This is equal to the number of physical processor cores in every node of our cluster: each of two CPUs has 12 cores, so we ask exactly one thread per physical core. In case OMP_NUM_THREADS is not explicitly set up, the Open MP runtime library will use all processors visible to the OS, which, in the case of enabled Hyper Threading, will lead to assignment of two Open MP threads to each physical core. The OMP_PLACES environment variable instructs Intel OpenMP runtime to distribute threads between the cores in the system, so that two different threads will not run on one physical core. Now we're ready to start the test using the mpirun command that requests eight ranks (using the -np 8 option), with only one rank per node (-ppn 1):

```
$ mpirun -np 8 -ppn 1 -hosts esg003,esg004,esg005,esg006,esg007,esg008,esg00
9,esg010 ./nodeperf
```

■ **Note** The -hosts option for the mpirun command explicitly lists the names of hosts allocated for our job by the scheduler, and we provide it here for illustration purposes. More convenient is to provide the list of hosts the program will run on in a separate file; or in a majority of cases, Intel MPI can pick it up automatically from the resource manager of the job scheduling system. Please consult your cluster documentation to see how the MPI jobs are to be run on your cluster.

The output of nodeperf run is shown in Listing 4-3.

Listing 4-3. Example Output of nodeperf (Cluster, 8 Nodes)

```
Multi-threaded MPI detected

The time/date of the run... at Mon May 12 06:11:29 2014

This driver was compiled with:
        -DITER=4 -DLINUX -DNOACCUR -DPREC=double
Malloc done. Used 827090096 bytes
(0 of 8): NN lda=10000 ldb= 168 ldc=10000 0 0 0 519260.972 esg003
(1 of 8): NN lda=10000 ldb= 168 ldc=10000 0 0 0 506726.008 esg004
(2 of 8): NN lda=10000 ldb= 168 ldc=10000 0 0 0 517275.263 esg005
(3 of 8): NN lda=10000 ldb= 168 ldc=10000 0 0 0 519160.998 esg006
(4 of 8): NN lda=10000 ldb= 168 ldc=10000 0 0 0 512007.115 esg007
(5 of 8): NN lda=10000 ldb= 168 ldc=10000 0 0 0 513921.217 esg008
(6 of 8): NN lda=10000 ldb= 168 ldc=10000 0 0 0 530959.117 esg009
(7 of 8): NN lda=10000 ldb= 168 ldc=10000 0 0 0 515852.598 esg010
```

The last two columns present the achieved performance of the DGEMM routine in MFLOPS and the respective host name where the nodeperf was run. We immediately find that node esg004 is the slowest one and esg009 is the fastest, and the performance difference between the fastest and the slowest nodes is about 4.8 percent.

EXERCISE 4-1

Taking into account that our computational nodes are built using two Intel Xeon E5-2697 v2 processors (each with 12 cores and 2700 MHz nominal clock frequency), with support of the Intel AVX instruction set (so each core is capable of delivering up to 8 Flops/cycle in double precision), compare the performance achieved on every node as a ratio between the achieved performance and the peak performance.

After completing Exercise 4-1, you should have found that three nodes demonstrate performance higher than the theoretical peak. How is this possible? This happens because the peak performance was calculated using the nominal rated frequency of the processor (2.7 GHz). But by default, Intel Turbo Boost technology is enabled. This allows for processors running at a higher frequency than the nominal one when the CPU power consumption stays within the specification and the cooling system can cool the processor package below its critical temperature. An Intel Xeon E5-2697 v2 processor can run at a up to 300 MHz higher clock speed in the Turbo Boost, thus reaching up to 3 GHz. When Turbo Boost is disabled in BIOS settings, though, the processor clock frequency cannot exceed the nominal 2.7 GHz, and consequently the performance reported by nodeperf is lower, while still above 90 percent from the peak performance, as shown in Listing 4-4.

Listing 4-4. Output of nodeperf with Turbo Boost Disabled (Cluster, 8 Nodes)

```
Multi-threaded MPI detected

The time/date of the run... at Mon May 12 06:25:39 2014

This driver was compiled with:
        -DITER=4 -DLINUX -DNOACCUR -DPREC=double
Malloc done. Used 827090096 bytes
(0 of 8): NN lda=10000 ldb= 168 ldc=10000 0 0 0 482853.191 esg003
(1 of 8): NN lda=10000 ldb= 168 ldc=10000 0 0 0 469475.454 esg004
(2 of 8): NN lda=10000 ldb= 168 ldc=10000 0 0 0 469658.038 esg005
(3 of 8): NN lda=10000 ldb= 168 ldc=10000 0 0 0 480475.968 esg006
(4 of 8): NN lda=10000 ldb= 168 ldc=10000 0 0 0 469907.603 esg007
(5 of 8): NN lda=10000 ldb= 168 ldc=10000 0 0 0 479765.330 esg008
(6 of 8): NN lda=10000 ldb= 168 ldc=10000 0 0 0 480635.807 esg009
(7 of 8): NN lda=10000 ldb= 168 ldc=10000 0 0 0 469960.729 esg010
```

One final observation: this result also shows that the performance difference between the fastest and the slowest nodes in the cluster is only 2.8 percent and is lower than the case when the Turbo Boost is enabled. Turbo Boost can help achieve better performance results; however, the observed performance variations between the nodes will be higher, depending on each node's conditions.

Testing Memory Subsystem Performance

Memory subsystem performance can be quickly characterized by measuring the main memory bandwidth and the latency, and comparing results to the good expected values and the values for different cluster nodes.

1. *Characterizing memory bandwidth*: The most famous test to check the memory bandwidth is the STREAM benchmark:[7] it is quick, easy to set up, and easy to run. It consists of just one source file that can be downloaded from the official benchmark site. After downloading the source code, you can compile it using the Intel compiler as follows:

   ```
   $ icc -O3 -xHost -mcmodel=medium -qopenmp stream.c -o stream
   ```

   Also, before compilation, you may consider increasing the STREAM_ARRAY_SIZE parameter to increase the size of the memory used during the benchmark from the default 0.2 GiB,[8] which may be too small to get reproducible results. For instance, setting the STREAM_ARRAY_SIZE to 800000000 elements will cause the benchmark to use 18 GiB of memory. In this case the compiler option -mcmodel=medium is required to remove the restriction of 2 GiB on the size of the arrays.

Out of the entire output of the STREAM benchmark you may pick just the values of the TRIAD component that executes the following computational kernel a(i) = b(i) + q*c(i). For convenience, we have put the stream command and necessary parsing of the results into a shell script with the file name 2run.sh, shown in Listing 4-5. In that script we assume the script with environment variables settings and compiled stream binary reside in the same folder as the 2run.sh script file. To keep the scripts portable, we have also used a dynamic way to calculate the number of physical cores in the server and set OMP_NUM_THREADS variable to that value.

Listing 4-5. Contents of 2run.sh Script to Run STREAM Benchmark and Output TRIAD Result

```
#/bin/sh
. `dirname $0`/0env.sh
export OMP_NUM_THREADS=$(cat /proc/cpuinfo| awk 'BEGIN{cpus=0}
/processor/{cpus++}
/cpu cores/{cpu_cores=$4}
/siblings/{siblings=$3}
END{print cpus*cpu_cores/siblings}')
export OMP_PLACES=cores
`dirname $0`/stream | awk -v host=$(hostname) '/Triad:/{printf
"%s: %s\n",host,$2}'
```

You can run this script using the following command, assuming the current working directory where the script resides is accessible from all nodes.

```
$ mpirun -np 8 -ppn 1 ./2run.sh
```

■ **Note**   In this command, we omitted listing hostnames to run the test on, and depending on your cluster setup, you may or may not have to do it explicitly in the mpirun command.

This will produce the output presented in Listing 4-6.

Listing 4-6. Example Output of the STREAM Benchmark (Cluster, 8 Nodes)

```
esg145: 84845.0
esg215: 85768.2
esg281: 85984.2
esg078: 85965.3
esg150: 85990.6
esg084: 86068.5
esg187: 86006.9
esg171: 85789.7
```

The measured memory bandwidth around 85 GB/s represents approximately 83 percent of the peak memory bandwidth achieved by a dual-socket platform with quad channel DDR3 memory running at 1600 MHz. The above scores represent very good efficiency. The STREAM TRIAD benchmark should achieve values of 80 to 85 percent from the peak memory bandwidth on Xeon E5 platforms.

2. *Measuring memory latency*: The second component of the memory performance is the memory access latency. Unlike bandwidth, latency is much harder to measure correctly and to get results that make sense.

First, you need to decide on the conditions of the environment in which to measure latency, such as whether *idle latency* (when no other significant workload is running) or *loaded latency* is to be measured (when multiple workloads run at the same time). The former is a lot easier to implement, but you may need to make sure that processor cores do not go into a sleep state while measuring the idle latency. The latter will require additional applications executing to stress the memory bus and quantify the intensity of that workload.

a. While measuring memory latency you need to ensure the results are really *not including the caching effects*. The processor caches become larger and more sophisticated with each generation, and the tools must be updated to keep up with the improvements in the cache logic.

b. Finally, the more advanced characterization of the system will require a tool measuring not only memory latency but also cache access latency. And considering multi-socket systems, this tool should measure latency for accessing local and remote memory when systems with *non-uniform memory architecture* (NUMA) are benchmarked.

Several Intel engineers came together to write a memory latency checker tool that is designed to help quantify latency for accessing main memory and caches. Intel Memory Latency Checker[9] prints out a matrix of the latencies and bandwidths (for various read:write ratios) when accessing the local and remote memory nodes from all the sockets in a multi-socket system, as shown in Listing 4-7 for a dual-socket system. The advanced usages include options to measure specific configurations, such as cache latencies, loaded latency (to produce charts similar to Figure 2-15), bandwidth matrices, and so on. In order to precisely measure latency and bandwidth, the tool requires access to the processor's internal performance counters. To gain access to these counters, the tool must be run with root privileges. We achieved that via the sudo command.

Listing 4-7. Example Output of Intel Memory Latency Checker for a Dual-Processor Server

```
$ sudo ./mlc --latency_matrix

Intel(R) Memory Latency Checker - v2.1
Command line parameters: --latency_matrix

Using buffer size of 200.000MB
Measuring idle latencies (in ns)...
        Memory node
Socket    0      1
    0   69.7   123.7
    1   124.5   70.3
```

The results of the local and remote memory latencies allow measuring the NUMA factor between the NUMA nodes in the system; for our specific system, this yields a value around 1.77 between sockets 0 and 1 (calculated as the ratio between 123.7 and 69.7, taken from the output in Listing 4-7). This quantifies the impact of the wrong memory pinning on the memory access latency, which is specifically important for the OpenMP programs that we will discuss in Chapter 6.

EXERCISE 4-2

Run the STREAM benchmark and Intel Memory Latency Checker on your system to determine maximum achievable memory bandwidth and access latency. What share of the peak memory throughout is achieved on the STREAM test? If your system has NUMA architecture, what NUMA factor does it have?

Testing I/O Subsystem Performance

The input and output (I/O) subsystem deals with everything the computational node has to send to or receive from other computational or storage nodes in the HPC cluster. In many clusters, computational nodes use at least two interconnects: Gigabit Ethernet for general TCP/IP traffic supporting management and monitoring services (for instance, secure shell and Ganglia) and high-speed fabrics, such as InfiniBand, for low-latency and high-bandwidth remote direct memory access (RDMA) traffic of the user applications. Since an InfiniBand link is usually dedicated to the performance-critical data transfers, such as Message Passing Interface (MPI) or access to the parallel file systems, its performance is of main concern. (In Chapter 5 we will cover performance benchmarks using Intel MPI library, and the special suite of tests to validate MPI functions performance: Intel MPI Benchmarks (IMB).) For a basic platform I/O validation, and specifically for understanding if the system delivers expected RDMA performance between two nodes, there are a couple of simple tests available with any InfiniBand installation.

For instance, the software stack coming along with the InfiniBand network drivers usually contains a package called perftest with a set of low-level performance tests. These tests allow for measuring bandwidth and latency for typical RDMA commands, such as

- The read and write operations between two nodes: ib_read_bw, ib_write_bw, ib_read_lat, ib_write_lat,

- The send command and atomic transactions: ib_send_bw, ib_atomic_bw, ib_send_lat, ib_atomic_lat.

The tests require a server to be started on one of the nodes and the client on another. Let's take two nodes in our cluster (say, esg012 and esg013), and start a server on the node named esg012 as follows:

```
[esg012]$ ib_read_lat -d mlx4_0
```

Here, the option -d will request a specific InfiniBand device to be used (alternatively, the tool will select the first device found). The list of available RDMA devices can be obtained using the ibv_devices command, and for our cluster this list looks like this:

```
$ ibv_devices
    device             node GUID
    ------             ----------------
    scif0              001b68fffe3d7f7a
    mlx4_0             0002c903002f18b0
```

By providing the mlx4_0 argument in the command, we select that InfiniBand adapter. The same has to be done on client node, esg013, where in addition the hostname of the server should be given. The RDMA read latency test command executed on the client node esg013 and its output are presented in Listing 4-8.

Listing 4-8. Example Output of the RDMA Read Latency Test (Cluster)

```
[esg013]$ ib_read_lat -d mlx4_0 esg012
---------------------------------------------------------------------------
                      RDMA_Read Latency Test
Dual-port        : OFF            Device : mlx4_0
Number of qps    : 1
Connection type  : RC
TX depth         : 1
Mtu              : 4096B
Link type        : IB
Outstand reads   : 16
rdma_cm QPs      : OFF
Data ex. method  : Ethernet
---------------------------------------------------------------------------
```

```
local address: LID 0x130 QPN 0x0733 PSN 0xe892fa OUT 0x10 RKey 0x3010939
VAddr 0x00000000f60000
remote address: LID 0x179 QPN 0x06fe PSN 0x5afd2 OUT 0x10 RKey 0x010933
VAddr 0x000000015c8000
---------------------------------------------------------------------
#bytes  #iterations  t_min[usec]   t_max[usec]  t_typical[usec]
2       1000         1.85          20.96        1.91
---------------------------------------------------------------------
```

Here, the measured latency for the 2-bytes messages is equal to 1.91 microseconds. Note that remote direct memory access to a different node takes approximately 15 times longer than access to the memory of the remote socket, and it takes 27 times longer than access to the local memory.

The bandwidth tests are run in a similar way. It may be interesting to see bandwidth for different message sizes, which can be measured by adding the -a command option. Listing 4-9 contains a typical output produced on a client compute nodes for a unidirectional write bandwidth test to the server on the node esg012.

Listing 4-9. Output of the Unidirectional RDMA Read Bandwidth Test (Cluster)

```
[esg013]$ ib_read_bw -a -d mlx4_0 esg012
---------------------------------------------------------------------
                     RDMA_Read BW Test
Dual-port        : OFF          Device : mlx4_0
Number of qps    : 1
Connection type  : RC
TX depth         : 128
CQ Moderation    : 100
Mtu              : 4096B
Link type        : IB
Outstand reads   : 16
rdma_cm QPs      : OFF
Data ex. method  : Ethernet
---------------------------------------------------------------------
local address: LID 0x130 QPN 0x0730 PSN 0x7540e6 OUT 0x10 RKey 0x18010939
VAddr 0x02b15b6bcf000
remote address: LID 0x179 QPN 0x06fc PSN 0x56dc8e OUT 0x10 RKey 0xf0010932
VAddr 0x02b826895800
```

#bytes	#iterations	BW peak[MB/sec]	BW average[MB/sec]	MsgRate[Mpps]
2	1000	8.11	7.82	4.098211
4	1000	16.56	16.55	4.337238
8	1000	33.12	33.07	4.334843
16	1000	66.13	66.07	4.329837
32	1000	132.47	132.43	4.339469
64	1000	264.09	254.07	4.162761
128	1000	517.41	509.61	4.174733
256	1000	1059.77	1059.05	4.337851
512	1000	2119.55	2116.35	4.334286
1024	1000	4205.29	4203.23	4.304106
2048	1000	5414.21	5410.27	2.770060
4096	1000	4939.99	4939.20	1.264436
8192	1000	5251.12	5250.99	0.672127
16384	1000	5267.51	5267.00	0.337088
32768	1000	5256.68	5256.65	0.168213
65536	1000	5263.24	5262.24	0.084196
131072	1000	5264.72	5262.55	0.042100
262144	1000	5271.87	5271.63	0.021087
524288	1000	5272.98	5270.55	0.010541
1048576	1000	5274.57	5273.48	0.005273
2097152	1000	5272.47	5271.77	0.002636
4194304	1000	5271.72	5270.81	0.001318
8388608	1000	5272.14	5270.38	0.000659

Using the default settings for the benchmark, we see that the maximum bandwidth achieved on this test is equal to 5.4 GB/s, which represents approximately 80 percent from the peak bandwidth of the InfiniBand link speed of around 6.8 GB/s.

EXERCISE 4-3

Run the perftest benchmarks on your favorite system to determine the maximum achievable interconnect bandwidth and the latency for RDMA network traffic. What share of the peak network speed is achieved on the bandwidth tests?

Characterizing Application System-Level Issues

System-level bottlenecks determine the performance of well-written and optimized applications. Improving the system characteristics, then, that are in direct relation to the application's slowest path, such as increasing CPU frequency for a compute bound code, will result in improved performance. But how does one find out what system feature is limiting the application performance? And what is the knowledge this investigation will give us?

The second question is rather easy to answer: finding out that an application is memory bandwidth or I/O bandwidth bound (that is, it spends most of the time transferring data to and from memory or over interconnect) will lead to decisions on how to improve performance. Taking into account Amdahl's Law and the roofline model discussed in Chapter 2, an understanding of the share of I/O or memory dependent execution time may guide you to a quantitative assessment of potential improvements and provide ideas for improving the algorithms.

Selecting Performance Characterization Tools

Historically, performance issues were qualified as system-level bottlenecks when a specific device—for instance, a disk or a network card—took a significant amount of time to process data requested by the application. When this happened, the system time (as opposite to the user time) consumed by the application was rather high. Thus, it was enough to look at the utilization and notice high system time, sometimes accompanied by low overall processor utilization, to conclude that an application had a system-level bottleneck. And this observation still holds: high system time reported by the standard UNIX/Linux time command still means that the respective application has bottlenecks at the system level. However, the opposite is not always true: an application may have no visible system time reported but still be limited in performance by system characteristics. To characterize system-level bottlenecks and identify what components of the system limit application performance, then, some additional tools are needed besides the simple observations done using the top or time commands.

Operating systems, such as Linux, have a rich set of tools developed to analyze system behavior under stress. Most of them may be found useful for system-level analysis and beyond. In general, the tools differ by how they gather information about system behavior: software-based counters or special performance counters built into the hardware. For example, in Linux, the perf utility embedded in the Linux kernel has great support and monitoring capabilities based on the software counters from the Linux kernel and the hardware counters in the processor. Many other monitoring tools generally shipped with the operating system—for instance, vmstat, iostat, and top—rely on the software counters from the operating system kernel.

Intel processors have many performance counters integrated in hardware that can report resource utilization and occurrence of specific run-time events. Since modern Intel processors for server applications contain integrated memory and I/O controllers, measuring the memory subsystem and I/O bus utilization has become a lot easier. However, the presence of counters themselves will not ensure the measurements are done. Special tools are required to access these counters and present their values in a meaningful way.

One of the easiest tools to use to characterize processor utilization is the Intel Performance Counter Monitor (Intel PCM).[10] In fact, today PCM is a "Swiss army knife" for system-level performance analysis and for quantifying the utilization of various system resources. In addition to the pcm command's characterizing compute core utilization, you will find tools for memory and PCI Express (PCIe) bus utilization, and even a power analyzer. Most of the PCM tools provide both interactive, top-like output and output to the comma-separated list (CSV) files for subsequent analysis using Excel or other tools. PCM is written in C++ and is also available as a library that can be used to instrument third-party applications to generate a detailed summary that covers all important parts of the application code. The use of the Open Source Initiative (OSI) BSD license makes them usable even inside commercial closed-source products. The tool is available on Linux, Microsoft Windows, FreeBSD, and Apple MacOS operating systems running on Intel Xeon, Core, and Atom processors.

Let's review a typical example of the I/O and memory utilization analysis done using Intel PCM tools. After downloading the source code of the tool from the Intel's website, you need to unpack the archive using the unzip command and then compile it. A simple make command will do all that is needed, based on the supplied Makefile, to produce several PCM tools:

- pcm.x: A command line PCM utility for monitoring core utilization, including counting the number of executed instructions, cache misses, and core temperature and per-core energy consumption.

- pcm-memory.x: A tool for reading memory throughout utilization.

- pcm-numa.x: A performance counter monitoring utility for NUMA, providing results for remote and local memory accesses.

- pcm-pcie.x: A command-line utility for monitoring PCIe bus utilization (for processors with an integrated PCIe I/O controller).

- pcm-power.x: A power-monitoring utility, reporting the power drawn by the cores and the memory, frequency residencies and transition statistics, and the number of cycles the processor was throttled, as well as many other power-related events.

- pcm-tsx.x: A performance- monitoring utility for Intel Transactional Synchronization Extensions, available in processors with Haswell microarchitecture.

In addition to the command-line monitoring tools, you will find a utility to view and change the values of the processor model specific registers (MSRs) called pcm-msr.x, and the pcm-sensor.x to produce visual plots using the KSysGuard utility from KDE. All PCM tools require direct access to the processor's MSRs, and thus call for administrative privileges; for that purpose, the PCM tools should be started using the sudo command.

Intel VTune Amplifier XE[11] (we refer to it as "VTune" throughout this chapter) provides access to the processor performance counters and has a rich user interface for data visualization and analysis. We will talk more about VTune for multithreaded application analysis in Chapter 6 and microarchitecture-level tuning in Chapter 7, but it is also useful for some system-level bottleneck characterization that we outline in this chapter. (In the following chapters of this book we will provide examples of how VTune could help you to extract knowledge about your application behavior and to pinpoint potential areas for performance improvement.)

Monitoring the I/O Utilization

One of the major innovations in the Intel processor microarchitecture, codenamed "Sandy Bridge," was integration of the PCI Express (PCIe) bus into the CPU. Together with the integrated PCIe logic on the processor die, respective performance counters were made available in the same way as were the ones for the core and the memory controller in previous generations of Intel microprocessors. Intel PCM added reading PCIe bus utilization counters in a tool called pcm-pcie.x, which is available for Intel Sandy Bridge and following microarchitectures. Since all the input/output devices are connected to the PCIe bus, by reading the PCIe bus utilization you can now gauge specific I/O utilization rates. These measurements may be complementary to the well-known ones in Linux utilities like iostat or iotop, or other vendor-specific tools designed for the network and storage controllers.

Let's look at how a basic I/O characterization can be made using the IOR benchmark.[12] We chose this benchmark because it provides a simple and straightforward way to test local and parallel file systems, accessing them via popular HPC interfaces such as MPI I/O and HDF5,[13] and via portable operating system interface (POSIX).[14] After downloading and unpacking the latest version, you may need to edit the file src/C/Makefile.config to specify the Intel MPI wrapper for the C-compiler by setting the variable CC.Linux to mpiicc. In the course of our demonstrations, we will use only MPI I/O interface, so a command make mpiio should produce a binary named IOR in the src/C folder. Then, you need to set up a sample test script with the contents shown in Listing 4-10:

Listing 4-10. Contents of the test_script File for the IOR Benchmark

```
IOR START
# MPIIO shared file test
    reordertasksconstant=1 # defeat buffer cache for read after write by
reordering tasks
    fsync=1 # call fsync for POSIX I/O before close
    intraTestBarriers=1 # use barriers between open/read/write/close
    repetitions=2
    verbose=2
    keepFile=0
    segmentCount=10000
    blockSize=1000000

    fsync=0
    filePerProc=0
    api=MPIIO # Compare MPIIO to POSIX shared
    collective=1 # enables data shipping optimization
    testFile = IOR_MPIIO_Test # File name
    transferSize=100000 # I/O call size
    RUN
IOR STOP
```

You should adjust the segmentCount parameter to ensure that the IOR benchmark files are not cached in the memory. The value of the segmentCount should be chosen so that the total amount of data written is greater than 1.5 times the available physical memory in the compute clients involved in the test, so as to avoid OS caching effects. The total size of the produced file, filesize, is given by the following formula:

```
filesize = segmentCount × blocksize × number of clients
```

Now you are ready to run the IOR benchmark. Let's start it on workstation with two local disks set up in a mirror. Launch the following command:

```
$ mpirun -np 24 ./IOR -f test_script
```

It will execute the IOR benchmark using 24 client processes with the input configuration file called test_script. IOR will execute both read and write tests for each run, doing two repetitions of each and calculating the maximum values. The bandwidth numbers of interest are the results listed as the *Max Write* and *Max Read* measured in *MB/s*.

While the benchmark is running, let's see a couple of tools to measure bandwidth stress on the I/O subsystem that is being created by the IOR benchmark. A very rough idea can be obtained by running the following command:

```
$ vmstat 1
```

It will print every second (or whatever interval you provide in the command line) statistics, as shown in Listing 4-11.

Listing 4-11. Output of vmstat Utility for 3 Seconds

```
procs -----------memory------------ --swap-- ---io--- --system-- -----cpu-----
 r  b  swpd free      buff   cache      si  so  bi bo    in    cs   us sy id wa st
12  4  4584 25969780 330260 94560032  0   0    0  88474 13029 3982 24 1  70 5  0
22  4  4584 24923576 330260 95468896  0   0    0  91750 12395 3892 22 1  70 7  0
 8  4  4584 23479916 330264 96865168  0   0    0  91750 10919 3599 20 1  73 6  0
```

The most interesting columns are labeled *bi* ("bytes in," or read from the I/O devices) and *bo* ("bytes out," or written to the I/O devices), showing I/O load in KiB (that is, multiples of 1024 bytes). The above example shows that around 90 megabytes were written in the last second. Another key system statistic is the number of interrupts (labeled *in*) processed every second, which in this example is over 10,000, and that accounts for the 6 percent wait time reported in the column *wa*.

■ **Note**   For a successful system-level performance characterization, it is essential to have an in-depth understanding of other capabilities of the vmstat and other standard tools provided by the operating system. An introduction to all these tools goes beyond the scope for this book; we strongly recommend you become familiar with the following standard Linux tools:

top - displays Linux tasks

ps - produces snapshot of the current processes

iostat - shows CPU, disk I/O, and NFS statistics

vmstat - displays virtual memory usage

mpstat - reports processors related information

sysctl - configures Linux kernel parameters at runtime

A very nice tool to capture I/O utilization statistics and see them per process in a top-like output is the iotop.[15] It has to be run as root as follows:

```
$ sudo iotop
```

The output of the iotop is presented in Figure 4-2. This output shows both the total disk bandwidth (around 60 MB/s) and the sustained I/O bandwidth per application process, such as 2.3 MB/s for the IOR instances.

```
Total DISK READ: 0.00 B/s | Total DISK WRITE: 61.35 M/s                    ▲
  TID  PRIO  USER      DISK READ  DISK WRITE  SWAPIN     IO>    COMMAND
 3728 be/3 root        0.00 B/s    0.00 B/s   0.00 % 99.31 % [jbd2/dm-5-8]
22102 be/4 book        0.00 B/s    2.31 M/s   0.00 % 69.67 % ./IOR -f test_script
 1447 be/4 root        0.00 B/s    0.00 B/s   0.00 % 61.17 % [kmirrord]
22116 be/4 book        0.00 B/s    2.28 M/s   0.00 % 12.24 % ./IOR -f test_script
22122 be/4 book        0.00 B/s    2.21 M/s   0.00 %  6.13 % ./IOR -f test_script
22115 be/4 book        0.00 B/s    2.28 M/s   0.00 %  5.99 % ./IOR -f test_script
22103 be/4 book        0.00 B/s    2.38 M/s   0.00 %  5.97 % ./IOR -f test_script
22119 be/4 book        0.00 B/s    2.28 M/s   0.00 %  0.29 % ./IOR -f test_script
22109 be/4 book        0.00 B/s    2.37 M/s   0.00 %  0.00 % ./IOR -f test_script
22111 be/4 book        0.00 B/s    2.28 M/s   0.00 %  0.00 % ./IOR -f test_script
22099 be/4 book        0.00 B/s    2.37 M/s   0.00 %  0.00 % ./IOR -f test_script
22100 be/4 book        0.00 B/s    2.28 M/s   0.00 %  0.00 % ./IOR -f test_script
22101 be/4 book        0.00 B/s    2.37 M/s   0.00 %  0.00 % ./IOR -f test_script
22104 be/4 book        0.00 B/s    2.38 M/s   0.00 %  0.00 % ./IOR -f test_script
22105 be/4 book        0.00 B/s    2.29 M/s   0.00 %  0.00 % ./IOR -f test_script
22106 be/4 book        0.00 B/s    2.38 M/s   0.00 %  0.00 % ./IOR -f test_script
22107 be/4 book        0.00 B/s    2.28 M/s   0.00 %  0.00 % ./IOR -f test_script
22108 be/4 book        0.00 B/s    2.37 M/s   0.00 %  0.00 % ./IOR -f test_script
22110 be/4 book        0.00 B/s    2.38 M/s   0.00 %  0.00 % ./IOR -f test_script
22112 be/4 book        0.00 B/s    2.38 M/s   0.00 %  0.00 % ./IOR -f test_script
22113 be/4 book        0.00 B/s    2.29 M/s   0.00 %  0.00 % ./IOR -f test_script
22114 be/4 book        0.00 B/s    2.28 M/s   0.00 %  0.00 % ./IOR -f test_script
22117 be/4 book        0.00 B/s    2.29 M/s   0.00 %  0.00 % ./IOR -f test_script
22118 be/4 book        0.00 B/s    2.28 M/s   0.00 %  0.00 % ./IOR -f test_script
22120 be/4 book        0.00 B/s    2.38 M/s   0.00 %  0.00 % ./IOR -f test_script
22121 be/4 book        0.00 B/s    2.28 M/s   0.00 %  0.00 % ./IOR -f test_script
 4096 be/4 root        0.00 B/s    0.00 B/s   0.00 %  0.00 % [kondemand/38]
    1 be/4 root        0.00 B/s    0.00 B/s   0.00 %  0.00 % init
    2 be/4 root        0.00 B/s    0.00 B/s   0.00 %  0.00 % [kthreadd]       ▼
```

Figure 4-2. Output of the iotop utility obtained while running the IOR write performance test

The IOR disk test takes almost an hour on our workstation and completes with the performance summary showing an average sustained write and read bandwidth of 82.93 MiB/s and 60.76 MiB/s, respectively:

```
access bw(MiB/s) block(KiB) xfer(KiB) open(s)  wr/rd(s) close(s) total(s) iter
------ --------- ---------- --------- -------- -------- -------- -------- ----
write  82.93     976.56     97.66     0.001178 2760.02  0.000192 2760.02  0
read   50.76     976.56     97.66     0.000257 4509     0.000111 4509     1
```

Let us now see a more complex example, when vmstat and other tools reading the operating system state will not help. Specifically, when a parallel file system is connected using a high-speed fabric such as InfiniBand, the file system also often provides its own set of drivers and tools to manage the mount points. Such an example would be a high-performance IBM General Parallel File System (GPFS).[16] In our next example, we run the same IOR benchmark and measure performance during its read test.

The parameter testFile in the test_script file is changed to a new location residing in the GPFS storage. The vmstat command executed on one of the compute nodes participating in the IOR test showed no I/O activity at all. However, the presence of large I/O happening on the node is indicated by around 20,000 interrupts processed every second:

```
$ vmstat 1
procs ----------memory----------  --swap--  --io-- ---system-- ------cpu------
 r  b   swpd free     buff  cache   si  so   bi  bo  in    cs    us sy id wa st
17  0   0    62642488 4692  118004  0   0    0   0   20701 73598 69 7  25 0  0
15  0   0    62642244 4692  118004  0   0    0   0   19221 66678 70 7  23 0  0
14  0   0    62642932 4692  118004  0   0    0   0   21165 77092 69 6  25 0  0
```

To quantify the rate of data transfer, better tools are needed. We know that on this cluster, the compute nodes use the InfiniBand network to access the storage servers, and that the InfiniBand adapter is connected to the Intel Xeon processor via the PCI Express bus. By analyzing the amount of traffic going via the PCIe bus, we could estimate the bandwidth achieved by each node. Using the pcm-pcie.x tool from the Intel PCM toolset will help us quantify the I/O load on the client nodes. The tool uses performance counters to report the number of cache lines read and written by the I/O controller integrated into the processors. So, to see the PCIe bus load, execute the following command:

```
$ sudo ./pcm-pcie.x -B 1
```

In this command, the option -B instructs the tool not only to report the number of written cache lines but also to estimate the bandwidth, while the number provided as the command-line option indicates the required refresh interval. The tool produced output every second, as shown in Figure 4-3:

```
Skt | PCIePRd | PCIeRdCur | PCIeNSRd | PCIeWiLF | PCIeItoM | PCIeNSWr | PCIeNSWrF | PCIe Rd (B) | PCIe Wr (B)
 0      0        12 M        0          0          2779       0          0           820 M         177 K
 1      0        0           0          0          0          0          0           0             0
-----------------------------------------------------------------------------------------------------------
 *      0        12 M        0          0          2779       0          0           820 M         177 K
```

Figure 4-3. Output of the pcm-pcie.x tool

In Figure 4-3, we clearly see the estimated read bandwidth of 820 MB/s, via over 12 million of 64 byte cache-line transfers done every second through the integrated I/O controller of one of the sockets (specifically, the processor socket 0). This observation gives us a clear indication of the system I/O utilization by the IOR benchmark. Previously we had found that the InfiniBand network can transfer data at rates exceeding 5.4 GB/s, so the IOR benchmark consumes approximately 15 percent of the available bandwidth; the bottleneck in this particular case is not in the network but, rather, likely in the storage servers or the disk shelves. As another observation, the bandwidth to read data from a shared parallel file system is over 16 times higher than for a standard SATA spinning disk.

```
                          EXERCISE 4-4
```

Characterize your favorite application to measure the consumed I/O bandwidth using
the different tools described above. How much bandwidth is used from the peak
throughput? Note: you may need to additionally consult the datasheets for your local
disks if the local file I/O is used.

Analyzing Memory Bandwidth

The memory traffic intensity can be observed using the pcm-memory.x tool from the
Intel Performance Counter toolset. As an example, let's look at how to monitor the
STREAM benchmark. STREAM is a small kernel benchmark that is good for reference, as
it prints its own performance, so the monitoring tool can be calibrated this way. Launch
STREAM benchmark as we described in the earlier section "Testing Memory Subsystem
Performance" and in a separate terminal window start the pcm-memory.x using the
following command:

```
$ sudo ./pcm-memory.x
```

The output produced with the default refresh of 1 second is shown in Listing 4-12.
The tool measures memory bandwidth observed for every channel (four, in case of Intel
Xeon E5-2600 series), reporting separately throughput for reads from the memory and
writes to the memory. We see that each memory channel is utilized to approximately
11 GB/s and that the total memory utilization is around 87832.62 MB/s, which is close
to the benchmark's own report of around 86,000 MB/s (as presented in Listing 4-3). The
PCM tool tends to report values slightly higher than the application's own measurement
because the PCM measures *all* memory traffic, not only that specific to the application or
specific to the arrays being monitored inside the benchmark.

Listing 4-12. Output of PCM Memory Monitoring Tool while Characterizing the STREAM Benchmark

```
---------------------------------------||---------------------------------------
--            Socket 0              --||--            Socket 1              --
---------------------------------------||---------------------------------------
---------------------------------------||---------------------------------------
---------------------------------------||---------------------------------------
--  Memory Performance Monitoring   --||--  Memory Performance Monitoring   --
---------------------------------------||---------------------------------------
--  Mem Ch 0: Reads (MB/s): 6847.91 --||--  Mem Ch 0: Reads (MB/s): 6829.25 --
--           Writes(MB/s): 4137.15 --||--           Writes(MB/s): 4133.35 --
--  Mem Ch 1: Reads (MB/s): 6855.36 --||--  Mem Ch 1: Reads (MB/s): 6834.53 --
--           Writes(MB/s): 4136.61 --||--           Writes(MB/s): 4128.56 --
--  Mem Ch 4: Reads (MB/s): 6847.00 --||--  Mem Ch 4: Reads (MB/s): 6828.56 --
--           Writes(MB/s): 4138.83 --||--           Writes(MB/s): 4134.27 --
--  Mem Ch 5: Reads (MB/s): 6864.27 --||--  Mem Ch 5: Reads (MB/s): 6844.44 --
--           Writes(MB/s): 4139.95 --||--           Writes(MB/s): 4132.56 --
-- NODE0 Mem Read (MB/s): 27414.54  --||-- NODE1 Mem Read (MB/s): 27336.79  --
-- NODE0 Mem Write (MB/s): 16552.54 --||-- NODE1 Mem Write (MB/s): 16528.75 --
-- NODE0 P. Write (T/s): 49936444   --||-- NODE1 P. Write (T/s): 49307477   --
-- NODE0 Memory (MB/s): 43967.07    --||-- NODE1 Memory (MB/s): 43865.54    --
---------------------------------------||---------------------------------------
--          System Read Throughput(MB/s): 54751.32                          --
--          System Write Throughput(MB/s): 33081.29                         --
--          System Memory Throughput(MB/s): 87832.62                        --
---------------------------------------||---------------------------------------
```

Another way to observe sustained memory utilization is to use Intel VTune Amplifier XE. VTune provides a graphical interface and, among many other things, reports memory bandwidth utilization of the application. Let's consider a quick example of the memory bandwidth analysis using the graphical interface of VTune.

First, in a terminal window under the X-window system, source the environment settings for Bash compatible shells as:

```
$ source /opt/intel/vtune_amplifier_xe/amplxe-vars.sh
```

and for C-shell variants as:

```
$ source /opt/intel/vtune_amplifier_xe/amplxe-vars.csh
```

These scripts will update all the necessary environment variables. For convenience, you can change your working directory to the folder where the STREAM benchmark is located. Now, start the VTune graphical user interface (GUI) using the amplxe-gui command, create a project, and specify the path to the STREAM benchmark script that was presented earlier. Go to the New Analysis, select Bandwidth analysis, and click the Start button. VTune will start the benchmark and will wait until the application finishes. You can always press the Stop button to interrupt the benchmark and proceed to analysis; VTune will terminate the application then. After VTune finishes parsing the performance profile, you will be able to find the consumed bandwidth timeline per processor package in the Bottom-up tab, as shown in Figure 4-4.

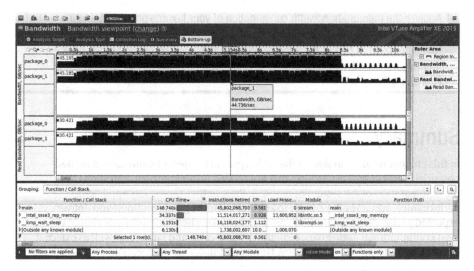

Figure 4-4. *Memory bandwidth analysis for the STREAM benchmark with Intel VTune Amplifier XE 2015*

The values of the sustained memory bandwidth observed in VTune are similar to those presented by PCM: around 44 GB/s for each processor socket, where approximately 30 GB/s are taken by the memory read traffic. The graphical representation of the timeline in VTune provides additional information, such as a clearly defined memory allocation phase, followed by 10 iterations of four benchmark kernels (called COPY, SCALE, ADD, and TRIAD), and finally the verification stage. The visual representation of the memory bandwidth over time helps you to see immediately what part of the application is memory bandwidth bound.

Of course, VTune provides a great set of additional features beyond counting certain event occurrences, such as finding that the average number of the processor clocks per instruction (CPI) for the STREAM is over 9.5. Based on the statistical event sampling, VTune allows you to drill down to the specific parts of your code and correlate the performance of many simultaneously collected events with the time taken by the specific code path.

In the following chapters you will find many more examples of using VTune to analyze applications performance, with a detailed introduction to VTune in Chapter 6.

EXERCISE 4-5

Analyze the memory bandwidth consumption of your favorite program using the different tools described above. How much bandwidth is used from the peak throughput? What part of the application consumes over 80 percent of the peak memory bandwidth available in your specific system, found as the result of doing Exercise 4-2?

Summary

In this chapter we have looked at the main types of bottlenecks and have classified potential issues at the system level that are related to environment conditions or the configuration of the system operations. Prior to fine-tuning any application performance, you want the system to achieve a known good condition and deliver expected performance on basic kernel benchmarks. These microkernels should cover at least computational performance, memory bandwidth and latency, as well as external interconnect bandwidth and latency. Good candidates for such tests are:

- DGEMM, with the nodeperf program coming with Intel Math Kernel Library, to test computational performance.

- STREAM benchmark to measure memory bandwidth, and Intel Memory Latency Checker to assess memory latency.

- For RDMA-capable high-performance interconnects such as InfiniBand, the perftest to find maximum achievable bandwidth and minimum latency.

The application performance dependency on the system-level characteristics can be understood by monitoring the resource utilization using tools that rely on the software performance counters (top, vmstat, iostat) and the utilities that collect data from the built-in hardware performance counters (Intel VTune, Intel PCM, perf).

References

1. "MCElog project," http://freecode.com/projects/mcelog.

2. Intel Open Source Technology Center, "PowerTOP Home," http://01.org/powertop.

3. Intel Corporation, "Intelligent Platform Management Interface," http://www.intel.com/content/www/us/en/servers/ipmi/ipmi-home.html.

4. "lm_sensors - Linux hardware monitoring," http://lm-sensors.org.

5. "Ganglia Monitoring System," http://ganglia.sourceforge.net.

6. "The Industry Standard In IT Infrastructure Monitoring," http://www.nagios.org.

7. John D. McCalpin, "Memory Bandwidth and Machine Balance in Current High Performance Computers", *IEEE Computer Society Technical Committee on Computer Architecture (TCCA) Newsletter*, p. 19-25, December 1995.

8. "Orders of Magnitude (data)," http://en.wikipedia.org/wiki/Orders_of_magnitude_(data).

9. Intel Corporation, "Intel Memory Latency Checker," https://software.intel.com/en-us/articles/intelr-memory-latency-checker.

10. Intel Corporation, "Intel Performance Counter Monitor: A better way to measure CPU utilization," https://software.intel.com/en-us/articles/intel-performance-counter-monitor-a-better-way-to-measure-cpu-utilization.

11. Intel Corporation, "Intel VTune Amplifier XE," https://software.intel.com/en-us/intel-vtune-amplifier-xe.

12. "IOR HPC benchmark," http://sourceforge.net/projects/ior-sio/.

13. HDF Group, "HDF5 Home Page," http://www.hdfgroup.org/HDF5/.

14. "POSIX," http://en.wikipedia.org/wiki/POSIX.

15. G. Chazarain, "Iotop," http://guichaz.free.fr/iotop/.

16. IBM, "IBM Platform Computing Elastic Storage," www-03.ibm.com/systems/platformcomputing/products/gpfs/.

■ ■ ■

## CHAPTER 5

Addressing Application Bottlenecks: Distributed Memory

The first application optimization level accessible to the ever-busy performance analyst is the distributed memory one, normally expressed in terms of the Message Passing Interface (MPI).[1] By its very nature, the distributed memory paradigm is concerned with communication. Some people consider all communication as *overhead*—that is, something intrinsically harmful that needs to be eliminated. We tend to call it "investment." Indeed, by moving data around in the right manner, you hope to get more computational power in return. The main point, then, is to optimize this investment so that your returns are maximized.

The time spent on the problem analysis and solution is an integral part of the overall investment. Hence, it is important to detect quickly what direction may be successful and what is going to be a waste of time, and to focus on the most promising leads. Following this pragmatic approach, in this chapter we will show how to detect and exploit optimization opportunities in the realm of communication patterns. Further chapters will step deeper into the increasingly local optimization levels. "And where are the algorithms?" you may ask. Well, we will deal with them as we go along, because algorithms will cross our path at every possible level. If you have ever tried to optimize bubble sort and then compared the result with the quick sort, you will easily appreciate the importance of algorithmic optimization.

Algorithm for Optimizing MPI Performance

Here is the algorithm we will use to optimize MPI performance, inspired in part by the work done by our friends and colleagues:[2]

1. Comprehend the underlying MPI performance.

2. Do an initial performance investigation of the application.

3. If the initial investigation indicates that performance may
    be improved, do an in-depth MPI analysis and optimization
    using the closed-loop approach, as follows:

    a. Get an overview of the application scalability and
        performance.

    b. If a load imbalance exceeds the cost of communication,
        address the load imbalance first or else perform MPI
        optimization.

    c. Repeat while performance improves and you still have
        time left.

4. Proceed to the node-level MPI optimization.

Let's go through these steps in detail.

Comprehending the Underlying MPI Performance

About the only sure way to grasp what is happening with application performance is to do benchmarking. Occasionally, you can deduce a performance estimate by plugging numbers into an analytical model that links, say, the estimated execution time to certain factors like the number of processes and their layout. However, this is more often the exception than the rule.

Recalling Some Benchmarking Basics

The first rule in benchmarking is to have a clean system setup. You have learned how to achieve that in Chapter 4. It may not always be possible to get to the ideal, no-interference situation, especially if you are doing your measurements on a system that is being utilized by many users at the same time, as they normally are. In this case, you will have to do several runs per parameter combination, possibly at different times of the day and week, and then apply statistical methods—or at least common sense—to estimate how reliable your data is.

To estimate the system variability, as well as to learn more about the underlying MPI performance, you may want to run Intel MPI Benchmarks (IMB).[3] Once started on a number of processes, this handy MPI benchmark will output timings, bandwidths, and other relevant information for several popular point-to-point and collective exchange patterns. You can also use any other benchmark you trust, but for now we will concentrate on the IMB, which was developed with the specific goal of representing typical application-level MPI use cases.

Gauging Default Intranode Communication Performance

Let us look first into the intranode communication—that is, data transfers done within one node. It is fairly easy to get started on IMB. The binary executable file IMB-MPI1 is provided as part of the Intel MPI library distribution. Having set up the Intel MPI environment as described in Chapter 4, you can run this MPI program now in the way you probably know better than we do. On a typical system with the Intel MPI library installed, this would look as follows:

```
$ mpirun -np 2 ./IMB-MPI1 PingPong
```

By default, the Intel MPI library will try to select the fastest possible communication path for any particular runtime configuration. Here, the most likely candidate is the shared memory channel. On our workstation, this leads to the output (skipping unessential parts) shown in Listing 5-1:

Listing 5-1. Example IMB-MPI1 Output (Workstation, Intranode)

```
#-----------------------------------------------------
# Benchmarking PingPong
# #processes = 2
#-----------------------------------------------------
      #bytes #repetitions      t[usec]   Mbytes/sec
           0         1000         1.16         0.00
           1         1000         0.78         1.22
           2         1000         0.75         2.53
           4         1000         0.78         4.89
           8         1000         0.78         9.77
          16         1000         0.78        19.55
          32         1000         0.88        34.50
          64         1000         0.89        68.65
         128         1000         0.99       123.30
         256         1000         1.04       234.54
         512         1000         1.16       420.02
        1024         1000         1.38       706.15
        2048         1000         1.63      1199.68
        4096         1000         2.48      1574.10
        8192         1000         3.74      2090.00
       16384         1000         7.05      2214.91
       32768         1000        12.95      2412.56
       65536          640        14.93      4184.94
      131072          320        25.40      4921.88
      262144          160        44.55      5611.30
      524288           80        91.16      5485.08
     1048576           40       208.15      4804.20
     2097152           20       444.45      4499.96
     4194304           10       916.46      4364.63
```

The PingPong test is an elementary point-to-point exchange pattern, in which one MPI process sends a message to another and expects a matching response in return. Half of the turnaround time measured is dubbed "latency" in this case, and the message size divided by latency is called "bandwidth." These two numbers constitute the two most important characteristics of a message-passing communication path for a particular message size. If you want to reduce this to just two numbers for the whole message range, take the zero-byte message latency and the peak bandwidth at whatever message size it is achieved. Note, however, that IMB performance may differ from what you see in a real application.

From the output shown here we can deduce that zero-byte message latency is equal to 1.16 microseconds, while the maximum bandwidth of 5.6 GB/s is achieved on messages of 256 KiB. This is what the shared memory communication channel, possibly with some extra help from the networking card and other MPI implementor tricks, is capable of achieving in the default Intel MPI configuration. Note that the default intranode MPI latency in particular is 7 to 20 times the memory access latency, depending on the exact communication path taken (compare Listing 5-4). This is the price you pay for the MPI flexibility, and this is why people call all communication "overhead." This overhead is what may make threading a viable option in some cases.

■ **Note**   The Intel MPI Library is tuned by default for better bandwidth rather than for lower latency, so that the latency can easily be improved by playing a bit with the process pinning. We will look into this in due time.

The general picture of the bandwidth values (the last column in Listing 5-1) is almost normal: they start small, grow to the L2 cache peak, and then go down stepwise, basically reaching the main memory bandwidth on very long messages (most likely, well beyond the 4 MiB cutoff selected by default).

However, looking a little closer at the latency numbers (third column), we notice an interesting anomaly: zero-byte latency is substantially larger than that for 1-byte messages. Something is fishy here. After a couple of extra runs we can be sure of this (anomalous values are highlighted in italic; see Table 5-1):

Table 5-1. *Small Message Latency Anomaly (Microseconds, Workstation)*

#bytes	Run 1	Run 2	Run 3	Min
0	*1.16*	*1.31*	*1.28*	*1.16*
1	0.78	*1.03*	*1.27*	0.78
2	0.75	0.77	*1.04*	0.75
4	0.78	0.79	0.71	0.71

This may be a measurement artifact, but it may as well be something worth keeping in mind if your application is strongly latency bound. Note that doing at least three runs is a good idea, even though your Statistics 101 course told you that this is not enough to get anywhere close to certainty. Practically speaking, if you indeed have to deal with outliers, you will be extremely unlucky to get two or all three of them in a row. And if just one outlier is there, you will easily detect its presence and eliminate it by comparison to other two results. If you still feel unsafe after this rather unscientific passage, do the necessary calculations and increase the number of trials accordingly.

Let us try to eliminate the artifact as a factor by increasing tenfold the number of iterations done per message size from its default value of 1000:

```
$ mpirun -np 2 ./IMB-MPI1 -iter 10000 PingPong
```

The option -iter 10000 requests 10,000 iterations to be done for each message size. This is what we get this time (again, skipping unessential output); see Listing 5-2.

Listing 5-2. Modified IMB-MPI1 Output (Workstation, Intranode, with 10,000 Iterations)

```
#----------------------------------------------------
# Benchmarking PingPong
# #processes = 2
#----------------------------------------------------
       #bytes #repetitions     t[usec]   Mbytes/sec
            0        10000        0.97         0.00
            1        10000        0.80         1.20
            2        10000        0.80         2.39
            4        10000        0.78         4.87
            8        10000        0.79         9.69
           16        10000        0.79        19.33
           32        10000        0.93        32.99
           64        10000        0.95        64.06
          128        10000        1.06       115.61
          256        10000        1.05       232.74
          512        10000        1.19       412.04
         1024        10000        1.40       697.15
         2048        10000        1.55      1261.09
         4096        10000        1.98      1967.93
         8192         5120        3.21      2437.08
        16384         2560        6.27      2493.14
        32768         1280       11.38      2747.05
        65536          640       13.35      4680.56
       131072          320       24.89      5021.92
       262144          160       44.77      5584.68
       524288           80       91.44      5467.92
      1048576           40      208.23      4802.48
      2097152           20      445.75      4486.85
      4194304           10      917.90      4357.78
```

From this, it does look like we get a measurement artifact at the lower message sizes, just because the machine is lightning fast. We can increase the iteration count even more and check that out.

EXERCISE 5-1

Verify the existence of the IMB short message anomaly on your favorite platform. If it is observable, file an issue report via Intel Premier Support.[4]

As before, the peak intranode bandwidth of 5.6 GiB/s at 256 KiB is confirmed, and we can deduce that the intranode bandwidth stabilizes at about 4.4 GB/s for large messages. These are quite reasonable numbers, and now we can proceed to investigate other aspects of the baseline MPI performance.

Before we do this, just to be sure, we will do two extra runs (oh, how important it is to be diligent during benchmarking!) and drive the new data into a new table (anomalous values are highlighted in italic again); see Table 5-2:

Table 5-2. *Small Message Latency Anomaly Almost Disappears (Microseconds, Workstation, with 10,000 Iterations)*

#bytes	Run 1	Run 2	Run 3	Min
0	*0.90*	*0.86*	*0.85*	*0.85*
1	0.69	0.72	0.72	0.69
2	0.70	0.71	0.73	0.70
4	0.70	0.71	0.72	0.70

Alternatively, if the observed anomaly can be attributed to the warm-up effects (say, connection establishment on the fly, buffer allocation, and so on), running another benchmark before the PingPong in the same invocation may eliminate this. The command would look as follows:

```
$ mpirun -np 2 ./IMB-MPI1 -iter 10000 PingPing PingPong
```

Listing 5-3 shows the effect we see on our workstation:

Listing 5-3. Modified IMB-MPI1 Output: PingPong after PingPing (Workstation, Intranode, with 10,000 Iterations)

```
#-----------------------------------------------------
# Benchmarking PingPong
# #processes = 2
#-----------------------------------------------------
       #bytes #repetitions      t[usec]   Mbytes/sec
            0        10000         0.56         0.00
            1        10000         0.56         1.69
            2        10000         0.57         3.37
            4        10000         0.57         6.73
```

8	10000	0.58	13.27
16	10000	0.58	26.49
32	10000	0.69	44.49
64	10000	0.69	88.48
128	10000	0.78	155.68
256	10000	0.81	300.65
512	10000	0.93	527.47
1024	10000	1.13	861.66
2048	10000	1.50	1305.38
4096	10000	2.14	1824.66
8192	5120	3.73	2094.46
16384	2560	6.48	2412.18
32768	1280	11.83	2642.52
65536	640	11.72	5334.40
131072	320	22.33	5598.75
262144	160	39.44	6338.08
524288	80	76.32	6551.55
1048576	40	183.25	5456.98
2097152	20	402.50	4968.89
4194304	10	783.05	5108.23
8388608	5	1588.30	5036.84
16777216	2	3417.25	4682.12

You can see not only that now the anomaly is gone but also that the numbers have changed quite substantially. This is in part why an application may behave differently from the most carefully designed benchmark. It is arguable whether doing special preconditioning of the benchmark like the one described earlier is valid all the time, so we will refrain from this approach further on.

Of course, we will keep all the log files, clearly named, safe and sound for future reference. The names like IMB-MPI1-n1p2-PingPong.logN, where N stands for the run number, will do just fine in this case. The notation n1p2 tells us that the results have been obtained on one node using two MPI processes.

Gauging Default Internode Communication Performance

If you are addressing a cluster rather than a single node or a workstation, you will want to perform a comparable investigation of the internode performance. The principle is similar to the one explained in the previous section. Let's start again with the two-process IMB PingPong benchmark.

Since in this case we are going to use more than one node, MPI startup will of necessity be a bit more complicated, because the MPI library should be made aware of the identity of the nodes we intend to run on. By far the easiest way that also leaves a clear log trace of what exactly was done is to specify those nodes explicitly in the IMB invocation command. For instance, on our example system:

```
$ mpirun -host esg054 -np 1 ./IMB-MPI1 PingPong : -host esg055 -np
1 ./IMB-MPI1 PingPong
```

Here, esg054 and esg055 stand for the respective node hostnames. They are very likely to be rather different in your installation. If you're in doubt, ask your friendly systems administrator.

■ **Note**   There are certainly more elegant and powerful ways of selecting the target nodes for an Intel MPI run. Do not worry; we will learn them one by one in due time. This precise inline method is just what we need right now.

Of course, your cluster may be controlled by a job-management system like PBS Pro, LSF, Torque, or one of half a dozen other alternative products. The chances are that mpirun will recognize any of them and allow a job to be started anyway, but this is a topic we would need to devote a whole chapter to. Just ask one of the local experts you know, and he or she will tell you what is needed to submit multiple node jobs.

Another conceptual complication that we will deal with is the way in which both nodes will communicate with each other. Normally, as in the intranode case, Intel MPI library will automatically try to select the fastest available communication path. Most likely, this will be InfiniBand on a dedicated HPC cluster and some Gigabit Ethernet on a general purpose cluster. In the case of InfiniBand, we get the following output on our test cluster introduced in Chapter 4; see Listings 5-4 and 5-5:

Listing 5-4. IMB-MPI1 Output (Cluster, Intranode)

```
#------------------------------------------------------
# Benchmarking PingPong
# #processes = 2
#------------------------------------------------------
       #bytes #repetitions    t[usec]   Mbytes/sec
            0         1000       0.67         0.00
            1         1000       0.67         1.42
            2         1000       0.68         2.82
            4         1000       0.68         5.62
            8         1000       0.70        10.85
           16         1000       0.71        21.54
           32         1000       0.86        35.63
           64         1000       0.88        69.40
          128         1000       0.98       124.95
```

256	1000	0.99	246.72
512	1000	1.15	426.27
1024	1000	1.42	685.35
2048	1000	1.78	1095.41
4096	1000	2.79	1400.88
8192	1000	4.64	1685.16
16384	1000	8.20	1904.89
32768	1000	15.10	2069.54
65536	640	16.79	3721.45
131072	320	31.61	3954.93
262144	160	57.92	4316.18
524288	80	107.18	4665.26
1048576	40	238.57	4191.58
2097152	20	503.15	3974.94
4194304	10	1036.91	3857.63

Listing 5-5. IMB-MPI1 Output (Cluster, Internode)

```
#------------------------------------------------------
# Benchmarking PingPong
# #processes = 2
#------------------------------------------------------
    #bytes #repetitions    t[usec]   Mbytes/sec
         0         1000       1.09         0.00
         1         1000       1.09         0.88
         2         1000       1.09         1.75
         4         1000       1.10         3.47
         8         1000       1.10         6.91
        16         1000       1.11        13.74
        32         1000       1.15        26.44
        64         1000       1.16        52.71
       128         1000       1.23        98.97
       256         1000       1.87       130.55
       512         1000       1.98       246.30
      1024         1000       2.30       425.25
      2048         1000       2.85       685.90
      4096         1000       3.42      1140.67
      8192         1000       4.77      1639.06
     16384         1000       7.28      2145.56
     32768         1000      10.34      3021.38
     65536         1000      16.76      3728.35
    131072         1000      28.36      4407.30
    262144          800      45.51      5493.00
    524288          400      89.05      5614.98
   1048576          200     171.75      5822.49
   2097152          100     338.53      5907.97
   4194304           50     671.06      5960.72
```

Several interesting differences between the shared memory and the InfiniBand paths are worth contemplating. Let's compare these results graphically; see Figures 5-1 and 5-2.

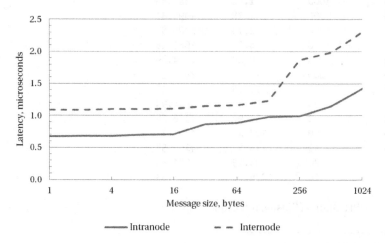

Figure 5-1. *IMB-MPI1 PingPong latency comparison: cluster, intranode vs internode (lower is better)*

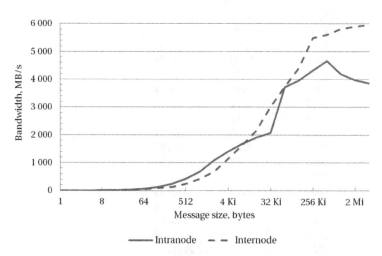

Figure 5-2. *IMB-MPI1 PingPong bandwidth comparison: cluster, intranode vs internode (higher is better)*

Now, let's enumerate the differences that may be important when we later start optimizing our application on the target cluster:

1. Intranode latency is substantially better than internode latency on smaller message sizes, with the crossover occurring at around 8 KiB. Hence, we should try to put onto the same node as many processes that send smaller messages to each other as possible.

2. Internode bandwidth is considerably higher than intranode bandwidth on larger messages above 8 KiB, with the exception of roughly 64 KiB, where the curves touch again. Hence, we may want to put onto different nodes those MPI ranks that send messages larger than 8 KiB, and surely larger than 64 KiB, to each other.

3. It is just possible that InfiniBand might be beating the shared memory path on the intranode bandwidth, as well. Since Intel MPI is capable of exploiting this after a minor adjustment, another small investigation is warranted to ascertain whether there is any potential for performance improvement in using InfiniBand for larger message intranode transfers.

Discovering Default Process Layout and Pinning Details

Is there an opportunity to further improve the underlying MPI performance? Certainly there are quite a few, starting with improving process pinning. Let's look at the output of the cpuinfo utility that is provided with the Intel MPI library; see Listing 5-6:

Listing 5-6. Cpuinfo Utility Output (Workstation)

```
Intel(R) processor family information utility, Version 5.0 Update 1 Build
20140709
Copyright (C) 2005-2014 Intel Corporation. All rights reserved.

=====  Processor composition  =====
Processor name    : Genuine Intel(R)   E2697V
Packages(sockets) : 2
Cores             : 24
Processors(CPUs)  : 48
Cores per package : 12
Threads per core  : 2
```

```
=====  Processor identification  =====
```

Processor	Thread Id.	Core Id.	Package Id.
0	0	0	0
1	0	1	0
2	0	2	0
3	0	3	0
4	0	4	0
5	0	5	0
6	0	8	0
7	0	9	0
8	0	10	0
9	0	11	0
10	0	12	0
11	0	13	0
12	0	0	1
13	0	1	1
14	0	2	1
15	0	3	1
16	0	4	1
17	0	5	1
18	0	8	1
19	0	9	1
20	0	10	1
21	0	11	1
22	0	12	1
23	0	13	1
24	1	0	0
25	1	1	0
26	1	2	0
27	1	3	0
28	1	4	0
29	1	5	0
30	1	8	0
31	1	9	0
32	1	10	0
33	1	11	0
34	1	12	0
35	1	13	0
36	1	0	1
37	1	1	1
38	1	2	1
39	1	3	1
40	1	4	1
41	1	5	1
42	1	8	1
43	1	9	1
44	1	10	1

```
45                1                11              1
46                1                12              1
47                1                13              1
===== Placement on packages  =====
Package Id.       Core Id.        Processors
0                                 0,1,2,3,4,5,8,9,10,11,12,13
                                  (0,24)(1,25)(2,26)(3,27)(4,28)(5,29)(6,30)
                                  (7,31)(8,32)(9,33)(10,34)(11,35)
1                                 0,1,2,3,4,5,8,9,10,11,12,13
                                  (12,36)(13,37)(14,38)(15,39)(16,40)(17,41)
                                  (18,42)(19,43)(20,44)(21,45)(22,46)(23,47)


===== Cache sharing  =====
Cache   Size               Processors
L1      32  KB             (0,24)(1,25)(2,26)(3,27)(4,28)(5,29)(6,30)(7,31)
                           (8,32)(9,33)(10,34)(11,35)(12,36)(13,37)(14,38)
                           (15,39)(16,40)(17,41)(18,42)(19,43)(20,44)(21,45)
                           (22,46)(23,47)
L2      256 KB             (0,24)(1,25)(2,26)(3,27)(4,28)(5,29)(6,30)(7,31)
                           (8,32)(9,33)(10,34)(11,35)(12,36)(13,37)(14,38)
                           (15,39)(16,40)(17,41)(18,42)(19,43)(20,44)(21,45)
                           (22,46)(23,47)
L3      30  MB             (0,1,2,3,4,5,6,7,8,9,10,11,24,25,26,27,28,29,30,31,
                           32,33,34,35)(12,13,14,15,16,17,18,19,20,21,22,23,
                           36,37,38,39,40,41,42,43,44,45,46,47)
```

This utility outputs detailed information about the Intel processors involved. On our example workstation we have two processor packages (sockets) of 12 physical cores apiece, each of them in turn running two hardware threads, for the total of 48 hardware threads for the whole machine. Disregarding gaps in the core numbering, they look well organized. It is important to notice that both sockets share the 30 MB L3 cache, while the much smaller L1 and L2 caches are shared only by the virtual cores (OS processors) that are closest to each other in the processor hierarchy. This may have interesting performance implications.

Now, let's see how Intel MPI puts processes onto the cores by default. Recalling Chapter 1, for this we can use any MPI program, setting the environment variable I_MPI_DEBUG to 4 in order to get the process mapping output. If you use a simple start/stop program containing only calls to the MPI_Init and MPI_Finalize, you will get output comparable to Listing 5-7, once unnecessary data is culled from it:

Listing 5-7. Default Process Pinning (Workstation, 16 MPI Processes)

```
[0] MPI startup(): Rank      Pid       Node name   Pin cpu
[0] MPI startup(): 0         210515    book        {0,1,24}
[0] MPI startup(): 1         210516    book        {2,25,26}
[0] MPI startup(): 2         210517    book        {3,4,27}
[0] MPI startup(): 3         210518    book        {5,28,29}
[0] MPI startup(): 4         210519    book        {6,7,30}
```

```
[0] MPI startup(): 5     210520   book   {8,31,32}
[0] MPI startup(): 6     210521   book   {9,10,33}
[0] MPI startup(): 7     210522   book   {11,34,35}
[0] MPI startup(): 8     210523   book   {12,13,36}
[0] MPI startup(): 9     210524   book   {14,37,38}
[0] MPI startup(): 10    210525   book   {15,16,39}
[0] MPI startup(): 11    210526   book   {17,40,41}
[0] MPI startup(): 12    210527   book   {18,19,42}
[0] MPI startup(): 13    210528   book   {20,43,44}
[0] MPI startup(): 14    210529   book   {21,22,45}
[0] MPI startup(): 15    210530   book   {23,46,47}
```

Comparing Listings 5-6 and 5-7, we can see that the first eight MPI processes occupy the first processor package, while the remaining eight MPI processes occupy the other package. This is good if we require as much bandwidth as we can get, for two parts of the job will be using separate memory paths. This may be bad, however, if the relatively slower intersocket link is crossed by very short messages that clamor for the lowest possibly latency. That situation would normally favor co-location of the intensively interacting processes on the cores that share the highest possible cache level, up to and including L1.

Gauging Physical Core Performance

What remains to be investigated is how much the virtual cores we have been using so far influence pure MPI performance. To look into this, we have to make Intel MPI use only the physical cores. The easiest way to do this is as follows:

```
$ export I_MPI_PIN_PROCESSOR_LIST=allcores
```

If you wonder what effect this will have upon performance, compare Listing 5-1 with Listing 5-8:

Listing 5-8. Example IMB-MPI1 Output (Workstation, Intranode, Physical Cores Only)

```
#---------------------------------------------------
# Benchmarking PingPong
# #processes = 2
#---------------------------------------------------
       #bytes #repetitions     t[usec]   Mbytes/sec
            0         1000        0.58         0.00
            1         1000        0.61         1.56
            2         1000        0.62         3.08
            4         1000        0.27        14.21
            8         1000        0.28        27.65
           16         1000        0.32        48.05
           32         1000        0.37        81.48
           64         1000        0.38       161.67
```

128	1000	0.42	293.83
256	1000	0.44	556.07
512	1000	0.50	975.70
1024	1000	0.59	1659.31
2048	1000	0.79	2470.82
4096	1000	1.21	3229.65
8192	1000	2.06	3799.85
16384	1000	3.77	4145.09
32768	1000	6.79	4605.72
65536	640	10.30	6066.17
131072	320	18.66	6699.50
262144	160	35.94	6956.02
524288	80	65.84	7593.73
1048576	40	125.46	7970.55
2097152	20	245.08	8160.72
4194304	10	482.80	8285.04

Note that we can still observe the small message latency anomaly in some form. This becomes outright intriguing. For the rest of it, latency is down by up to three times and bandwidth is up by 40 to 50 percent, with bandwidth in particular still going up, whereas it would sharply drop in prior tests. This is natural: in the absence of necessity to share both the core internals and the off-core resources typical of the virtual cores, MPI performance will normally go up. This is why pure MPI programs may experience a substantial performance hike when run on the physical cores.

Note also that the performance hike observed here has to do as well with the change in the process layout with respect to the processor sockets. If you investigate the process layout and pinning in both cases (not shown), you will see that in the default configuration, MPI ranks 0 and 1 occupy different processor sockets, while in the configuration illustrated by Listing 5-8, these ranks sit on adjacent physical cores of the same processor socket. That is, the observed difference is also the difference between the intersocket and intrasocket performance, respectively.

At this point we have discovered about 90 percent of what needs to be known about the underlying MPI performance. You might want to run more complicated IMB sessions and see how particular collective operations behave on more than two processes and so on. Resist this temptation. Before we go there, we need to learn a bit more about the target application.

EXERCISE 5-2

Compare the virtual and physical core performance of your favorite platform using the procedure described here. Try the `-cache_off` option of the IMB to assess the influence of the cache vs. memory performance at the MPI level. Consider how relevant these results may be to your favorite application.

Doing Initial Performance Analysis

Let us proceed to the next step of the performance investigation algorithm. When you optimize an application at the MPI level, it is not so interesting at first what is happening inside any particular process. What is more pertinent is how these processes interact, how much time is spent doing this, and whether this interaction can be improved to a noticeable degree. Thus, performance investigation of an MPI application starts with the initial benchmarking and a couple of estimates.

Is It Worth the Trouble?

This is the first question to answer, and this is not a trivial matter. One measurement is not likely to give the final answer here, since application behavior may depend on the run configuration (number of nodes, kind of the fabrics selected, MPI settings), as well as on the workload used and other, sometimes outright mysterious, factors.

Following the typical engineering practice of estimating upfront the problem by the order of magnitude, we recommend you do the following first:

1. Select one or two representative workloads.

2. Use the default Intel MPI settings and activate the built-in statistics gathering to collect vital profile information (export I_MPI_STATS=ipm).

3. Do several benchmarking runs at a low, medium, and high (but still practicable) number of processes, for any curve can connect two points, as they say.[5]

4. Analyze the statistics output files to find out whether it is worth bothering about the application's distributed memory performance, in particular.

By following this routine, you will not only understand whether there is a noticeable optimization potential at the distributed memory level but also learn how your application scales with the number of nodes and what MPI operations it uses most extensively. Moreover, you will establish a performance baseline that you will compare your results against every time you introduce a purported improvement into the application or the platform. All this information will flow directly into the further optimization process, and none of your time will be wasted.

Example 1: Initial HPL Performance Investigation

Let us revisit the High Performance Linpack Benchmark that we mentioned in Chapter 1, and practice a little on it.[6] To save time in configuring and building an executable with all the necessary optimizations and libraries inside, we will fetch Intel's pre-cooked HPL that we quietly used in Chapter 4.[7]

We do not have to select the workload because HPL generates it automatically during startup. What we need to change are a few workload parameters; see Listing 5-9:

Listing 5-9. HPL Input File (HPL.dat) with the Most Important Parameters Highlighted

```
HPLinpack benchmark input file
Innovative Computing Laboratory, University of Tennessee
HPL.out     output file name (if any)
6           device out (6=stdout,7=stderr,file)
1           # of problems sizes (N)
235520      Ns
1           # of NBs
256         NBs
1           PMAP process mapping (0=Row-,1=Column-major)
1           # of process grids (P x Q)
4           Ps
4           Qs
16.0        threshold
1           # of panel fact
2           PFACTs (0=left, 1=Crout, 2=Right)
1           # of recursive stopping criterium
4           NBMINs (>=1)
1           # of panels in recursion
2           NDIVs
1           # of recursive panel fact.
1           RFACTs (0=left, 1=Crout, 2=Right)
1           # of broadcast
0           BCASTs (0=1rg,1=1rM,2=2rg,3=2rM,4=Lng,5=LnM)
1           # of lookahead depth
1           DEPTHs (>=0)
0           SWAP (0=bin-exch,1=long,2=mix)
1           swapping threshold
1           L1 in (0=transposed,1=no-transposed) form
1           U  in (0=transposed,1=no-transposed) form
0           Equilibration (0=no,1=yes)
8           memory alignment in double (>0)
```

Some of the points to note from the script in Listing 5-8 are:

- *Problem size* (N) is normally chosen to take about 80 percent of the available physical memory by the formula *memory* $= 8N^2$ for double precision calculations.

- *Number of blocks* (NB) usually ranges between 32 and 256, with the higher numbers promoting higher computational efficiency while creating more communication.

- *Process grid dimensions* (P and Q), where both P and Q are typically greater than 1, P is equal to or slightly smaller than Q, and the product of P and Q is the total number of processes involved in the computation.

This and further details are well explained in the *HPL FAQ*.[8] As can be seen, Listing 5-9 was generated when the matrix size was set to 235,520, yielding total occupied memory of about 413 GiB. We used 256 blocks and the process grid dimensions 4 x 4. A quick look into the built-in statistics output given in Listing 1-1 that was obtained for this input data shows that MPI communication occupied between 5.3 and 11.3 percent of the total run time, and that the MPI_Send, MPI_Recv, and MPI_Wait operations took about 81, 12, and 7 percent of the total MPI time, respectively. The truncated HPL output file (see Listing 5-10) reveals that the run completed correctly, took about 40 minutes, and achieved about 3.7 TFLOPS.

Listing 5-10. HPL Report with the Most Important Data Highlighted (Cluster, 16 MPI Processes)

```
================================================================================
HPLinpack 2.1 -- High-Performance Linpack benchmark -- October 26, 2012
Written by A. Petitet and R. Clint Whaley,  Innovative Computing Laboratory, UTK
Modified by Piotr Luszczek, Innovative Computing Laboratory, UTK
Modified by Julien Langou, University of Colorado Denver
================================================================================

An explanation of the input/output parameters follows:

T/V    : Wall time / encoded variant.
N      : The order of the coefficient matrix A.
NB     : The partitioning blocking factor.
P      : The number of process rows.
Q      : The number of process columns.
Time   : Time in seconds to solve the linear system.
Gflops : Rate of execution for solving the linear system.

The following parameter values will be used:

N      :   235520
NB     :      256
PMAP   : Column-major process mapping
P      :        4
Q      :        4
PFACT  : Right
NBMIN  :        4
NDIV   :        2
RFACT  : Crout
BCAST  : 1ring
DEPTH  :        1
SWAP   : Binary-exchange
L1     : no-transposed form
U      : no-transposed form
EQUIL  : no
ALIGN  :        8 double precision words
```

```
--------------------------------------------------------------------------
- The matrix A is randomly generated for each test.
- The following scaled residual check will be computed:
      ||Ax-b||_oo / ( eps * ( || x ||_oo * || A ||_oo + || b ||_oo ) * N )
- The relative machine precision (eps) is taken to be 1.110223e-16
- Computational tests pass if scaled residuals are less than    16.0
Column=001280 Fraction=0.005 Mflops=4809238.67
Column=002560 Fraction=0.010 Mflops=4314045.98
...
Column=210944 Fraction=0.895 Mflops=3710381.21
Column=234496 Fraction=0.995 Mflops=3706630.12
============================================================================
T/V                N    NB    P    Q               Time            Gflops
----------------------------------------------------------------------------
WC10C2R4        235520  256   4    4              2350.76        3.70500e+03
HPL_pdgesv() start time Fri Feb 14 05:44:48 2014

HPL_pdgesv() end time   Fri Feb 14 06:23:59 2014
----------------------------------------------------------------------------
||Ax-b||_oo/(eps*(||A||_oo*||x||_oo+||b||_oo)*N)=   0.0028696 ...... PASSED
============================================================================
Finished     1 tests with the following results:
             1 tests completed and passed residual checks,
             0 tests completed and failed residual checks,
             0 tests skipped because of illegal input values.
----------------------------------------------------------------------------
End of Tests.
============================================================================
```

Now, let's document what we have found. The input and output files form the basis of this dataset that needs to be securely stored. In addition to this, we should note that this run was done on eight nodes with two Ivy Bridge processors, with 12 physical cores in turbo mode per processor and 64 GiB of memory per node.

The following tools were used for this run:

- Intel MPI 5.0.1

- Intel MKL 11.2.0 (including MP_LINPACK binary precompiled by Intel Corporation)

- Intel Composer XE 2015

The environment variables for this test were as follows:

```
export I_MPI_DAPL_PROVIDER=ofa-v2-mlx4_0-1
export I_MPI_PIN=enable
export I_MPI_PIN_DOMAIN=socket
export OMP_NUM_THREADS=12
export KMP_AFFINITY=verbose,granularity=fine,physical
export I_MPI_STATS=ipm
```

Some of these variables are set by default. However, setting them explicitly increases the chances that we truly know what is being done by the library. The first line indicates a particular communication fabric to be used by Intel MPI. The next four lines control the Intel MPI and OpenMP process and thread pinning. (We will look into why and how here, and in Chapter 6.) The last line requests the built-in, IPM-style statistics output to be produced by the Intel MPI Library.

This dataset complements the lower-level data about the platform involved that we collected and documented in Chapter 4. Taken together, they allow us to reproduce this result if necessary, or to root-cause any deviation that may be observed in the future (or in the past).

Since this program has not been designed to run on small problem sizes or small numbers of processes, it does not make much sense to continue the runs before we come to the preliminary conclusion. One data point will be sufficient, and we can decide what to do next. If we compute the efficiency achieved during this run, we see it comes to about 90 percent. This is not far from the expected top efficiency of about 95 percent. From this observation, as well as the MPI communication percentages shown here and Amdahl's Law explained earlier, we can deduce that there is possibly 2—at most 3—percent overall performance upside in tuning MPI. In other words, it makes sense to spend more time tuning MPI for this particular application only if you are after those last few extra drops of efficiency. This may very well be the case if you want to break a record, by the way.

Just for comparison, we took the stock HPL off the netlib.org and compared it to the optimized version presented here. The only tool in common was the Intel MPI library. We used the GNU compiler, BLAS library off the netlib.org, and whatever default settings were included in the provided Makefile.[9] First, we were not able to run the full-size problem owing to a segmentation fault. Second, the matrix size of 100,000 was taking so much time it was impractical to wait for its completion. Third, on the very modest matrix size of 10,000, with the rest of the aforementioned HPL.dat file unchanged (see Listing 5-9), we got 35.66 GFLOPS for the stock HPL vs. 152.07 GFLOPS for the optimized HPL, or a factor of more than *4.5 times* in favor of the optimized HPL. As we know from the estimates given, and a comparison of the communication statistics (not shown), most of this improvement does not seem to be coming from the MPI side of the equation. We will revisit this example in the coming chapters dedicated to other levels of optimization to find out how to get this fabulous acceleration.

All this may look to you like a very costly exercise in finding out the painfully obvious. Of course, we know that Intel teams involved in the development of the respective tools have done a good job optimizing them for one of the most influential HPC benchmarks. We also know what parameters to set and how, both for the application and for the Intel MPI Library. However, all this misses the point. Even if you had a different application at hand, you would be well advised to follow this simple and efficient routine before going any further. By the way, if you miss beautiful graphs here, you will do well to get used to this right away. Normally you will have no time to produce any pictures, unless you want to unduly impress your clients or managers. Well-organized textual information will often be required if you take part in the formal benchmarking efforts. If you would rather analyze data visually, you will have to find something better than the plain text tables and Excel graphing capabilities we have gotten used to.

EXERCISE 5-3

Do an initial performance investigation of the HPCG benchmark,[10] and determine whether it is desirable and indeed feasible to improve its distributed memory performance. Repeat this exercise with your favorite application.

Getting an Overview of Scalability and Performance

If an initial investigation suggests that there may be some improvement potential in the area of distributed memory performance, and if a couple of the simple tricks described in Chapter 1 do not yield a quick relief, it is time to start an orderly siege. The primary goal at this point is to understand whether the application is memory-bound or compute-bound, whether it scales as expected (if scaling is indeed a goal), and how the observed performance relates to the expected peak performance of the underlying platform.

Learning Application Behavior

Now, you are in for a lot of benchmarking. Proper selection of the representative workloads, application parameters, MPI process and OpenMP thread counts, and other relevant settings are paramount. Also desirable are scripting skills or a special tool that will help you run benchmarks and organize the pile of resulting data.

There is also a distinct temptation at this stage to follow the white rabbit down the hole. Try hard to resist this temptation because the first performance issue you observe may or may not be the primary one, both in its causal importance and in its relative magnitude. Only when you have a complete overview of the application behavior and its quirks will you be able to chart the most effective way of addressing the real performance issues, if indeed there are any. Let us look at a very good example of this view that we will keep revisiting as we go.

Example 2: MiniFE Performance Investigation

The miniFE application from the Mantevo suite represents a typical finite element method of solving implicit unstructured partial differential equations.[11] It includes all important solution stages, like the sparse matrix assembly and the solution of the resulting system of linear equations. Thus, whatever we learn here may be directly transferrable to the more involved packages that provide general finite element capabilities.

It is relatively easy to set up and run this application. Upon downloading the application archive and unpacking it recursively, you will end up with a number of directories, one of which is named miniFE-2.0_mkl. Note that we quite intentionally go for the Intel MPI and Intel MKL-based executable here, for we have learned earlier in the example of HPL that this gives us a head start on performance. In other words, by now we are almost past the recommendations of Chapter 1 and into the realm of the unknown.

First, you need to fetch and build the program. Upon unpacking, go to the directory miniFE-2.0-mkl/src, copy the Makefile.intel.mpi into the Makefile, change the -fopenmp flag there to -qopenmp so that the multithreaded Intel MPI Library is picked up by default, then type make and enjoy.

Next you need to find a proper workload. After a couple of attempts, with the system sizes of 10 and 100 being apparently too small, and the system size of 1000 leading to the operating system killing the job (results not shown), the following launch string looks adequate:

```
$ mpirun -np 16 ./miniFE.x nx=500
```

This command produces the output seen in Listing 5-11:

Listing 5-11. MiniFE Output (Workstation, Size 500, 16 MPI Processes)

```
      creating/filling mesh...0.377832s, total time: 0.377833
generating matrix structure...17.6959s, total time: 18.0737
          assembling FE data...13.5461s, total time: 31.6199
     imposing Dirichlet BC...11.9997s, total time: 43.6195
     imposing Dirichlet BC...0.47753s, total time: 44.0971
making matrix indices local...14.6372s, total time: 58.7342
Starting CG solver ...
Initial Residual = 501.001
Iteration = 20 Residual = 0.0599256
Iteration = 40 Residual = 0.0287661
Iteration = 60 Residual = 0.0185888
Iteration = 80 Residual = 0.121056
Iteration = 100 Residual = 0.0440518
Iteration = 120 Residual = 0.00938303
Iteration = 140 Residual = 0.00666799
Iteration = 160 Residual = 0.00556699
Iteration = 180 Residual = 0.00472206
Iteration = 200 Residual = 0.00404725
Final Resid Norm: 0.00404725
```

There is also a corresponding report file with the file extension .yaml, shown in Listing 5-12:

Listing 5-12. MiniFE Report (Workstation, Size 500, 16 MPI Processes)

```
Mini-Application Name: miniFE
Mini-Application Version: 2.0
Global Run Parameters:
  dimensions:
    nx: 500
    ny: 500
    nz: 500
  load_imbalance: 0
  mv_overlap_comm_comp: 0 (no)
  number of processors: 16
  ScalarType: double
  GlobalOrdinalType: int
  LocalOrdinalType: int
Platform:
  hostname: book
  kernel name: 'Linux'
  kernel release: '2.6.32-431.17.1.el6.x86_64'
  processor: 'x86_64'
Build:
  CXX: '/opt/intel/impi_latest/intel64/bin/mpiicpc'
  compiler version: 'icpc (ICC) 15.0.0 20140723'
  CXXFLAGS: '-O3 -mkl -DMINIFE_MKL_DOUBLE -qopenmp -DUSE_MKL_DAXPBY -mavx'
  using MPI: yes
Run Date/Time: 2014-05-27, 19-21-30
Rows-per-proc Load Imbalance:
  Largest (from avg, %): 0
  Std Dev (%): 0
Matrix structure generation:
  Mat-struc-gen Time: 17.6959
FE assembly:
  FE assembly Time: 13.5461
Matrix attributes:
  Global Nrows: 125751501
  Global NNZ: 3381754501
  Global Memory (GB): 38.731
  Pll Memory Overhead (MB): 28.8872
  Rows per proc MIN: 7812500
  Rows per proc MAX: 7938126
  Rows per proc AVG: 7.85947e+06
  NNZ per proc MIN: 209814374
  NNZ per proc MAX: 213195008
  NNZ per proc AVG: 2.1136e+08
```

```
CG solve:
  Iterations: 200
  Final Resid Norm: 0.00404725
  WAXPY Time: 21.2859
  WAXPY Flops: 2.2575e+11
  WAXPY Mflops: 10605.6
  DOT Time: 6.72744
  DOT Flops: 1e+11
  DOT Mflops: 14864.5
  MATVEC Time: 98.8167
  MATVEC Flops: 1.35947e+12
  MATVEC Mflops: 13757.4
  Total:
    Total CG Time: 126.929
    Total CG Flops: 1.68522e+12
    Total CG Mflops: 13276.9
  Time per iteration: 0.634643
Total Program Time: 185.796
```

From the last few lines of Listing 5-12, you can see that we achieve about
13.3 GFLOPS during the conjugate gradient (CG) solution stage, taking 185.8 seconds for
the whole job. Now we will look into whether this is the optimum we are after with respect
to the problem size, the number of the MPI processes, and the number of OpenMP
threads that are used implicitly by the Intel MKL. For comparison, we achieved only
10.72 MFLOPS for the problem size of 10 and 12.72 GFLOPS for the problem size of 100,
so that there is some dependency here.

For now, let's do a quick investigation of the MPI usage along the lines mentioned.
If we collect the Intel MPI built-in statistics, we get the output seen in Listing 5-13:

Listing 5-13. MiniFE Statistics (Workstation, Size 500, 16 MPI Processes)

```
###########################################################################
#
# command : ./miniFE.x (completed)
# host    : book/x86_64_Linux              mpi_tasks : 16 on 1 nodes
# start   : 05/27/14/17:21:30              wallclock : 185.912397 sec
# stop    : 05/27/14/17:24:35              %comm     : 7.34
# gbytes  : 0.00000e+00 total              gflop/sec : NA
#
```

```
######################################################################
# region  : * [ntasks] = 16
#
#                      [total]      <avg>        min          max
# entries              16           1            1            1
# wallclock            2974.58      185.911      185.91       185.912
# user                 3402.7       212.668      211.283      213.969
# system               20.6389      1.28993      0.977852     1.56376
# mpi                  218.361      13.6475      4.97802      20.179
# %comm                             7.3409       2.67765      10.8541
# gflop/sec            NA           NA           NA           NA
# gbytes               0            0            0            0
#
#
#                      [time]       [calls]      <%mpi>
<%wall>
# MPI_Allreduce        212.649      6512         97.38        7.15
# MPI_Send             2.89075      29376        1.32         0.10
# MPI_Init             1.81538      16           0.83         0.06
# MPI_Wait             0.686448     29376        0.31         0.02
# MPI_Allgather        0.269436     48           0.12         0.01
# MPI_Irecv            0.0444376    29376        0.02         0.00
# MPI_Comm_size        0.00278258   3360         0.00         0.00
# MPI_Bcast            0.00242162   32           0.00         0.00
# MPI_Comm_rank        1.62125e-05  176          0.00         0.00
# MPI_Finalize         5.24521e-06  16           0.00         0.00
# MPI_TOTAL            218.361      98288        100.00       7.34
######################################################################
```

This is positively interesting. One MPI operation—MPI_Allreduce–is taking almost 97.5 percent of the total MPI time that in turn accounts for from 2.67 to 10.85 percent of the overall application time. Do you feel the almost irresistible temptation to start playing with the MPI_Allreduce tuning settings right away? Be cool. We will show soon enough how wrong it would be to succumb to the tempation (to be continued).

Choosing Representative Workload(s)

Workload size—or more generally, the computational and memory load created by the workload—may dramatically affect application characteristics. To understand this, you have only to recall the memory hierarchy and the attending latencies mentioned at the beginning of Chapter 3.

You can imagine that at the very beginning, at a very low memory load, the application will be basically starving for data; the computations will consume all the data in the highest level of cache where it fits, and they will stop before it can achieve full computational performance. Moreover, interprocess and interthread synchronization will probably play a more noticeable role here than at higher memory loads. Finally, the program may even break if each of its computational units, be they processes or threads, receives less than the minimum amount of data that it can sensibly handle.

As the memory load continues to grow, the workload will start occupying the LLC pretty regularly. This is where you are likely to observe the maximum possible computational performance of a particular computational node. This point in the performance curve is very important because it may show to what degree the overall problem needs to be split into smaller parts, so that those parts can be computed with maximum efficiency by separate cluster nodes.

Further growth of the memory load will lead to part of the data spilling over into the main system memory. At this point the application may become memory bound, unless clever techniques or the built-in facilities of the platform, like prefetching, are able to alleviate the detrimental effects of the spilling.

Eventually, when the size of the workload exceeds the size of the physical memory available to the current process's working set, the virtual memory mechanism of the operating system will kick in and, depending on its quality and the speed of the offline storage (like hard disk drives [HDD] or solid state disks [SSD]), this may depress performance further.

Finally, the growing memory load will cause a job to exceed the limits of the virtual memory subsystem, and the job will start extensively swapping data in and out of the main memory. This effect is called *thrashing*. The program will effectively become strongly I/O bound. At this point, unless the program was designed to handle offload data gracefully (like so many off-core solvers of yore), all bets are off.

Another, no less important aspect of the workload selection is the choice of the typical target problem class that the benchmarking will address. For example, if the target application is intended for computing—as in car-to-car collisions—it may not make much sense to benchmark it on a test case that leads to no contact and deformation of the objects involved.

Benchmarking and a bit of back-of-the-envelope calculations can help in choosing the right *workload size*. Only your experience and knowledge of the standards, traditions, and expectations of the target area are going to help you to choose the right *workload class*. Fortunately, both selections are more often than not resolved by the clients, who tell you upfront what they are interested in.

Example 2 (cont.): MiniFE Performance Investigation

We ruffled through the selection of the workload in this example earlier and settled on the workload size of 500 after very few simple runs. Let's revisit this choice now that we know the program may have noticeable MPI optimization potential.

We know from the earlier attempts that the size of 10 is so low as to lead to some 10 MFLOPS. This is a clear indication of the problem size leading to the data starvation mentioned earlier. The size of 100 achieves some 12 GFLOPS, which is not so far from the 13 GFLOPS we can observe on the size of 500. Unfortunately, the size of 1000 is apparently too high, and the system protects itself by killing off the offending job.

What we should try to gauge now is how low we can go before we see data starvation, and how high we can go before we exhaust the system memory to the point of activating its self-protection instincts. Given the points of 100 and 500, as well as the desire to do as few experiments as possible, we find that four extra data points appear warranted, namely 50, 250, 375, and 750. If we do these extra measurements in the 16 MPI processes, three thread configurations used so far, we can add the new data to the data already obtained, and thus save a bit of time.

Table 5-3 shows what we get once we drive all the data together:

Table 5-3. *MiniFE Dependency on Problem Size (Workstation, 16 MPI Processes)*

Size	CG (GLOPFS)	Total Time (seconds)	Memory (GB)
10	36.052	0.145	0.00034
50	6578.06	0.35	0.039
100	12738.8	1.5	0.31
250	13213.7	22.9	4.9
375	13225.6	78.1	16.4
500	13335.9	187.6	38.7

Recalling the characteristics of the workstation at hand, we can deduce that the problem size of 250 is probably the last one to fit into the physical memory, although the virtual memory mechanism will kick in anyway long before that. It does not look as if the size of 500 was overloading the system unduly, so we can safely keep using it.

Being a proper benchmark, this program outputs a lot of useful data that can be analyzed graphically with relative ease. For example, Figure 5-3 illustrates the absolute contribution of various stages of the computation to the total execution time.

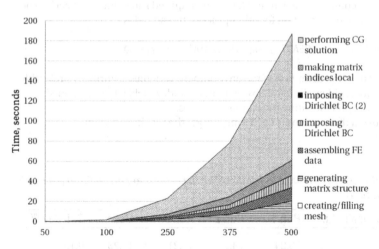

Figure 5-3. *MiniFE stage cummulative timing dependency on the problem size (16 MPI processes)*

These curves look like some power dependency to the trained eye, and this is what they should look like, given that the total number of mesh nodes grows as a cube of the problem size, while the number of the nonzero matrix elements grows as a quadrat of the problem size owing to the two-dimensional nature of the finite element interaction. This, however, is only a speculation until you can prove it (to be continued).

Balancing Process and Thread Parallelism

We started with the process/thread combination that looked reasonable for the earlier benchmarks, namely 16 MPI processes, each of them running three OpenMP threads if the application so desires. It is not clear, however, whether this is the optimum we are after. Threads have a lower context switch overhead and can use shared memory and synchronization primitives over it directly. It is not impossible that they may enjoy a slight performance advantage over the MPI processes owing to these features, at least as long as the number of threads per process is relatively low. On the other hand, the complexity of a hybrid program may actually lead to the threading adding extra overhead that detrimentally affects the overall program performance. About the only way to find out what is happening to a particular application is—you have guessed it—benchmarking.

Example 2 (cont.): MiniFE Performance Investigation

Let's do a couple of experiments to make sure that we strike the right balance between the processes and the threads. Given the total of 48 virtual cores per node, we can reasonably start not only 16 MPI processes of three OpenMP threads each but also 24 MPI processes with two OpenMP threads, and 12 MPI processes with four OpenMP threads each, and so on, up to the extreme combinations of 48 MPI processes or 48 threads that will still occupy all available computational units. Here is the required run string that needs to be changed according to the derivation for other process/thread ratios:

```
$ mpirun -genv OMP_NUM_THREADS 3 -np 16 ./miniFE.x nx=500
```

This method of inline definition of the environment variables is normally preferable because you cannot accidentally leave any of them behind, which, if that happened, could inadvertently spoil the future measurement series.

Doing our usual three attempts each time, we get the results shown in Tables 5-4 and 5-5:

Table 5-4. *MiniFE CG Performance Dependency on the Process to Thread Ratio (GFLOPS, Size 500, Workstation)*

MPI proc.	OpenMP thr.	Run 1	Run 2	Run 3	Mean	Std. dev, %
12	4	13.24	13.24	13.21	13.23	0.13
16	3	13.27	13.26	13.26	13.26	0.02
24	2	13.26	13.25	13.26	13.26	0.04

Table 5-5. *MiniFE Total Time Dependency on the Process to Thread Ratio (Seconds, Size 500, Workstation)*

MPI proc.	OpenMP thr.	Run 1	Run 2	Run 3	Mean	Std. dev, %
12	4	210.39	210.93	210.58	210.64	0.13
16	3	187.77	186.39	185.94	186.70	0.51
24	2	174.82	175.19	174.55	174.85	0.18

Although computational performance of the main CG block is equal for 16 and 24 processes, the overall time for 24 processes is lower. This is significant because the benchmark tries to approximate the behavior of a complete finite element application, and the total execution time is a more pertinent metrics here. We will focus on this wall-clock metric while keeping in mind that we do want to use the processor as efficiently as possible during the main computational step (to be continued).

Doing a Scalability Review

If you recall the treatise in Chapter 2, there are two major types of scalability: weak and strong. Weak scalability series increases the load proportionally to the number of processes involved. In other words, it keeps the per-node load constant and seeks to investigate the effect of the growing number of connections between the nodes. Strong scalability keeps the problem size constant while increasing the number of processes involved. This is what we are interested in primarily now. Just as in the case of intranode communication, here we want to see where the problem starts loading the machine so much as to make further increase in the computational resources allocated pointless or even counterproductive.

Example 2 (cont.): MiniFE Performance Investigation

First, let's look into strong scalability of the miniFE. We will put up to 48 MPI processes on one node and let the runtime decide how many threads to start. Further, we will try to load the nodes so that we get into the memory-bound state from the very beginning, and gradually move toward the compute-bound situation, looking for the knee of the graph. We will also incidentally check whether explicit setting of the OpenMP thread number is indeed helping instead of hurting performance. After a series of respective runs without the OMP_NUM_THREADS variable set, we get the data shown in Tables 5-6 and 5-7:

Table 5-6. *MiniFE CG Performance Dependency on the Process Number (GFLOPS, Size 500, Workstation, No OpenMP Threads)*

MPI proc.	OpenMP thr.	Run 1	Run 2	Run 3	Mean	Std. dev, %
8	undefined	11.95	11.83	12.04	11.94	0.90
12	undefined	13.02	13.00	13.00	13.00	0.11
16	undefined	13.32	13.32	13.32	13.32	0.01
24	undefined	13.36	13.36	13.36	13.36	0.03
48	undefined	13.19	13.20	13.20	13.19	0.04

Table 5-7. *MiniFE CG Total Time Dependency on the Process Number (Seconds, Size 500, Workstation, No OpenMP Threads)*

MPI proc.	OpenMP thr.	Run 1	Run 2	Run 3	Mean	Std. dev, %
8	undefined	257.41	254.92	257.63	256.65	0.59
12	undefined	212.77	212.80	212.28	212.61	0.14
16	undefined	185.80	185.72	185.43	185.76	0.03
24	undefined	173.37	173.71	173.65	173.58	0.11
48	undefined	160.92	160.91	160.69	160.84	0.08

By setting the environment variable KMF_AFFINITY to verbose, you can verify that more than one OpenMP thread is started even if its number is not specified. It is interesting that we get about 100 MFLOPS extra by not setting the OpenMP thread number explicitly, and that the total time drops still further if all 48 cores are each running MPI process Moreover, it drops between the process counts by as much as 16 and 24. This indicates that the application has substantial scaling potential in this strong scaling scenario.

The tendency toward performance growth with the number of MPI processes suggests that it might be interesting to see what happens if we use only the physical cores. Employing the recipe described earlier, we get 13.38 GFLOPS on 24 MPI processes put on the physical cores, taking 176.47 seconds for the whole job versus 173.58 for 24 MPI processes placed by default. So, there is no big and apparent benefit in using the physical cores explicitly.

Thus, we are faced with the question of what configuration is most appropriate for the following investigation. From Tables 5-4 through 5-7, it looks like 16 MPI processes running three threads each combine reasonable overall runtime, high CG block performance, and potential for further tweaks at the OpenMP level. One possible issue in the 16 MPI process, three OpenMP thread configuration is that every second core will contain parts of two different MPI processes, which may detrimentally affect the caching. Keeping this in mind, we will focus on this configuration from now on, and count on the 24 process, two thread configuration as plan B.

We could continue the scalability review by proceeding from the workstation to the cluster. In particular, the speedup $S(p)$ and efficiency $E(p)$ graphs can be used to track the expected and observed performance at different MPI process and OpenMP thread counts. For an ideal scaling program, $S(p) = p$ and $E(p) = 1$, so it will be easy to detect any deviation visually. This investigation can be done for the overall program execution time, which can be measured directly. It can also be done for the time used up by its components, be that computation versus communication, or particular function calls, or even code fragments. This more detailed information can be discovered by directly embedding the timing calls, like MPI_Wtime, into the program code; looking into the statistics output we have seen before; or using one of the advanced analysis tools described later in this book. However, the limited scope of this example does not make this investigation necessary. In any case, we have settled both the representative workload and the most promising run configurations, and this is good enough for now.

Note that there may be a certain interaction between the process: thread ratio, on one hand, and the workload size, on the other hand. So far, we have been basically ignoring this effect, hoping that we can change the respective coordinates independently or that at least this effect will be of the second order. This may or may not be true in the general case: it is conceivable that smaller workloads will lend themselves better to the higher thread counts. However, to gauge this effect, we would have to perform a full series of the measurements over all the MPI process and thread counts, as well as the problem sizes. That is, instead of probing this three-dimensional Cartesian space along two lines (the process:thread ratio at problem size of 500, and then the problem size at the process:thread ratio of 16:3), we would have to do a full search. The time required for this, as well as the amount of data produced, would probably be prohibitive for the scope of this book (to be continued).

EXERCISE 5-4

Perform a focused sampling around the point that we consider as the optimum for miniFE, to verify it is indeed at least the local maximum of performance we are after. Replace miniFE by your favorite application and repeat the investigation. If intranode scalability results warrant this, go beyond one node.

Analyzing the Details of the Application Behavior

There are many ways to analyze the behavior of parallel applications. That is, they differ in the way in which the data is collected. Three of them are most frequently used:

- *Printing* uses timestamp collection and output statements built into the program during its development or added specifically for debugging. Surprisingly enough, this is probably still the best way to understand the overall program behavior unless you are after an issue that disappears when observed (so-called Heisenbug).

- *Sampling* takes snapshots of the system, either at fixed time intervals or at certain points of the program or system lifecycle. Information collected this way comes in the form of hardware and software counters, register values, and so on, and it normally requires a tool to make sense of it.

- *Tracing* follows program execution and tracks all important events as they occur by creating a so-called application trace. Again, tools are nearly unavoidable if a nontrivial program is to be analyzed.

People will also just go through the application in an interactive debugger, but this mode is more suitable for debugging than for performance analysis per se. In any case, there are arguments in favor of each of these methods, as well as interesting cases when they may usefully complement each other. We will see some of them later.

The Intel Trace Analyzer and Collector (ITAC) we are going to use for the distributed memory performance analysis in this book is a tracing tool, one of many that can produce and visualize application trace files in various forms. Instead of trying to describe this very powerful program in general terms, we propose to simply use it for the example at hand.

Example 2 (cont.): MiniFE Performance Investigation

You can use ITAC to generate an application trace file and to inspect it visually. You enter the following commands to get the trace file miniFE.x.stf:

```
$ source /opt/intel/itac_latest/bin/itacvars.sh
$ mpirun -trace -np 16 ./miniFE.x -nx=500
```

The first command establishes the necessary environment. As usual, we added this command to the script 0env.sh included in the respective example archive, so if you have sourced that file already, you do not need to source the specific ITAC environment script. The -trace option in the mpirun invocation instructs the Intel MPI library link the executable at runtime against the ITAC dynamic library, which in turn creates the requested trace file. Application rebuilding is not required.

If you work on a cluster or another remote computer, you will have to ship all the files associated with the main trace file `miniFE.x.stf` (most of them are covered by the file mask `miniFE.x.stf*`) to a computer where you have the ITAC installed. To make this process a little easier, you can ask ITAC to produce a single trace file if you use the following command instead of the earlier `mpirun` invocation:

```
$ mpirun -trace -np 16 ./miniFE.x -nx=500 --itc-args --logfile-format
SINGLESTF --itc-args-end
```

You can learn more about the ways to control ITAC runtime configuration in the product online documentation.[12]

Now you can run the ITAC:

```
$ traceanalyzer miniFE.x.stf
```

This way or another, after a few splash screens, the ITAC summary chart shows up (see Figure 5-4; note that we maximized the respective view inside the ITAC window).

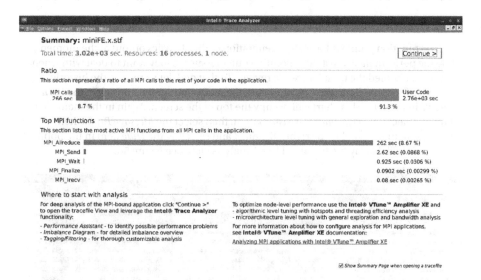

Figure 5-4. *MiniFE trace file in ITAC summary chart (Workstation, 16 MPI processes)*

This view basically confirms what we already know from the built-in statistics output. Press the *Continue* button at the upper right corner, and you will see the default ITAC screen that includes the function profile (left) and the performance assistant (right), with the rest of the screen occupied by the main program and view menus (very top), as well as the handy icons and the schematic timeline (below the top); see Figure 5-5, and note that we maximized the respective window once again.

Figure 5-5. *MiniFE trace file in ITAC default view (Workstation, 16 MPI processes)*

The function profile is basically a reiteration of the statistics output at the moment, while the performance assistant is pointing out an issue we may want to deal with when we have performed the initial trace file review. To that end, let us restore the historical ITAC trace file view. Go to the *Charts* item in the main chart menu and select the *Event Timeline* item there. This chart will occupy the top of the screen. Again in the main view menu, deselect the *Performance Assistant* item, then select the *Message Profile* item. Also, hide the schematic timeline by right-clicking it and selecting the *Hide* item in the popup menu. This will display the historical ITAC analysis view; see Figure 5-6.

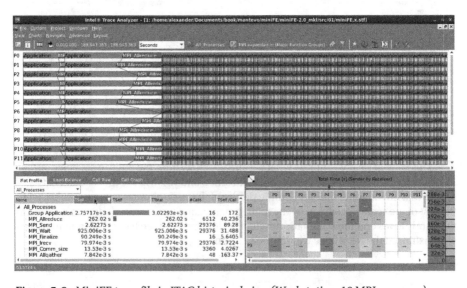

Figure 5-6. *MiniFE trace file in ITAC historical view (Workstation, 16 MPI processes)*

Nothing can beat this view in the eyes of an experienced analyst. The event timeline shows pretty clearly that the program is busy computing and communicating most of the time after setup. However, during setup there are substantial issues concerning one of the MPI_Allreduce calls that may need to be addressed. The message profile illustrates the neighbor exchanges between the adjacent processes that possess the respective adjacent slabs of the overall computation domain. These relatively short exchanges still differ in duration by approximately four times. To make sure this is indeed the case, you can scroll this view up and down using the scrollbar on the right. If you right-click on the *Group MPI* in the function profile, and select *Ungroup MPI* in the popup menu, this will show how MPI time is split between the calls. Again, this information is known to you from the built-in statistics. Some scrolling may be required here as well, depending on the size of your display. Alternatively, click on any column header (like *TSelf*) to sort the list.

Now, zoom in on a piece of the event timeline around the offending MPI_Allreduce; move the mouse cursor where you see fit, hold and drag to highlight the selected rectangle, and release to see the result. All charts will automatically adjust themselves to the selected time range (see Figure 5-7).

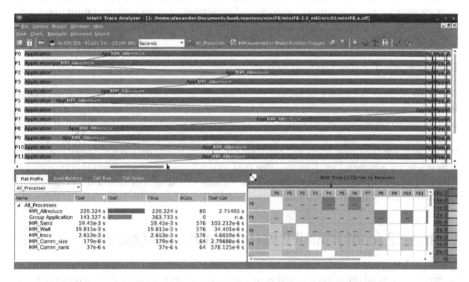

Figure 5-7. *MiniFE trace file in ITAC zoomed in upon the offending MPI_Allreduce operation (Workstation, 16 MPI processes)*

Well, this is exactly what we need to see if we want to understand the ostensibly main MPI-related performance issue in this program. The updated Functional Profile chart confirms that it is indeed this MPI_Allreduce operation that takes the lion's share of MPI communication time. On the other hand, the time spent for the actual data exchange is very low, as can be seen in the Message Profile chart, so the volume of communication cannot be the reason for the huge overhead observed. Therefore, we must assume this is load imbalance. Let us take this as a working hypothesis (to be continued).

EXERCISE 5-5

Analyze the behavior of your favorite application using the process described here. What operations consume most of the MPI communication time? Is this really communication time or load imbalance?

Choosing the Optimization Objective

If you recall, at the very beginning of this chapter we faced the decision as to what to address: load imbalance or MPI performance. The criteria for selecting one over the other are relatively soft, for the situation in real-life programs is rarely black and white. Normally there is some degree of load imbalance and some degree of MPI sloppiness. If one of them clearly dominates the other, the choice may seem obvious. However, you need to keep in mind that even a relatively small load imbalance may jog some collective operations off tune; alternatively, suboptimal performance of an MPI operation may lead to something that looks like load imbalance. How does one lighten this gray area?

Detecting Load Imbalance

Fortunately, there is a sure way to detect load imbalance in a distributed memory program. Imagine that you take out all the communication costs, essentially presuming that you run over an ideal communication fabric that has zero latency and infinite bandwidth. It is clear that, in this case, you cannot blame the network for any undue delays left in the program. Whatever is left behind is, then, the program's own fault rather than the network's or MPI's. This is why an advanced analysis tool like ITAC offers both an Ideal Interconnect Simulator (IIS) and a Load Imbalance Diagram that are broadly based on this idea and therefore help to pinpoint the load imbalance and its main victims.

Example 2 (cont.): MiniFE Performance Investigation

Let us get back to the miniFE application example, in which we came to the preliminary suspicion that load imbalance might be to blame for the extraordinarily bad observed behavior of one particular MPI_Allreduce operation.

There is a very good way to check out our working hypothesis. Go to the *Advanced* tab in the main menu, select the *Idealize* command and click OK in the respective popup to generate the ideal trace file. Now, open the ideal trace file using the *File* control in the main ITAC window, click on the *Advanced* tab, and select the *Imbalance Diagram* item. Then click *OK* in the resulting popup. Upon some meditation reflected by a progress bar, the program will visually confirm the initial suspicion: all of the MPI communication seems to be covered by load imbalance. Figure 5-8 shows that (note that we changed the default colors to make the difference more visible).

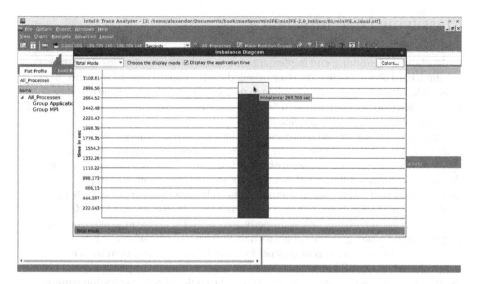

Figure 5-8. *MiniFE trace file in ITAC imbalance diagram (C version, Workstation, 16 MPI processes, 3 OpenMP threads)*

Of course, this may be an artifact of the model used to compute the load imbalance. However, this certainly indicates we should look into the load imbalance first, and only then look into further MPI communication details. Depending on this, we will decide where to go.

Referring back to the Performance Assistant chart (see Figure 5-5), we can conclude that the MPI_Wait issue most likely related to the internal workings of the MPI_Allreduce operation that might issue a call to the MPI_Wait behind the curtain. However, taken at face value, this indication itself is somewhat misleading until we understand what stands behind the reported issue. Indeed, if you switch to the *Breakdown Mode* in the view of Figure 5-8 (not shown), you will see that small message performance of the MPI_Wait call is the sole major contributor of the load imbalance observed (to be continued).

EXERCISE 5-6

Choose the primary optimization objective for your favorite application using the method described in this section. Is this load imbalance or MPI tuning? How can you justify your choice?

Dealing with Load Imbalance

Once the decision is made to address the load imbalance, it is necessary to understand what causes it and then devise an appropriate cure.

Classifying Load Imbalance

Load imbalance can come from different quarters. The first is from the *application itself*: its data layout, algorithms, and implementation quality. If the application developer did not think hard about dividing the data among the job components—be they processes or threads or tasks—fairly and according to their capabilities, there will be no other way to attack load imbalance than to fix the respective data layout, algorithmic, and implementation issues of the application.

This is where the second major source of load imbalance pops up: *platform heterogeneity*, especially heterogeneity that was not taken into account when the application was conceived. A typical example is the use of different processors across the machine, be they different CPUs or various accelerators. Another example of heterogeneity is the difference in communication characteristics of the underlying platform. Even the difference between shared memory, on the one hand, and fast network, on the other hand, unless properly accounted for, may lead to part of the job's lagging behind, waiting for the necessary data to come over the slower link.

These dependencies may or may not be explicit. It is relatively clear what is happening when two MPI processes send data to each other in the point-to-point fashion. As soon as any collective operation is involved, the choice of communication pattern is delegated to the MPI library, and ultimately, to the MPI implementor who created this library. In that case, it may be necessary to understand exactly what algorithm is being used, especially if there are more than two processes involved.

However, the situation may be substantially less transparent. Many libraries and language extensions (like offload) try to hide the actual data movement from the application programmer. In that case, it may be necessary to understand what exactly is happening beneath the hood, up to and including monitoring the activities of the underlying software and hardware components, or at least talking to someone in the know.

Addressing Load Imbalance

The treatment for load imbalances is basically determined by their source of the issue and the amount of time available.

Data partitioning and algorithmic issues may be the hardest to address, unless the program already possesses mechanisms that provide relatively easy control over these parameters. In some cases, the amount of data apportioned to each computational unit can be defined by the program input file. In other cases, the amount of work (rather than only data) apportioned to a program component may depend on its role. For example, if boundary conditions are involved, corner segments will have only two neighbors in the two-dimensional case, while internal segments will have four, and so on. If data or work partitioning is implicated in the load imbalance, a deep dive into the program may be required, up to and including reformulation of the data layout or work-partitioning strategy; replacement of the data-partitioning algorithm or component; selection of a more advanced, easier to parallelize algorithm; and so on. There is little by the way of general advice that can be given here.

Platform heterogeneity may pop up everywhere. In a modern heterogeneous cluster that uses Intel Xeon CPUs and Intel Xeon Phi coprocessors connected to the main processors by the PCI Express bus, with a fast network like InfiniBand connecting the nodes, there are so many way to get things wrong that, most likely, only proper application design upfront can "guarantee" success of the undertaking. Indeed, in such a cluster, you will have several effects uniting their forces to cause trouble:

1. Differences in the clock rate and functionality of the processors involved. These differences may go up to several times, especially as far as the clock rate is concerned. You will have to allocate proportionally less data to the weaker components.

2. Differences between the intranode communication over the shared memory and over the PCI Express bus. Again, the latency and bandwidth will vary greatly, and sometimes the relationship will not be linear. For example, PCI Express will normally lose to the shared memory on latency but may overtake it on bandwidth on certain message sizes, depending on the way in which the bus is programmed.

3. Differences between the intranode communication of any kind, on one hand, and internode communication over the fast network, on the other. In addition to this normal situation typical of any cluster, in a heterogeneous cluster with accelerated nodes, there may be the need to tunnel data from accelerator to accelerator via the PCI Express bus, over the network, and then over the PCI Express bus on the other side.

Of course, a properly implemented MPI library will handle all of this transfer transparently to your benefit, but you may still see big differences in the performance of the various communication links involved, and you will have to take this into account when partitioning the data.

On top of this, there is an interesting interaction between the component's computing capacity and its ability to push data to other components. Because of this interaction, in an ideal situation, it is possible that a relatively slower component sitting on a relatively slower interface may be loaded 100 percent of the time and cause no trouble across the job, provided the relatively faster components get larger pieces of data to deal with and direct the bulk data exchanges to the fastest available communication paths. However, it may be difficult to arrive at this ideal situation. This consideration applies, of course, to both explicit and implicit data-movement mechanisms.

Example 2 (cont.): MiniFE Performance Investigation

To complete the miniFE investigation at the MPI level, we need to understand what is causing the load imbalance detected earlier. Once again, ITAC is going to be of great help in finding that out.

First, rebuild your application so that the compiler adds debugging information to the files it produces. Adding the -g flag to the CFLAGS variable in the miniFE src/ Makefile, doing make clean there, and then make does the trick.

Now, set the environment variable VT_PCTRACE to 5 and rerun the miniFE, asking for the trace file to be produced. (You know how to do this.) Note, however, that call stack tracing requested this time is a relatively expensive procedure that will slow the execution, so it may make sense to take a rather low problem size, hoping that the program execution path does not depend on it. We used the size of 50.

Open the resulting file miniFE.x.stf in the ITAC, go to the offending MPI_Allreduce operation in the event timeline, right-click on it, and ask for details. When you click on the *View Source Code* item in the resulting popup window, you will see where the offending MPI_Allreduce was called from (see Figure 5-9).

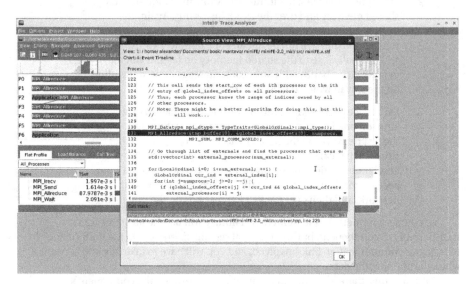

Figure 5-9. *Finding* MPI_Allreduce *source code location in miniFE (Workstation)*

If you browse the source code in this window, you will see that immediately prior to this MPI_Allreduce call, the program imposes Dirichlet boundary conditions. Very likely, the imbalance is coming from that piece of code. This is only a guess for now, so you will have to do more work before you can be sure of having found the culprit. However, if this guess is correct, and given that the program itself reports very low data imbalance as far as the distribution of nonzero matrix elements across the processes is concerned, it looks like an algorithmic issue. If you want to address it now, you know where to start. Later on, we will cover advanced techniques that will allow you to pinpoint the exact problematic code location in any situation, not only in presence of the conveniently placed and easily identifiable MPI operational brackets (to be continued in Chapter 6).

EXERCISE 5-7

Narrow down the search area by recalling from Figure 5-6 that, prior to the problematic MPI_Allreduce operation, there was another MPI_Allreduce operation that also synchronized the processes that were almost perfectly aligned at that moment. What remains to be done is to repeat this procedure and find out the other code location. Did you find the culprit?

Example 3: MiniMD Performance Investigation

Having looked into an algorithmically induced load imbalance in the case of miniFE, we can now take time to investigate another application from the same Mantevo suite, namely miniMD. This application is reported as representing, in a very lightweight form, the core of the typical molecular dynamics application LAMMPS.[13] Another useful feature is that this application (at least in its miniMD-Intel reincarnation) has been ported to the Intel Xeon Phi coprocessor, which may allow us to investigate heterogeneity-induced load imbalance issues without investing any time in the porting effort.

If you repeat all the steps mentioned here with the miniMD application, you will learn that this application shows admirable scalability intranode (see Table 5-8).

Table 5-8. *MiniMD Execution Time Dependency on the Process Number (Seconds, Workstation)*

MPI proc.	Run 1	Run 2	Run 3	Mean	Std. dev, %
1	6.402392	6.412376	6.401814	6.405527	0.075692
2	4.146758	3.884414	3.623191	3.884788	5.502115
4	1.739194	1.839692	1.683867	1.754251	3.676788
8	0.944237	0.951552	0.91314	0.93631	1.778618
16	0.518546	0.523697	0.504854	0.515699	1.541922
24	0.367219	0.365578	0.365644	0.366147	0.207156
32	0.409625	0.407031	0.397341	0.404666	1.306382
48	0.287009	0.28772	0.277317	0.284015	1.670798

The only hitch happens around 32 processes. It is probably caused by half of the MPI processes running on eight physical cores, with the other half occupying the other 16 cores for themselves. This is effectively a heterogeneous situation. Indeed, Listing 5-14 shows what the process pinning looks like:

Listing 5-14. Default Pinning for 32 MPI Processes (Workstation)

```
[0] MPI startup(): Rank      Pid       Node name    Pin cpu
[0] MPI startup(): 0         225142    book         0
[0] MPI startup(): 1         225143    book         24
[0] MPI startup(): 2         225144    book         1
[0] MPI startup(): 3         225145    book         25
[0] MPI startup(): 4         225146    book         2
[0] MPI startup(): 5         225147    book         26
[0] MPI startup(): 6         225148    book         3
[0] MPI startup(): 7         225149    book         27
[0] MPI startup(): 8         225150    book         4
[0] MPI startup(): 9         225151    book         5
[0] MPI startup(): 10        225152    book         6
[0] MPI startup(): 11        225153    book         7
[0] MPI startup(): 12        225154    book         8
[0] MPI startup(): 13        225155    book         9
[0] MPI startup(): 14        225156    book         10
[0] MPI startup(): 15        225157    book         11
[0] MPI startup(): 16        225158    book         12
[0] MPI startup(): 17        225159    book         36
[0] MPI startup(): 18        225160    book         13
[0] MPI startup(): 19        225161    book         37
[0] MPI startup(): 20        225162    book         14
[0] MPI startup(): 21        225163    book         38
[0] MPI startup(): 22        225164    book         15
[0] MPI startup(): 23        225165    book         39
[0] MPI startup(): 24        225166    book         16
[0] MPI startup(): 25        225167    book         17
[0] MPI startup(): 26        225168    book         18
[0] MPI startup(): 27        225169    book         19
[0] MPI startup(): 28        225170    book         20
[0] MPI startup(): 29        225171    book         21
[0] MPI startup(): 30        225172    book         22
[0] MPI startup(): 31        225173    book         23
```

Comparing this to Listing 5-5, we get the distribution of the MPI processes among the virtual processors, as shown in Figure 5-10.

0	2	4	6	8	9	10	11	12	13	14	15
0	1	2	3	4	5	6	7	8	9	10	11

1	3	5	7								
24	25	26	27	28	29	30	31	32	33	34	35

16	18	20	22	24	25	26	27	28	29	30	31
12	13	14	15	16	17	18	19	20	21	22	23

17	19	21	23								
36	37	38	39	40	41	42	43	44	45	46	47

Figure 5-10. Default process pinning (workstation, 32 MPI processes): MPI ranks (gray upper numbers) mapped upon processor identifiers (black lower numbers)

You could argue that this may not be the fairest mapping of all, but whatever you do, you will end up with some MPI processes out of 32 running two apiece on some physical cores. This probably explains the hitch we observed in Table 5-9.

Table 5-9. Intel MPI Library Communication Fabric Selection

I_MPI_DEVICE	I_MPI_FABRICS	Description
sock	tcp	TCP/IP-capable network fabrics, such as Ethernet and InfiniBand (the latter through IP over IB). Normally the slowest available fabric.
shm	shm	Shared memory only. Normally the fastest available fabric, but for very large messages where fast interconnects may win intranode.
ssm	shm:tcp	Shared memory + TCP/IP. Good for multicore clusters built on Ethernet.
rdma	dapl	Direct Access Programming Library (DAPL). Good for DAPL-capable network fabrics, such as InfiniBand or iWarp.
rdssm	shm:dapl	Shared-memory + DAPL. The default and fastest choice in most cases. See above for details.
N/A	ofa	Open Fabric Association (OFA)-capable network fabric including InfiniBand.* Comparable to DAPL but with some advantages, like multirail and checkpoint/restart support.

(*continued*)

Table 5-9. (*continued*)

I_MPI_DEVICE	I_MPI_FABRICS	Description
N/A	shm:ofa	Shared memory + OFA-capable network fabric. See above for details.
N/A	tmi	Tag Matching Interface (TMI)-capable network fabric including Intel True Scalue Fabric. Includes shared memory support internally, so there is no point in using the shm:tmi combination.

Next, you will observe that this application suffers from noticeable load imbalance *and* MPI overhead (called "interconnect" in the imbalance diagram; see Figure 5-11).

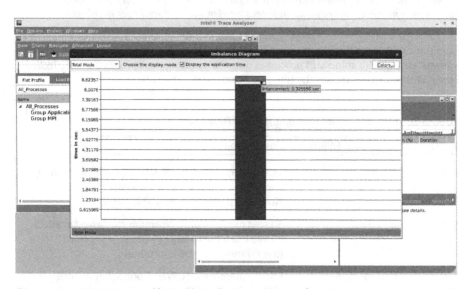

Figure 5-11. *MiniMD trace file in ITAC imbalance diagram (Workstation, 16 MPI processes)*

There is something to haul on the MPI side of the equation, at least on the default workload in.lj.miniMD. We can find out what exactly is contributing to this by comparing the real and ideal traces, ungrouping the *Group MPI* and sorting the list by *TSelf* (see Figure 5-12).

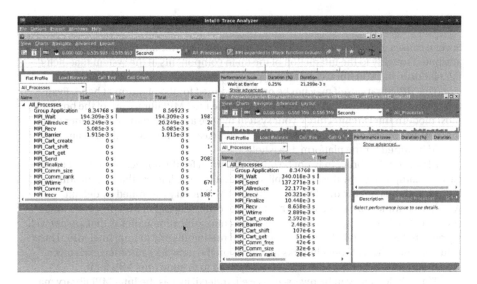

Figure 5-12. *MiniMD ideal and real traces compared (Workstation, 16 MPI processes)*

Compare the ideal trace in the upper left corner with the real trace in the lower right corner. The biggest part of the improvement comes from halving the time spent in the MPI_Wait. Most of the remaining improvement can be attributed to the reduction of the MPI_Send and MPI_Irecv durations to zero in the ideal trace, not to mention the MPI_Finalize. Contrary to this, the time spent in the MPI_Allreduce changes only slightly.

By the looks of it, MPI issues might be induced by the load imbalance rather than intrinsic communication overhead, but we cannot see this right now, for sure. Hence, we should look into the communication pattern first. This is even more the case because the relative portion of the MPI time is noticeable on this workload, and the increase of the time step parameter in the input file to the more representative value of 1000 drives this portion from 7 percent down to only 5.5 percent, on average (to be continued).

EXERCISE 5-8

Analyze and address the load imbalance in miniMD. What causes it? Replace miniMD with your favorite application and address the load imbalance there, provided this is necessary. What causes the imbalance?

Optimizing MPI Performance

If MPI overhead clearly dominates the overhead caused by the load imbalance, or if you simply do not see a practical way of addressing the load imbalance within the constraints of the target application and available time, you can still do well by addressing MPI performance issues.

Classifying the MPI Performance Issues

Several causes may lead to the MPI performance being lower than expected. They can be attributed roughly to the interaction of the main components of the system that include the platform, the MPI library, and the application involved.

The MPI library itself may not be optimally tuned for the platform at hand. Even though great care is taken to tune, for example, the Intel MPI library out of the box for the most modern Intel architectures, your system may be a bit different or a bit older than that covered by the default tuning process. In this case, the Intel MPI library can and should be tuned for the platform as a whole.

Also, the MPI library may not be optimally tuned for the application involved. The easiest example to show this is an application that is more latency than bandwidth bound, and thus not the one for which the Intel MPI library was tuned by default. Another example is an application that uses a specific number of MPI processes and several collective operations or point-to-point communication patterns that are not well represented by the Intel MPI Benchmarks used predominantly to tune Intel MPI. These would include the OSU benchmarks that focus on the network saturation exchanges.[14] If your application behaves like this, you may need to re-tune Intel MPI for it.

This relationship can be reversed, as well. Indeed, just as the Intel MPI library may be considered suboptimally tuned for a particular application, the application itself may be doing things that are bad for Intel MPI in particular and any MPI in general. Sometimes this involves interaction with the platform, sometimes it does not. For example, the MPI library usage of the cache may be competing with the application usage of it. Your methods will change depending on what you have to address.

If a MPI/platform interaction is involved, an application may be using intrinsically higher latency (e.g., internode) links for short messages. A high-quality MPI implementation like Intel MPI may sometimes be able to work around this by, say, rearranging collective operations so that the local part of the communication is done first. However, sometimes you will have to help it out.

If, however, the application is doing something intrinsically bad for any MPI, the main goal is to change the application to do the right thing. One fairly common example is a well-intentioned desire of some application developers to replace the collective operations that may not have been optimally tuned in the past by manual, point-to-point implementations thereof included into the application itself, sometimes in a pretty implicit form. This may indeed bring some performance improvement, but more often than not it does quite the opposite. Another example is the much beloved packing of noncontiguous data types into dense arrays and sending of them across and then unpacking them at the other end. Again, sometimes this makes sense, but more often it does not.

Addressing MPI Performance Issues

There is a bit of a chicken-and-egg problem once you turn toward optimizing MPI communication: what comes under scrutiny first—the platform, the MPI, or the application? The number of components and complexity of their direct and implicit interactions make it relatively difficult to give fast and ready advice for all possible situations. As a rule of thumb, keep in mind the following priorities:

1. *Map* the application upon the target platform. This includes, in particular, selection of the fastest communication fabrics, proper process layout and pinning, and other settings that affect the way application and platform interact via MPI mediation.

2. *Tune* the Intel MPI library for the platform and/or the application involved. If your application is bandwidth bound, you are likely to do well with the platform-specific tuning. If your application differs, you may need to cater to its particular needs.

3. *Optimize* the application for Intel MPI library. This includes typical MPI optimizations valid for any MPI implementation and specific Intel MPI tricks for varying levels of complexity and expected return on investment.

As usual, you will have to iterate until convergence or timeout. We will go through these steps one by one in the following sections. However, if in a particular case you perceive the need for bypassing some steps in favor of others, feel free to do so, but beware of spending a lot of time addressing the wrong problem first.

You will notice that we differentiate between optimization and tuning. *Optimization* is a wider term that may include tuning. *Tuning* normally concerns changing certain environment settings that affect performance of the target application. In other words, optimization may be more intrusive than tuning because deep optimization may necessitate source code modifications.

Mapping Application onto the Platform

Before you start the process of MPI optimization in earnest, you have to make sure that you are actually trying to optimize the application configuration that is suitable for the platform involved. The biggest potential problem here is improper process layout and pinning that may exercise slow communication paths where fast paths are needed and indeed possible.

Understanding Communication Paths

Intranode communication paths are typically the fastest the closer to the processor you get, with the shared memory ruling the realm, intranode busses like PCI Express coming next, and networking equipment bringing up the rear. However, in some cases the situation may be different, and the seemingly slower paths, like InfiniBand, may offer better bandwidth (see Figures 5-1 and 5-2), even intranode. You should definitely make yourself familiar with the quirks of the platform involved via extensive low-level benchmarking described earlier in this chapter.

A very important aspect of tuning is the selection of a proper communication fabrics combination for a particular job. Even though Intel MPI will try to choose the fastest possible fabrics automatically, in certain situations you will have to help it out. This is particularly true of the heterogeneous installations with the Intel Xeon Phi coprocessor involved, where there are so many paths to explore.

Beyond that, you have already seen several examples of one simple pinning setting's dramatically changing the behavior of certain benchmarks and applications. Generally speaking, if your application is latency bound, you will want its processes to share as much of the memory and I/O subsystem paths as possible. This means, in part, that you will try to put your processes onto adjacent cores, possibly even virtual ones. If your application is bandwidth bound, you will do better sharing as little of the memory subsystem paths as possible. This means, in part, putting your MPI processes on different processor sockets, and possibly even different nodes, if you use a cluster.

Selecting Proper Communication Fabrics

The Intel MPI Library selects reasonable communication fabric(s) by default. You can always find out what has been selected by setting the environment variable I_MPI_DEBUG to 2. If the default selection does not look right, you can change this by using one of the two environment variables, the older I_MPI_DEVICE and the newer I_MPI_FABRICS environment variables, and their respective relations. Table 5-9 gives a brief overview of what you can do.

Using Scalable Datagrams

Note that when you use a DAPL-capable fabric, with or without shared memory involvement, you can select a scalable connectionless DAPL UD transport by setting the environment variable I_MPI_DAPL_UD to enable. This may make sense if your job runs on thousands of processes. Pure connection-oriented DAPL will normally be faster below this threshold.

Specifying a Network Provider

In certain situations, you will have to specify further details of the lower-level networking configuration. This is most often the case when you have more than one version of the DAPL stack installed on the system. You will probably have to ask around to determine whether or not you need to set the I_MPI_DAPL_PROVIDER and I_MPI_DAPL_UD_PROVIDER variables, and if so, what values to use when.

Using IP over IB

Another trick is to switch over to IP over IB (IPoIB) when using the TCP transport over InfiniBand. Here is how you can do this:

```
$ export I_MPI_TCP_NETMASK=ib0               # for IP over IB or
$ export I_MPI_TCP_NETMASK=192.169.0.0       # for a particular subnet
```

Controlling the Fabric Fallback Mechanism

A word of caution for benchmarking: Intel MPI library will normally fall back upon the TCP communication if the primary fabric refuses to work, for some reason. This is a useful feature out in the field, where running a program reliably may be more important than running it fast. If you want to control the fallback path, enter this:

```
$ mpirun -genv I_MPI_FABRICS_LIST dapl,tcp -np <number of processes> ./your_app
```

However, this feature may be outright misleading during benchmarking. To make sure you are indeed using the fabric you selected, you may want to disable the Intel MPI built-in fallback mechanism by setting the environment variable I_MPI_FALLBACK to disable.

Using Multirail Capabilities

If your installation supports multirail capability, which modern InfiniBand hardware normally does by providing more than one port and possibly even InfiniBand adapter per node, you can exploit this over the OFA fabric. Just enter these magic commands depending on the number of adapters and ports you have:

```
$ export I_MPI_FABRICS=shm:ofa
$ export I_MPI_OFA_NUM_ADAPTERS=<n>    # e.g. 2 (1 by default)
$ export I_MPI_OFA_NUM_PORTS=<n>       # e.g. 2 (1 by default)
```

Detecting and Classifying Improper Process Layout and Pinning Issues

It is relatively easy to detect signs of improper process layout. Once you fire up ITAC on a trace file, you may either see exchange volumes spread very unevenly between the processes in the Message Profile chart (which by itself might be a sign of load imbalance that we have addressed), or you may notice overly long message lines crisscrossing substantial portions of the application event timeline. Normally, these latter messages will also lead to exorbitant wait times that may be picked up by the Performance Assistant and shown in the respective chart. This kind of problem can be observed both intra- and internode, as well as in the mixed configurations.

Now, any of these nice pictures will not tell you what is actually *causing* the observed issues. You will have to find that out yourself. In general, there are several ways of attacking this problem once you understand the root cause:

1. Rearrange the MPI processes and/or change their pinning at job startup to make offending messages go along the fastest possible communication path. This is the least intrusive method, which we will concentrate on below.

2.   Use virtual process topologies to make MPI rearrange the process ranks according to the expected intensity of the interprocess communication. This implies that the MPI implementation does rearrange processes when asked to do so. Intel MPI does not do this at the moment, so we will basically gloss over this approach.

3.   Rewrite the application to use a different communication pattern, or choose an alternative algorithm for the offending MPI collective operation. This is a more intrusive approach that we will consider when dealing with the MPI tuning and application modification later in this chapter.

Process pinning acts one level below the process layout. When you choose the process layout, you basically tell Intel MPI what node to put any particular MPI process on. Where exactly it lands on this node is decided by the process pinning. The ways to detect issues arising from improper process pinning are basically comparable to those recommended for the process layout investigation.

In the presence of NUMA, you will also have to mind the relationship between the processes and their memory. If the memory is located "close" to the process (in the NUMA sense), performance may be substantially better compared to when the process memory sits a few processor interconnect hops away. In the latter case, you will notice the platform latency and bandwidth limitations biting in much sooner than expected from the theoretical estimates and the low-level MPI benchmarking.

Finally, and less obviously, NUMA considerations may apply not only to the memory but also to the peripherals, like networking cards or interconnect busses. Again, if a card used for communication by a given process sits next to it in the node hierarchy, respective communication will most likely be noticeably faster compared to when the card sits several hops away. Add to this the unavoidable relationship between the memory and the networking cards, and you will get a pretty mess to clean up.

The overall picture gets even more complicated once you add dynamic processes to the mix. This includes process spawning and process attachment, especially in the heterogeneous environments. As it's still a relatively rarely used set of features, we will only touch upon them in this book.

Controlling Process Layout

The default process layout induced by the Intel MPI library is the so-called group round robin. This means that, by default, consecutive MPI ranks are placed on one node until all the available virtual cores are occupied. Once one node is fully loaded, the next node is dealt with in the same manner if it is available. Otherwise, the processes wraps around back to the very first node used, and so on.

There are several ways to control the process layout. The first of them acts *a priori*, at the job startup. The other method kicks in when the processes have been started. It uses the so-called virtual topologies defined by the MPI standard—the communicators created by using the MPI_Cart_create, MPI_Graph_create, and friends. This latter method presumes that the underlying MPI implementation indeed rearranges the MPI process ranks when asked to do so by the application programmer.

Controlling the Global Process Layout

Several methods exist to specify the process layout at startup, with varying degrees of brevity and precision. The easiest of them is use of the -ppn option and friends, including the environment variable I_MPI_PERHOST. You set the I_MPI_PERHOST environment variable to control process layout in the following manner:

```
$ export I_MPI_PERHOST=1          # makes round-robin distribution
$ export I_MPI_PERHOST=all        # maps processes to all virtualCPUs
                                  # on a node (default)
$ export I_MPI_PERHOST=allcores   # maps processes to all physicalCPUs
                                  # on a node
```

Alternatively, you can use one of the following mpirun options:

```
-perhost <number>    # group round-robin distribution with number of
                     # processes per node
-ppn <number>        # "group round-robin", same as '-perhost <number>'
-grr <number>        # "group round-robin", same as '-perhost <number>'
-rr                  # round-robin distribution, same as '-perhost 1'
```

For example, this will put only two processes on each node:

```
$ mpirun -ppn 2 -np <number of processes> ./your_app
```

You will normally want to use the default process layout for pure MPI applications. For hybrid programs, you may want to decrease the number of processes per node accordingly, so as to leave enough cores for the OpenMP or another threading library to use. Finally, and especially in benchmarking the internode rather than the intranode communication, you will need to go down to one process per node.

Controlling the Detailed Process Layout

More detailed process layout control methods include the so-called long mpirun notation and the -hostfile, -machinefile, and, in the case of the scalable Hydra process manager only, the hosts options. Each of them essentially prescribes what processes to put where. The long notation is probably the most illustrative of all, so we will briefly review it here. You can look up the rest of the control possibilities in the *Intel MPI Library Reference Manual*.[15] Note that use of specific process placement is very common in benchmarking when you really want to make sure rank 0 sits here, rank 1 sits there, and so on. This may contribute substantially to the reproducibility of the results.

In normal operational mode, you will probably use the long notation more often when dealing with Intel Xeon Phi co-processor than otherwise, so let's demonstrate it in that case (here and elsewhere we split the overly long run strings into several lines by using the shell backslash/new line notation):

```
$ mpirun -genv I_MPI_MIC enable \
          -host `hostname` -np 2 ./your_app : \
          -host `hostname`-mic0 -np 16 ./your_app.mic
```

You can see that the run string is separated into two parts by the colon (:). The first half prescribes two MPI processes to be started on the host CPU. The second half puts 16 MPI processes upon the Intel Xeon Phi coprocessor connected to this CPU. This coprocessor conventionally bears the name of the host node plus the extension -mic0.

Setting the Environment Variables at All Levels

Note that you can set environment variables, such as those controlling the process pinning, either generally for all parts using the -genv option *before* the first -host option or individually in each part using the -env option, preferably *after* the respective -host option. Here is a good mixed example:

```
$ mpirun -genv I_MPI_MIC enable \
          -host `hostname` -env I_MPI_PIN_DOMAIN 4 -np 2 ./your_app : \
          -host `hostname`-mic0 -env I_MPI_PIN_DOMAIN 16 -np 4 ./your_app.mic
```

This particular command will turn on the Intel Xeon Phi coprocessor support, and then create OpenMP domains of four cores on the host processes and 16 cores on the Intel Xeon Phi coprocessor.

Controlling the Process Pinning

The Intel MPI library ships in several variants. The main ones are the sequential optimized library and the multithreaded optimized library. In the former library, the maximum supported thread level is MPI_THREAD_SINGLE. In the latter library, the maximum supported thread level is MPI_THREAD_MULTIPLE, with the default being MPI_THREAD_FUNNELED. More than one library is shipped so as to achieve maximum possible performance in each use case. Owing to Intel MPI development's constant work on optimization, it is not impossible that only the multithreaded library will be included in the delivery in the future, so we will concentrate on that right away.

The default process pinning imposed by the Intel MPI library is geared toward hybrid applications. It is roughly described by the following settings:

```
I_MPI_PIN=on
I_MPI_PIN_MODE=pm
I_MPI_PIN_DOMAIN=auto,compact
I_MPI_PIN_RESPECT_CPUSET=on
I_MPI_PIN_RESPECT_HCA=on
I_MPI_PIN_CELL=unit
I_MPI_PIN_ORDER=compact
```

There are several important aspects to keep in mind:

1. Process pinning is turned on by default. You may want to control this by setting the environment variable I_MPI_PIN to the values of disable or enable (likewise, off and on, or false and true, or just 0 and 1, respectively).

2. The default process pinning is imposed by the process management infrastructure rather than the library itself. This has some far-reaching ramifications with respect to the memory and peripherals affinity we are going to consider in the next section. You probably do not want to interfere with this unless your job manager starts making trouble here.

3. There are two major methods of controlling the pinning, one of which focuses on hybrid ones (via the I_MPI_PIN_DOMAIN and friends) while the other is better suited for pure MPI programs (via the I_MPI_PIN_PROCESSOR_LIST and friends). If the former method is used, it normally overrides the latter if that is used as well.

4. The default I_MPI_PIN_DOMAIN value auto means that the domain size is defined by the formula *size=#cpu/#proc*, where *#cpu* is the number of virtual processors on the node and *#proc* is the number of the MPI processes started on the node. It is this domain into which all the threads belonging to the respective MPI process are placed. The qualifier compact above leads to the domains' being put as close to each other as possible in the sense of sharing the processor resources like caches. If you do not want this, you can try values of scatter and platform to go for the least possible resource sharing and the platform-specific thread ordering, respectively.

5. The default pinning takes into account the platform affinity setting (cf. cpuset command) and the locality of the InfiniBand networking cards (called host channel adapter, or HCA). It also prescribes targeting the virtual cores (unit) and compact domain ordering (compact) in the absence of respective qualifiers in the values of the I_MPI_PIN_PROCESSOR_LIST and I_MPI_PIN_DOMAIN environment variables.

There may be small deviations between the description given and the realities of the default pinning, so you should look into the aforementioned *Intel MPI Library Reference Manual* to learn all the details.

If you want to use OpenMP in your program, you better change the value auto to omp, in which case the size of the domain will be defined by the OpenMP specific means, like the value of the environment variable OMP_NUM_THREADS or KMP_NUM_THREADS. Likewise, the pinning inside the domain will be determined according to the OpenMP specific settings like KMP_AFFINITY, which we will consider in detail in Chapter 6.

Like the I_MPI_PIN_DOMAIN, the I_MPI_PIN_PROCESSOR_LIST has many possible values. The most practical values are as follows:

```
$ export I_MPI_PIN_PROCESSOR_LIST=all         # all virtual cores
$ export I_MPI_PIN_PROCESSOR_LIST=allcores     # all physical cores
$ export I_MPI_PIN_PROCESSOR_LIST=allsocks      # all processor sockets
```

When you start playing with exact process placement upon specific cores, both I_MPI_PIN_DOMAIN and I_MPI_PIN_PROCESSOR_LIST will help you by providing the list-oriented, bit mask–based, and symbolic capabilities to cut the cake exactly the way you want, and if you wish, by using more than one method. You will find them all fully described in the *Intel MPI Library Reference Manual*.

Controlling Memory and Network Affinity

There are no special means of controlling memory affinity in the Intel MPI library per se. However, as mentioned in the previous section, the library facilitates the operating system doing the right thing by setting the process pinning before the process launch. Under normal conditions, this means that the processor running a particular process will be located closely to the memory this process uses. At the same time, it is possible to use the system and third-party tools to affect the memory affinity (cf. numactl command), which will be reviewed in Chapter 6.

Contrary to this, networking affinity enjoys some level of support in Intel MPI Library, as represented by the I_MPI_PIN_RESPECT_HCA setting mentioned here. There are other settings available, but they are considered experimental at the moment and are reserved for the MPI implementors until better times.

Example 4: MiniMD Performance Investigation on Xeon Phi

Let's see what happens to the miniMD application and its mapping on the platform if we add Intel Xeon Phi coprocessors to the mix. First, you will need to get access to a machine that has them. In our case, we used the same cluster that happens to have several Intel Xeon Phi equipped nodes. Running the application on Intel Xeon Phi is only a bit more complicated than on the normal Xeon. You need to build the executable program separately for Intel Xeon and for Intel Xeon Phi. In the case of the miniMD, this is accomplished by the following commands (see also 1build.sh):

```
$ make intel            # for Intel Xeon
$ mv ./miniMD_intel ./miniMD_intel.host
$ make clean
$ make intel KNC=yes    # for Intel Xeon Phi
$ mv ./miniMD_intel ./miniMD_intel.mic
```

Here, we renamed both executables to keep them separate and distinguishable from each other and from the plain Xeon executable we may need to rebuild later on. This way we cannot spoil our executable programs by accident.

Running the program is similar to the workstation:

```
$ export I_MPI_MIC=enable
$ mpiexec.hydra \
      -env LD_LIBRARY_PATH /opt/intel/impi_latest/mic/lib:$MIC_LD_LIBRARY_PATH \
      -host `hostname`-mic0 -np 16 ./miniMD_intel.mic
```

These environment settings make sure that the Intel Xeon Phi coprocessor is found and that the path settings there are correct. If we compare performance of the programs on Intel Xeon and Intel Xeon Phi at different process counts, we get the results shown in Table 5-10:

Table 5-10. *MiniMD Execution Time on Intel Xeon or Intel Xeon Phi (Seconds, Cluster)*

MPI proc.	Xeon	Xeon Phi	Ratio, times
1	8.13	52.72	6.48
2	4.08	26.90	6.60
4	2.08	14.22	6.85
8	1.06	7.02	6.62
16	0.56	3.85	6.92
24	0.38	2.65	6.90
32	0.43	2.04	4.77
48	0.30	1.47	4.82
64		1.38	
96		1.12	
128		1.18	

As usual, we performed three runs at each process count and analyzed the results for variability, which was all below 1 percent in this case. You have certainly gotten used to this procedure by now, so that we can skip the details. From this table we can derive that a Xeon is roughly 6.5 to 6.9 times faster than Xeon Phi for the same number of MPI processes, as long as Xeon cores are not saturated. Note that this relationship holds for the core-to-core comparison (one MPI process results) and for MPI-to-MPI comparison (two through 24 MPI processes). So, you will need between 6.5 and 12 times more Xeon Phi processes to beat Xeon. Note that although Xeon Phi saturates later, at around 64 to 96 MPI processes, it never reaches Xeon execution times on 48 MPI processes. The difference is again around six times.

It may be interesting to see how speedup and efficiency compare to each other in the case of Xeon and Xeon Phi platforms; see Figure 5-13.

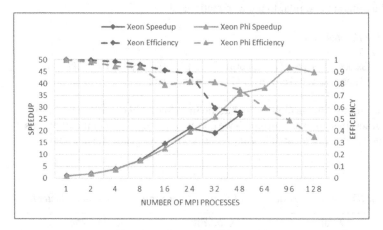

Figure 5-13. *MimiMD speedup and efficiency on Xeon and Xeon Phi platforms (cluster)*

Here, speedup is measured by the left-hand vertical axis, while efficiency goes by the right-hand one. Looking at this graph, we can draw a number of conclusions:

1. We can see that Xeon efficiency surpasses Xeon Phi's and goes very much along the ideal speedup curve until Xeon efficiency drops dramatically when we go beyond 24 MPI processes and start using virtual rather than physical cores. It then recovers somewhat by sheer weight of the resources applied.

2. Since this Xeon Phi unit has 61 physical cores, we observe a comparable effect at around 61 MPI processes as well.

3. Xeon surpasses Xeon Phi on efficiency until the aforementioned drop, when Xeon Phi takes over.

4. Xeon Phi becomes really inefficient and stops delivering speedup growth on a large number of MPI processes. It is possible that OpenMP threads might alleviate this somewhat.

5. There is an interesting dip in the Xeon Phi efficiency curve at around 16 MPI processes. What it is attributed to may require extra investigation.

If you try to use both Xeon and Xeon Phi at once, you will have to not only balance their respective numbers but also keep in mind that the data traversing the PCI Express bus may move slower than inside Xeon and Xeon Phi, and most likely will move slower most of the time, apart from large messages inside Xeon Phi. So, if you start with the aforementioned proportion, you will have to play around a bit before you get to the nearly ideal distribution, not to mention doing the process pinning and other tricks we have explored. A good spot to start from would probably be 16 to 24 MPI processes on Xeon and 64 to 96 MPI processes on Xeon Phi.

The required command will look as follows:

```
$ export I_MPI_MIC=1
$ export I_MPI_DAPL_PROVIDER_LIST=ofa-v2-mlx4_0-1u,ofa-v2-scif0
$ mpiexec.hydra -host `hostname` -np 16 ./miniMD_intel.host : \
    -env LD_LIBRARY_PATH /opt/intel/impi_latest/mic/lib:$MIC_LD_LIBRARY_PATH \
    -host `hostname`-mic0 -np 96 ./miniMD_intel.mic
```

Table 5-11 shows a result of our quick testing on the same platform:

Table 5-11. *MiniMD Execution Time on Intel Xeon and Intel Xeon Phi with Local Minima Highlighted (Seconds, Cluster)*

Xeon/Phi	48	64	96	128
8	1.396	1.349	1.140	1.233
16	1.281	1.324	*1.133*	1.134
24	1.190	1.256	1.137	1.222
48	*0.959*	1.219	1.157	1.093

We placed Xeon process counts along the vertical axis and Xeon Phi process counts along the horizontal axis. This way we could obtain a sort of two-dimensional data-distribution picture represented by numbers. Also, note that we prudently under- and overshot the guesstimated optimal process count ranges, just in case our intuition was wrong. And as it happens, it was wrong! We can observe two local minima: one for the expected 16:96 Xeon to Xeon Phi process count ratio. However, the better global minimum is located in the 48:48 corner of the table. And if we compare it to the best we can get on 48 Xeon–based MPI processes alone, we see that Xeon Phi's presence draws the result *down* by more than three times.

One can use ITAC to see what exactly is happening: is this imbalance induced by the aforementioned Xeon to Xeon Phi core-to-core performance ratio that has not been taken into account during the data distribution? Or is it by the communication overhead basically caused by the PCI Express bus? It may be that both effects are pronounced to the point of needing a fix. In particular, if the load imbalance is a factor, which it most likely is because the data is likely split between the MPI processes proportional to their total number, without accounting for the relative processor speed, one way to fight back would be to create a bigger number of OpenMP threads on the Xeon Phi part of the system. Quite unusually, you can control the number of threads using the program's own -t option. For example, the following command uses one of the better miniMD configurations while generating a valid ITAC trace file:

```
$ mpiexec.hydra -trace -host `hostname` -np 2 ./miniMD_intel.host -t 12 :\
    -env LD_LIBRARY_PATH \ /opt/intel/impi_latest/mic/lib:/opt/intel/itac_
latest/mic/lib:$MIC_LD_LIBRARY_PATH \
    -host `hostname`-mic0 -np 6 ./miniMD_intel.mic -t 32
```

Even a quick look at the resulting trace file shows that load imbalance caused by the platform heterogeneity is indeed the root cause of all the evil here, as shown in Figure 5-14.

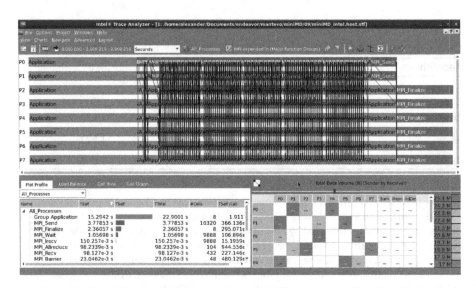

Figure 5-14. *MiniMD trace file in ITAC (cluster, 2 Xeon processes, 6 Xeon Phi processes)*

Here, processes *P0* and *P1* sit on the Xeon, while the rest of them sit on the Xeon Phi. The difference in their relative speed is very clear from the direct visual comparison of the corresponding (blue) computing sections. We can discount the MPI_Finalize duration because it is most likely caused by the ITAC data post-processing. However, the MPI_Send and MPI_Wait times are out of all proportion.

Further analysis of the data-exchange pattern reveals that two closely knit groups take four processes each, with somewhat lower exchange volumes between the groups (not shown). Moreover, a comparison of the transfer rates that can be done by clicking on the *Message Profile* and selecting *Attribute to show/Maximum Transfer Rate* shows that the PCI Express links achieve at most 0.2 bytes per tick while up to 2 bytes per tick are possible inside Xeon and up to 1.1 bytes per tick inside Xeon Phi (not shown). This translates to about 0.23 GiB/s, 2.3 GiB/s, and 1.1 GiB/s, respectively, with some odd outliers.

Hence, we can hope for performance improvement if we do the following:

1. Split the Xeon and Xeon Phi portions into equal-size process groups (say, 4 vs. 4). This should match the data split performed by the program because currently the first two processes of the first group sit on Xeon and the other two are on Xeon Phi.

2. Use up to 12 times fewer threads on Xeon than on Xeon Phi (say, 4 vs. 48). This should compensate for the relative difference in processor speed.

3. Pray that the lower exchange volume in the fringes will not overload the PCI Express links. The difference in volumes (25 MiB vs. 17 MiB) is, however, rather small and may not suffice.

Indeed, if we follow these recommendations and change the run string accordingly, we get a substantial reduction in the program execution time (from 1.58 seconds to 1.26 seconds) despite the fact that we used *fewer* cores on Xeon and the same number of cores on Xeon Phi. This is, however, only the beginning of the journey, because we are still far away from the best Xeon-only result obtained so far (0.3 seconds; see Table 5-10). Given the prior treatise in this book, and knowing how to deal with the load imbalance in general, you can read other sources dedicated to Intel Xeon Phi programming if you want to pursue this path.[16] If, after that, the heterogeneity still shows through the less than optimal data-exchange paths, especially across the PCI Express lane, you can address this in other ways that we will discuss further along in this chapter.

EXERCISE 5-9

Find out the optimal MPI process to the OpenMP thread ratio for miniMD using a heterogeneous platform. Quantify this ratio in comparison to the relative component speeds. How much of the effect can be attributed to the computation and communication parts of the heterogeneity?

Example 5: MiniGhost Performance Investigation

Let's take on a beefier example this time. Instead of going for the realistic but relatively small workloads we used in the case of miniFE and miniMD earlier, we'll deal with the miniGhost from the NERSC-8 Trinity benchmark set.[17] This finite difference calculation will nicely complement the finite element and molecular dynamics programs we have considered so far. However, for Trinity, being a record-setting procurement, even the smallest configuration of its miniGhost benchmark will certainly overwhelm our workstation, so we will first have to reduce the size of the workload in order to make sense of it.

Using the benchmarking methods described earlier, you will find that setting the domain size to 200 cubed will do the trick. Moreover, you will learn that the best performance is achieved by taking 12 processes per node and running four OpenMP threads per process, and by splitting the task into 1:3:4 slabs in the X, Y, and Z directions, respectively. By the way, for the program to build, you will have to change the Makefile to reference Intel compilers, and also add the -qopenmp flag to the OPT_F and add the -lifcore library to the LIBS variables there. It is quite usual that some minor adjustments are necessary.

Long story made short, here is the run string we used for the workstation launch:

```
$ export OMP_NUM_THREADS=4
$ mpirun -np 12 ./miniGhost.x --scaling 1 --nx 200 --ny 200 --nz 200
    --num_vars 40 \
    --num_spikes 1 --debug_grid 1 --report_diffusion 21 --percent_sum 100 \
    --num_tsteps 20 --stencil 24 --comm_method 10 --report_perf 1 --npx 1
        --npy 3 --npz 4 \
    --error_tol 8
```

Built-in statistics output shows the role distribution among the top three MPI calls, as illustrated in Listing 5-15:

Listing 5-15. MiniGhost Statistics (Workstations, 12 MPI Processes, 4 OpenMP Threads per Process)

#	[time]	[calls]	<%mpi>	<%wall>
# MPI_Allreduce	3.17148	9600	54.74	3.47
# MPI_Waitany	2.23135	1360	38.51	2.44
# MPI_Init	0.371742	12	6.42	0.41

High relative cost of the MPI_Allreduce makes it a very attractive tuning target. However, let us try the full-size workload first. Once we proceed to run this benchmark in its "small" configuration on eight cluster nodes and 96 MPI processes, we will use the following run string inspired in part by the one we used on the workstation (here, we highlighted deviations from the original script run_small.sh):

```
$ export OMP_NUM_THREADS=4
$ export I_MPI_PERHOST=12
$ mpirun -np 96 ./miniGhost.x --scaling 1 --nx 672 --ny 672 --nz 672
    --num_vars 40 \
    --num_spikes 1 --debug_grid 1 --report_diffusion 21 --percent_sum 100 \
    --num_tsteps 20 --stencil 24 --comm_method 10 --report_perf 1 --npx 4
        --npy 4 --npz 6 \
    --error_tol8
```

The irony of benchmarking in the context of a request for proposals (RFP) like NERSC-8 Trinity is that we cannot change the parameters of the benchmarks and may not be allowed to change the run string, either. This means that we will probably have to go along with the possibly suboptimal data split between the MPI processes this time; although looking at the workstation results, we would prefer to leave as few layers along the X axis as possible. However, setting a couple of environment variables upfront to ask for four instead of one OpenMP threads, and placing 12 MPI processes per node, might be allowed. Thus, our initial investigation did influence the mapping of the application to the platform, and we know that we may be shooting below the optimum in the data-distribution sense.

Further, it is interesting to see what is taking most of the MPI time now. The built-in statistics show a slightly different distribution; see Listing 5-16:

Listing 5-16. MiniGhost Statistics (Cluster, 8 Nodes, 12 MPI Processes per Node, 4 OpenMP Threads per Process)

```
#                      [time]     [calls]    <%mpi>    <%wall>
# MPI_Init             149.771    96         44.95     4.17
# MPI_Allreduce        96.3654    76800      28.92     2.68
# MPI_Waitany          79.7788    17920      23.94     2.22
```

The sharp hike in relative MPI_Init cost is probably explained by the presence of the relatively slower network. It may also be explained by all the threads being busy when the network stack itself needs some of them to process the connection requests. Whatever the reason, this overhead looks abnormally high and certainly deserves further investigation.

This way or another, the MPI_Init, MPI_Allreduce, and MPI_Waitany take about 99 percent of all MPI time, between them. At least the first two calls may be amenable to the MPI-level tuning, while the last one may indicate some load imbalance (to be continued).

EXERCISE 5-10

Find the best possible mapping of your favorite application on your favorite platform. Do you do better with the virtual or the physical cores? Why?

Tuning the Intel MPI Library

Once you are certain that the application is properly mapped onto the platform, it makes sense to turn to the way the MPI Library is exploiting this situation. This is where MPI tuning for the platform comes into play. As mentioned above, you are likely to go this way if your application falls into the wide class of bandwidth-bound programs. In the case of latency-bound applications, you will probably want to use the application-specific tuning described later in this section.

Tuning Intel MPI for the Platform

There are two ways to tune Intel MPI for the platform: automatically by using the mpitune utility or manually.

If you elect to use the mpitune utility, run it once after installation and each time after changes in cluster configuration. The best configuration of the automatically selected Intel MPI tuning parameters is recorded for each combination of the communication device, the number of nodes, the number of MPI ranks, and the process layout. The invocation string is simple in this case:

```
$ mpitune
```

Be aware that this can take a lot of time, so it may make sense to run this job overnight. Note also that for this mode to work, you should have the writing permission for the etc subfolder of the Intel MPI Library installation directory, or use the -od option to select a different output directory.

Once the mpitune finishes, you can reuse the recorded values in any run by adding the -tune option to the normal mpirun invocation string; for example:

```
$ mpirun -tune -np 32 ./your_app
```

You can learn more about the mpitune utility in the *Tutorial: MPI Tuner for Intel MPI Library for Linux* OS*.[18] If you elect to do the tuning manually, you will have to dig into the MPI internals quite a bit. There are several groups of tuning parameters that you will need to deal with for every target fabric, number of processes, their layout, and the pinning. They can be split into point-to-point, collective, and other magical settings.

Tuning Point-to-Point Settings

Point-to-point operations form the basis of most MPI implementations. In particular, Intel MPI uses point-to-point communication extensively for the collective and (however counterintuitive this may seem) one-sided communications. Thus, the tuning should start with the point-to-point settings.

■ **Note** You can output some variable settings using the I_MPI_DEBUG value of 5.

Adjusting the Eager and Rendezvous Protocol Thresholds

MPI implementations normally support two communication protocols:

- *Eager protocol* sends data immediately regardless of the availability of the matching receive request on the other side. This protocol is used normally for short messages, essentially trading better latency on the sending side for the danger of having to allocate intermediate buffers on the receiving side when the respective receive operation has not yet been posted.

- *Rendezvous protocol* notifies the receiving side on the data pending, and transfers it only once the matching receive request has been posted. This protocol tries to avoid the cost of the extra buffer allocation on the receiving side at the sacrifice of, typically, two extra short messages used for the notification and acknowledgment.

The protocol switchover point is controlled by the environment variable I_MPI_EAGER_THRESHOLD. Below and at this integral value that currently defaults to 256 KiB, the eager protocol is used. Above it, the rendezvous protocol kicks in. As a rule of thumb, the longer the messages you want to send immediately, the higher will be your optimal eager threshold.

Changing DAPL and DAPL UD Eager Protocol Threshold

Specifics of the Intel MPI Library add another, lower-level eager/rendezvous protocol threshold to the DAPL and DAPL UD communication paths. This has to do with how messages are sent between the processes using Remote Direct Memory Access (RDMA) methods. Basically, the lower-level eager protocol tries to avoid the cost of extra memory registration, while the rendezvous protocol goes for this registration to speed up the resulting data transfer by bypassing any intermediate buffers.

As in the case of the high-level eager threshold, each of the fabrics has its own threshold, called I_MPI_DAPL_DIRECT_COPY_THRESHOLD and I_MPI_DAPL_UD_DIRECT_COPY_THRESHOLD, respectively. When setting these environment variables, you will have to balance the desire to send messages off immediately with the increase in memory consumption associated with the raised value of the respective threshold.

Bypassing Shared Memory for Intranode Communication

It may happen on certain platforms that fabric performance overtakes the shared memory performance intranode. If it happens at all, it normally occurs at around 350 KiB message size. If your preliminary benchmarking reveals this situation, set the environment variable I_MPI_SHM_BYPASS to enable. This will make Intel MPI use the DAPL or TCP fabrics, if selected, for message sizes larger than the value of the environment variable I_MPI_INTRANODE_EAGER_THRESHOLD that currently defaults to 256 KiB for all fabrics but shm.

Bypassing the Cache for Intranode Communication

As a final note on point-to-point thresholds, there is a way to control what variant of the memory copying is used by the shared memory communication path. If you set the environment variable I_MPI_SHM_CACHE_BYPASS to enable, Intel MPI Library will use the normal, cache-mediated memory for messages below the values of the I_MPI_SHM_CACHE_BYPASS_THRESHOLDS and special non-temporal memory copy for larger messages. If activated, this feature may prevent the so-called cache pollution by data that will be pushed out of cache by additional incoming message segments anyway.

This last is a fairly advanced control, so you should approach it with care and read the respective part of the *Intel MPI Library Reference Manual*. The default values set to half of the size of L2 cache are normally adequate, but you may want to set them to the size of the L1 cache if you feel adventurous; for example:

```
$ export I_MPI_SHM_CACHE_BYPASS_THRESHOLDS=16384,16384,-1,16384,-1,16384
$ mpirun -np 2 -genv I_MPI_FABRICS shm IMB-MPI1 PingPong
```

Choosing the Best Collective Algorithms

Now that you are sure of your fabric selection and the most important point-to-point thresholds, it is the right time to proceed to tuning the collective operations. Certainly, you should make a list of operations that are relevant to your task. Looking into the built-in statistics output by the Intel MPI Library is a good first step here.

As it happens, Intel MPI Library provides different algorithms for each of the many MPI collective operations. Each of these algorithms has its strengths and weaknesses, as well as its possible limitations on the number of processes and message sizes it can sensibly handle.

■ **Note**   You can output default collective settings using the I_MPI_DEBUG value of 6.

You can use the environment variables named after the pattern I_MPI_ADJUST_<opname>, where the <opname> is the name of the respective collective operation. This way you come to the variable names like I_MPI_ADJUST_ALLREDUCE.

If we consider the case of the MPI_Allreduce a little further, we will see that there are no less than eight different algorithms available for this operation alone. Once again, the *Intel MPI Library Reference Manual* is your friend. Here, we will only be able to give some rules of thumb as to the algorithm selection by their class. To see how this general advice fits your practical situation, you will have to run a lot of benchmarking jobs to determine where to change the algorithm, if at all. A typical invocation string looks as follows:

```
$ mpirun -genv I_MPI_ADJUST_ALLREDUCE 4 -np 16 IMB-MPI1 Allreduce
```

You can certainly use any other benchmark, or even application, you want for this tuning. We will stick to the IMB here, out of sheer weight of experience. This way or another, you will end up with pretty fancy settings of the following kind that will have to be put somewhere (most likely, a configuration file):

```
$ export I_MPI_ADJUST_ALLGATHER= \
  '1:4-11;4:11-15;1:15-27;4:27-31;1:31-32;2:32-51;3:51-5988;4:5988-13320'
```

Well, it's your choice. Now, going through the most important collective operations in alphabetical order, in Table 5-12, we issue general recommendations based on extensive research done by Intel engineers.[19] You should take these recommendations with a grain of salt, for nothing can beat your own benchmarking.

Table 5-12. *Intel MPI Collective Algorithm Recommendations*

Operation	Algorithm	Small msgs	Large msgs	Rec. PPN
MPI_Allgather	(1) Recursive Doubling	+	+	1*
	(2) Bruck's	+	+	1*
	(3) Ring		+	any
	(4) Topological Gatherv/Bcast	+		>1
MPI_Allreduce	(1) Recursive Doubling	+		
	(2) Rabenseifner's	+	+	
	(3) Reduce/Bcast		+**	1
	(4) Topological Reduce/Bcast		+**	>1
	(5) Binomial Tree	+		1
	(6) Topological Binomial Tree	+		>1
	(7) Shumilin's Ring		+**	
	(8) Ring		+	
MPI_Alltoall	(1) Bruck's	+		
	(2) Isend/Irecv		+	
	(3) Pairwise Exchange		+	
	(4) Plum's	+	+	

(continued)

Table 5-12. (*continued*)

Operation	Algorithm	Small msgs	Large msgs	Rec. PPN
MPI_Barrier	(1) Dissemination	N/A	N/A	1
	(2) Recursive Doubling	N/A	N/A	1
	(3) Topology Dissemination	N/A	N/A	>1
	(4) Topology Recursive Doubling	N/A	N/A	>1
	(5) Binominal Gather/Scatter	N/A	N/A	1
	(6) Topology Binominal Gather/Scatter	N/A	N/A	>1
MPI_Bcast	(1) Binomial Tree	+		1
	(2) Recursive Doubling	+	+	1
	(3) Ring		+	1
	(4) Topological Binomial Tree	+		>1
	(5) Topological Recursive Doubling	+	+	>1
	(6) Topological Ring		+	>1
	(7) Shumilin's		+**	
MPI_Gather &	(1) Binomial Tree	+	+	1
MPI_Scatter	(2) Topological Binomial Tree	+	+	>1
	(3) Shumilin's		+	
MPI_Reduce	(1) Shumilin's		+**	1
	(2) Binomial Tree	+		1
	(3) Topological Shumilin's		+**	>1
	(4) Topological Binomial Tree	+		>1
	(5) Rabenseifner's	+	+	1
	(6) Topological Rabenseifner's	+	+	>1

*Only for large messages, otherwise any PPN.

**For buffers larger than the number of processes times the algorithm specific segment size.

Tuning Intel MPI Library for the Application

Again, you can tune Intel MPI for a particular application either automatically using the mpitune utility or manually. The mpitune invocation string is a little more complicated in this case (the use of backslashes and quotes is mandatory):

```
$ mpitune --application \"mpiexec -np 32 ./my_app\" --of ./my_app.conf
```

This way you can tune Intel MPI for any kind of MPI application by specifying its command line. By default, performance is measured as the inverse of the program execution time. To reduce the overall tuning time, use the shortest representative application workload (if applicable). Again, this process may take quite a while to complete.

Once you get the configuration file, you can reuse it any time in the following manner:

```
$ mpirun -tune ./my_app.conf -np 32 ./my_app
```

Note that here you not only mention the file name but also use the same number of processes and generally the same run configuration as in the tuning session. (You can learn more about this tuning mode in the aforementioned tuning tutorial.)

If you elect to tune Intel MPI manually, you will basically have to repeat all that you did for the platform-specific tuning described in the previous section, with the exception of using your application or a set of representative kernels instead of the IMB for the procedure. Certainly, you will do better instead by addressing only those point-to-point patterns and collective operations at the number of processes, their layout and pinning, and message sizes that are actually used by the target application. The built-in statistics and ITAC output will help you in finding out what to go for first.

Using Magical Tips and Tricks

Sometimes you will have to foray beyond the normal tuning of the point-to-point and collective operations. Use the following expert advice sparingly: the deeper you get into this section, the closer you are moving toward Intel MPI open heart surgery.

Disabling the Dynamic Connection Mode

Intel MPI establishes connections on demand if the number of processes is higher than 64. This saves some time at startup and may diminish the total number of connections established, so it is an important scalability feature. However, it may also lead to certain delays during the first exchange that require a new connection to be set up. Set the environment variable I_MPI_DYNAMIC_CONNECTION to disable in order to establish all connections upfront.

Applying the Wait Mode to Oversubscribed Jobs

Sometimes applications do a lot of I/O and may profit from running in the so-called oversubscribed mode—that is, in the mode with the number of processes that exceeds the number of the available cores. In these rare cases, try to set the environment variable I_MPI_WAIT_MODE to enable so as to make MPI processes wait for an interrupt to be delivered to them instead of polling the fabrics for the new messages. Even though Intel MPI possesses a rather elaborate back-off strategy in the default polling mode, going for the outright wait mode (also called event-driven mode) may bring a quantum leap in performance under some circumstances.

Fine-Tuning the Message-Passing Progress Engine

Deep inside any MPI implementation there sits a vital component called the *progress engine*. It is this component that actually pushes bytes into the fabric layers and makes sure they proceed to their respective destinations, reach them, and are put into the user buffers on the other side.

Typically, this component is called (or, in implementor speak, "kicked") every time there is a substantial call into the MPI Library that can be implicated in moving data across the wires. Examples of this class include the MPI_Send, MPI_Recv, MPI_Wait, MPI_Test, MPI_Probe, all collective operations, their multiple friends and relations, and some other calls. This approach is called *synchronous invocation of the progress engine*. On a level with this, an MPI implementation can offer asynchronous capabilities by, say, running part of the progress engine in a background thread.

This way or another, this component is faced with a difficult existential dilemma. On one hand, it needs to be reactive to new messages coming and going, in order to achieve acceptable latency. On the other hand, it should try to avoid using up too much of the processor's time, for this would make the overall system performance go down. To address this dilemma, various MPI implementations offer so-called back-off strategies that try to find the right balance between reactivity and resource consumption. Of course, there are multiple settings that control this strategy, and the default tuning tries to select them so that a typical application will do alright.

Intel MPI has elaborate and finely tuned back-off mechanisms. Should you become dissatisfied with the default settings, however, try to increase the I_MPI_SPIN_COUNT value from the default of 1 for one process per node and 250 for more than one process per node. This will change the number of times the progress engine spins, waiting for a message or connection request, before the back-off strategy kicks in. Higher values will favor better latency, to a degree. If you raise this value too much, you will start burning too many CPU cycles, polling the memory needlessly.

If you run more than one process per node that use the shared memory channel for data exchange, try to increase the I_MPI_SHM_SPIN_COUNT value above its default of 100. This may benefit multicore platforms when the application uses topological algorithms for collective operations.

Reducing the Pre-reserved DAPL Memory Size

Large-scale applications may experience memory resource pressures due to a big number of pre-allocated buffers pinned to the physical memory pages. If you do not want to go for the DAPL UD mode, use the environment variable I_MPI_DAPL_BUFFER_NUM to decrease the number of buffers for each pair in a process group. The default value is 16.

If you increase this value, you may notice better latency on short messages (see the low-level eager protocol threshold mentioned earlier). In addition, if your application mostly sends short messages, you can try to reduce the DAPL buffer size by changing the environment variable I_MPI_DAPL_BUFFER_SIZE. The default value is 23808.

Finally, you can try to set the environment variable I_MPI_DAPL_SCALABLE_PROGRESS to enable for high process count. This is done automatically for more than 128 processes, though.

What Else?

Here is an assorted mix of tips and tricks you may try in your spare time:

- I_MPI_SSHM=1 Turns on the scalable shared memory path, which might be useful on the latest multicore Intel Xeon processors and especially on the many-core Intel Xeon Phi coprocessor.

- I_MPI_OFA_USE_XRC=1 Turns on the extensible reliable connection (XRC) capability that may improve scalability for several thousand nodes.

- I_MPI_DAPL_UD_RDMA_MIXED=1 Makes DAPL UD use connectionless datagrams for short messages and connection-oriented RDMA for long messages.

- I_MPI_DAPL_TRANSLATION_CACHE_AVL_TREE=1 May be useful for applications sending a lot of long messages over DAPL.

- I_MPI_DAPL_UD_TRANSLATION_CACHE_AVL_TREE=1 Same for DAPL UD.

Of course, even this does not exhaust the versatile toolkit of tuning methods available. Read the Intel MPI documentation, talk to experts, and be creative. This is what this work is all about, right?

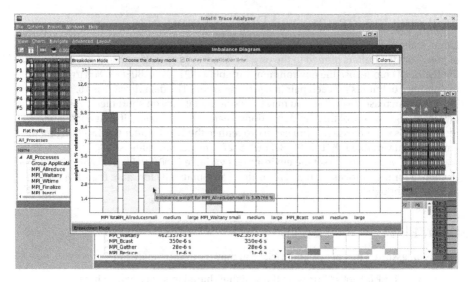

Figure 5-15. *MiniGhost trace file in ITAC imbalance diagram breakdown mode (Workstation, 12 MPI processes, 4 OpenMP threads)*

Example 5 (cont.): MiniGhost Performance Investigation

Figure 5-15 shows the split of the MPI and load imbalance issues in the breakdown mode.

So, the total MPI overhead is evenly split between the MPI_Allreduce and the MPI_Waitany. Most of the MPI_Allreduce overhead is induced by load imbalance on small messages, while most of the MPI_Waitany overhead is caused by actual communication that we will analyze later on. We can assume that the picture will be qualitatively the same on the cluster. So, if you decide to address the MPI_Allreduce performance right away, which is not recommended, you can do some benchmarking at the target node counts for all MPI_Allreduce algorithms to see whether there is anything to haul there. Given several MPI processes per node and short messages dominating the MPI_Allreduce overhead, topology-aware algorithm number 6 is going to be your first preference (see Table 5-12). Such a trial is very easy to perform. Just enter the following command before the launch:

```
$ export I_MPI_ADJUST_ALLREDUCE=6
```

A quick trial we performed confirmed that algorithm number 6 was among the best for this workload. However, algorithms 1 and 2 fared just as well and were only 0.2 seconds below the default one. Hence, most likely, optimization of the program source code aimed at reduction of the irregularity of the exchange pattern will bring more value if done upfront here. That may include both load imbalance correction and tuning of the communication per se, because they may be interacting detrimentally with each other (to be continued).

EXERCISE 5-11

Try your hand at both platform- and application-specific Intel MPI tuning, using your favorite platform and application. Gauge the overall performance improvement. Identify the cases where platform-specific tuning goes against the application-specific one.

Optimizing Application for Intel MPI

At last, it is time to turn to the application itself. That is, unless you noticed much earlier a grave and apparent problem that went against all good MPI programming practices. In that case, you may want to try and fix that problem first, provided you make double sure it is that problem that is causing trouble—as usual.

You can sensibly apply the advice contained in this section only if you have access to the application source code. It may be way out of reach in most industrial situations in the field. This situation is, however, different if you are using open-source software or have been graciously granted a source code license to a piece of closed-source code. Thus, we are talking about real optimization rather than tuning here, and real optimization takes time—a luxury that you most likely will not have under real conditions.

There are quite a few things that can go wrong. This book is not a guide to MPI programming per se, so we will be brief and will focus on the most important potential issues.

Avoiding MPI_ANY_SOURCE

Try to make your exchanges deterministic. If you have to use the MPI_ANY_SOURCE, be aware that you may be paying quite a bit on top for every message you get. Indeed, instead of waiting on a particular communication channel, as prescribed by a specific receive operation, in the case of MPI_ANY_SOURCE the MPI Library has to poll all existing connections to see whether there is anything matching on input. This means extensive looping and polling, unless you went for the wait mode described earlier. Note that use of different message tags is not going to help here, because the said polling will be done still.

Generally, all kinds of nondeterminism are detrimental and should be avoided, if possible. One way this cannot be done is when a server process distributes some work among the slave processes and waits to them to report back. However the work is apportioned, some will come back earlier than others, and enforcing a particular order in this situation might slow down the overall job. In all other cases, though, try to see whether you can induce order and can benefit from doing that.

Avoiding Superfluous Synchronization

Probably the worst thing application programmers do, over and over again, is superfluous synchronization. It is not uncommon to see, for example, iterations of a computational loop separated by an MPI_Barrier. If you program carefully and remember that MPI guarantees reliable and ordered data delivery between any pair of processes, you can skip this synchronization most of the time. If you are still afraid of missing things or mixing them up, start using the MPI message tags to instill the desired order, or create a communicator that will ensure all messages sent within it will stay there.

Another aspect to keep in mind is that, although collective operations are not required to synchronize processes by the MPI standard (with the exception of the aforementioned MPI_Barrier, of course), some of them may do this, depending on the algorithm they use. This may be a boon in some cases, because you can exploit this side effect to your ends. You should avoid doing so, however, because if the algorithm selection is changed for some reason, you may end up with no synchronization point where you implied one, or vice versa.

About the only time when you may want to introduce extra synchronization points is in the search for the load imbalance and its sources. In that case, having every iteration or program stage start at approximately the same time across all the nodes involved may be beneficial. However, this may also tilt the scale so that you will fail to see the real effect of the load imbalance.

Using Derived Datatypes

There are a few more controversial topics besides the one related to the derived datatypes (one word, as it appears in the MPI standard). As you may remember, these are opaque MPI objects that basically describe the data layout in memory. They can be used almost without limitation in any imaginable data-transfer operation in MPI.

Unfortunately, they suffer from a bad reputation. In the early days of MPI, the implementors could not always make data transfer efficient in the presence of the derived datatypes. This may still be the case now in some implementations, especially if the datatype involved is, well, too involved. Owing to this mostly ungrounded fear, application programmers try to use contiguous data buffers; and if they have to work with noncontiguous data structures, they do the packing in and out themselves by hand or by using the MPI_Pack/MPI_Unpack calls.

For most of the time, though, this is a thing of the past. You can actually win quite a bit by using the derived datatypes, especially if the underlying MPI implementation provides native support for them. Modern networks and memory controllers can do scatter, gather, and some other manipulations with the data processed on the fly, without any penalty you would need to take care of at this level. Moreover, buffer management done inside the MPI library, as well as packing and unpacking if that ever becomes necessary, is implemented using techniques that application programmers may simply have no everyday access to. Of course, if you try hard enough, you will write your own specific memory copy utility or a datatype unrolling loop that will do better than the generic procedure used by your MPI implementation. Before you go to this trouble, however, make sure you prove it's worth doing.

Using Collective Operations

Another rudimentary fear widespread among application programmers is that of suboptimal collective operations. Especially, older codes will go to great pains tore-implement all collective operations they need on the basis of the earlier status of MPI implementations.

Again, this is mostly a thing of the past. Unless you know a brilliant new algorithm that beats, hands down, all that can be extracted by the MPI tuning described earlier, you should try to avoid going for the point-to-point substitute. Moreover, you may actually win big by replacing the existing homegrown implementations with an equivalent MPI collective operation. There may be exceptions to this recommendation, but you will have to justify any efforts very carefully in this case.

Betting on the Computation/Communication Overlap

Well, don't. Most likely you will lose out. That is, there is some overlap in certain cases, but you have to measure its presence and real effect before you can be sure. Let's look into a couple of representative cases where you can hope to get something in return for the effort of converting mostly deterministic blocking communication into the controlled chaos of nonblocking transfers (again, this is the way the MPI standard decided to refer to these operations).

This method may be effective if you notice that blocking calls make the program stall and you have eliminated all other possible reasons for this happening. That is, your program is soundly mapped onto the platform, is well load balanced, and runs on top of a tuned MPI implementation. If in this case you still see that some processes stall in vastly premature receive operations; or, on the contrary, you can detect an inordinately high amount of unexpected receives (that is, messages arrive before the respective receive operation is posted); or if your sending processes are waiting for the data to be pumped out, you may need to act. A particular case of unnecessary serialization that happens when processes wait for each other in turn is well described in the *Tutorial: Detecting and Removing Unnecessary Serialization*.[20]

The replacement per se is rather trivial, at least at first. Every blocking send operation is replaced by its nonblocking variant, like MPI_Send by MPI_Isend or MPI_Recv by MPI_Irecv, with the closing call like MPI_Wait or MPI_Test issued later in the program. You can also group several operations by using the MPI_Waitall, MPI_Waitsome, and MPI_Waitany, and their MPI_Test equivalents. Here, you will do well by ordering the requests passed to these calls so that those most likely to be completed first come first. Normally, you want to post a receive operation just in time for the respective send operation to match it on the other side. You may even go for special variations on the send operations, like buffered, synchronous, or ready sends, in case this is warranted by your application and it brings a noticeable performance benefit. This can be done with or without making them nonblocking, by the way. Moreover, you can even generate so-called generic requests or use persistent operations to represent these patterns, provided doing so brings the desired performance benefit.

What is important to understand before you dive in is that the standard MPI_Send can be mapped onto any blocking send operation depending on the message size, internal buffer status in the MPI library, and some other factors. Most often, small messages will be sent out eagerly in order to return control back to the application as soon as possible. To this end, even a copy of the user buffer may be made, as in the buffered send, if the message passing machinery appears overloaded at the moment. In any case, this is almost equivalent to a nonblocking send operation, with the very next MPI call implicated in the data transfer in any way actually kicking the progress engine and doing what an MPI_Isend and/or MPI_Test would have done at that moment. Changing this blocking operation to a nonblocking one would probably be futile, in many cases.

Likewise, large messages will probably be sent using the rendezvous protocol mentioned above. In other words, the standard send operation will effectively become a synchronous one. Depending on the MPI implementation details, this may or may not be equivalent to just calling the MPI_Ssend. Once again, in absence of a noticeable computation/communication overlap, you will not see any improvement if you replace this operation with a nonblocking equivalent.

More often than not, what does make sense is trying to do bilateral exchanges by replacing a pair of sends and receives that cross each other by the MPI_Sendrecv operation. It may happen to be implemented so that it exploits the underlying hardware in a way that you will not be able to reach out for unless you let MPI handle this transfer explicitly. Note, however, that a careless switch to nonblocking communication may actually introduce extra serialization into the program, which is well explained in the aforementioned tutorial.

Another aspect to keep in mind is that for the data to move across, something or someone—in the latter case, you—will need to give the MPI library a chance to help you. If you rely on asynchronous progress, you may feel that this matter has been dealt with. Actually, it may or it may not have been, and even if it has been addressed, doing some relevant MPI call in between, be aware that even something apparently pointless, like an MPI_Iprobe for a message that never comes, may speed up things considerably. This happens because synchronous progress is normally less expensive than asynchronous.

Once again, here the MPI implementation faces a dilemma, trading latency for guarantee. Synchronous progress is better for latency, but it cannot guarantee progress unless the program issues MPI calls relatively often. Asynchronous progress can provide the necessary guarantee, especially if there are extra cores or cards in the system doing just this. However, the context switch involved may kill the latency. It is possible that in the future, Intel MPI will provide more controls to influence this kind of behavior. Stay tuned; until then, be careful about your assumptions and measure everything before you dive into chaos.

Finally, believe it or not, blocking transfers may actually help application processes self-organize during the runtime, provided you took into account their natural desires. If your interprocess exchanges are highly regular, it may make sense to do them in a certain order (like north-south, then east-west, and so on). After initial shaking in, the processes will fall into lockstep with each other, and they will proceed in a beautifully synchronized fashion across the computation, like an army column marching to battle.

Replacing Blocking Collective Operations by MPI-3 Nonblocking Ones

Intel MPI Library 5.0 provides MPI-3 functionality while maintaining substantial binary compatibility with the Intel MPI 4.x product line that implements the MPI-2.x standards.[21] Thus, you can start experimenting with the most interesting features of the MPI-3 standard right away. We will review only the nonblocking collective operations here, and bypass many other features.[22] In particular, we will not deal with the one-sided operations and neighborhood collectives, for their optimization is likely to take some time yet on the implementor side. Of course, if you want to experiment with these new features, nobody is going to stop you. Just keep in mind that they may be experimenting with you in return.

Contrary to this, nonblocking collective operations are relatively mature, even if their tuning may still need to be improved. You can replace any blocking collective operation (including, surprisingly, the MPI_Barrier) by a nonblocking version of it, add a corresponding closing call later in the program, and enjoy—what?

Let's see in more detail what you may hope to enjoy. First, your program will become more complicated, and you will not be able to tell what is happening with the precision afforded by the blocking collectives. This is a clear downside. Even in the case of the MPI_Ibarrier, you will not be able to ascertain when exactly the synchronization happens, whether in the MPI_Ibarrier call itself (which is possible) or in the matching closing call (which is probably desired). All depends on the algorithm selected by the implementation, and this you can control only externally, if at all.

Next, tuning of the settings for the blocking collectives may not influence the nonblocking ones and vice versa. Indeed, tuning of the nonblocking operations may not be controllable by you at this moment, at all. In addition, the MPI standard specifically clarifies that the blocking and nonblocking settings may be independent of each other, for the sake of making proper choices on the actual performance benefits observed. This is another clear downside.

On the bright side, you can use more than one nonblocking collective at a time over any communicator, and hope to exploit the computation/communication overlap in as much as is supported by the MPI library involved. In the Intel MPI Library, you may profit from setting the environment variable MPICH_ASYNC_PROGRESS to enable.

EXERCISE 5-12

If your application fares better with the MPI-3 nonblocking collectives inside, let us know; we are looking for good application examples to justify further tuning of this advanced MPI-3 standard feature.

Using Accelerated MPI File I/O

If your program relies on MPI file I/O, you can speed it up by telling Intel MPI what parallel file system you are using. If this is PanFS,[23] PVFS2,[24] or Lustre,[25] you may obtain noticeable performance gain because Intel MPI will go through a special code path designed for the respective file system. To achieve this, enter the following commands:

```
$ export I_MPI_EXTRA_FILE_SYSTEM=on
$ export I_MPI_EXTRA_FILE_SYSTEM_LIST=panfs,pvfs2,lustre
```

You can mention only those file systems that interest you in the second line, of course.

Example 5 (cont.): MiniGhost Performance Investigation

Analysis of the full miniGhost trace file done on the "small" problem size on the cluster basically confirms all findings observed on the workstation (not shown). Surprisingly, ITAC traces do not show MPI_Init anomaly in either case. Possibly, we have to do with a so-called Heisenbug that disappears due to observation.

That phenomenon aside, if we can fix the substantially smaller workstation variant, we should see gains in the bigger cluster case. This can be further helped by adjusting the workstation run configuration so that it fully resembles the situation within one node of the "small" cluster run by 12 MPI processes, four OpenMP threads, and respective process layout and grid size. Thus, the problems to be addressed, in order of decreasing importance, are as follows:

1. MPI_Init overhead visible only in the built-in statistics output.

2. Load imbalance that hinders proper MPI_Allreduce performance. This is the biggest issue at hand.

3. Communication related to the MPI_Waitany that may be interacting with the load imbalance and detrimentally affecting the MPI_Allreduce as well.

The MPI_Init overhead may need to be confirmed by repeated execution and independent timing of the MPI_Init invocation using the MPI_Wtime to be embedded into the main program code for this purpose (see file main.c). If this confirms that the effect manifested by the statistics output is consistently observable in other ways, we can probably discount the ITAC anomaly as a Heisenbug. At the moment of this writing, however, our bets were on the involuntary change of the job manager queue that may have contributed to this effect.

The earlier statistics measurements were done in a queue set up for larger jobs, while the later ITAC measurements used another queue set up for shorter jobs, because the larger queue became overloaded and nothing was moving there, as it usually does under time pressure. This resulted in the later jobs being put onto another part of the cluster, with comparable processors but with a possibly better connectivity. This once again highlights the necessary of keeping your environment unchanged throughout the measurement series, and of doing the runs well ahead of the deadlines.

Load imbalance aside, we may have to deal with the less than optimal process layout (4x4x6) prescribed by the benchmark formulation. Indeed, when we tried other process layouts within the same job manager session, we observed that the communication along the X axis was stumbling—and more so as more MPI processes were placed along it; see Table 5-13:

Table 5-13. *MiniGhost Performance Dependency on the Process Layout (Cluster, 8 Nodes, 96 MPI Processes, 4 OpenMP Threads per Process)*

Layout, XxYxZ	Performance, GFLOPS	Time, Sec
4x4x6	3.69E+03	3.55E+01
1x8x12	3.72E+03	3.52E+01
8x1x12	3.55E+03	3.69E+01
8x12x1	3.41E+03	3.85E+01
1x1x96	3.10E+03	4.23E+01
1x96x1	3.11E+03	4.21E+01
96x1x1	1.72E+03	7.62E+01

Let's try to understand what exactly is happening here. If you view a typical problematic patch of the miniGhost trace file in ITAC, you will notice the following picture replicated many times across the whole event timeline, at various moments and at different time scales, as shown in Figure 5-16.

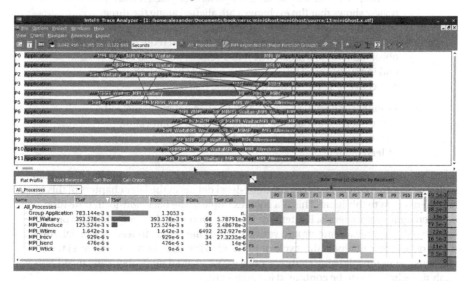

Figure 5-16. *Typical MiniGhost exchange pattern (Workstation, 12 MPI processes, 4 OpenMP threads)*

This patch corresponds to the very first and most expensive exchange during the program execution. Rather small per se, it becomes a burden due to endless replication; all smaller MPI communication segments after this one follow the same pattern or at least have a pretty imbalanced MPI_Allreduce inside (not shown). It is clear that the first order of the day is to understand why the MPI_Waitany has to work in such irregular circumstances, and then try to correct this. It is also possible that the MPI_Allreduce will recover its dignity when acting in a better environment.

By the looks of it, the pattern in Figure 5-16 resembles a typical neighbor exchange implemented by nonblocking MPI calls. Since the very first MPI_Allreduce is a representative one, we have no problem identifying where the prior nonblocking exchange comes from: a bit of source code and log file browsing lead us to the file called MG_UNPACK_BSPMA.F, where the waiting is done using the MPI_Waitany on all MPI_Request items filled by the prior calls to MPI_Isend and MPI_Irecv that indeed represent a neighbor data exchange. In addition to this, as the name of the file suggests and the code review confirms, the data is packed and unpacked using the respective MPI calls. From this, at least three optimization ideas of different complexity emerge:

1. *Relatively easy*: Use the MPI_Waitall or MPI_Waitsome instead of the fussy MPI_Waitany. The former might be able to complete all or at least more than one request per invocation, and do this in the most appropriate order defined by the MPI implementation. However, there is some internal application statistics collection that is geared toward the use of MPI_Waitany, so more than just a replacement of one call may be necessary technically.

2. *Relatively hard*: Try to replace the nonblocking exchange with the properly ordered blocking MPI_Sendrecv pairs. A code review shows that the exchanges are aligned along the three spatial dimensions, so that a more regular messaging order might actually help smoothe the data flow and reduce the observed level of irregularity. If this sounds too hard, even making sure that all MPI_Irecv are posted shortly before the respective MPI_Isend might be a good first step.

3. *Probably impossible*: Use the MPI derived datatypes instead of the packing/unpacking. Before this deep modification is attempted, it should be verified that packing/unpacking indeed matters.

This coding exercise is only sensible once the MPI_Allreduce issue has been dealt with. For that we need to look into the node-level details in the later chapters of this book, and then return to this issue. This is a good example of the back-and-forth transition between optimization levels. Remember that once you introduce any change, you will have to redo the measurements and verify that the change was indeed beneficial. After that is done, you can repeat this cycle or proceed to the node optimization level we will consider in the following chapters, once we've covered more about advanced MPI analysis techniques (to be continued in Chapter 6).

EXERCISE 5-13

Investigate the miniGhost MPI_Init overhead and clarify whether this is a Heisenbug or not. If it is, contact Intel Premier and report the matter.

EXERCISE 5-14

Return here once the MPI_Allreduce load imbalance has been dealt with, and implement one of the proposed source code optimizations. Gauge its effect on the miniGhost benchmark, especially at scale. Was it worth the trouble?

Using Advanced Analysis Techniques

We have barely scratched the surface of capabilities offered by the Intel MPI and Intel Trace Analyzer and Collector. This section introduces more advanced features that you may need in your work, but you will have to read more about them before you can start to use them.

Automatically Checking MPI Program Correctness

We started with the premise of a correctly written parallel application. Here's the truth, though: there are none. That is, there are some applications that manifest no apparent errors at the moment. Even as we were writing this book, we detected several errors in candidate programs of various levels of maturity, from our own naïve code snippets to the venerable, internationally recognized, and widely used benchmarks. Some programs would not build, some would not run, some would break on ostensibly valid input data, and so on. This is all a fact of life.

Fortunately, if you use Intel MPI and ITAC, you can mitigate at least some of the risk in trying to optimize an erroneous program. Just add option -check_mpi to your application build string or the mpirun, run string, and the ITAC correctness checking library will start watching all MPI transfers and checking them for many issues, including incorrect parameters, potential or real deadlocks, race conditions, data corruption, and more.

This may cost quite some a bit at runtime, especially if you ask for the buffer check sums to be computed and verified, or you used the valgrind in addition to check the memory access patterns. However, in return you will get at least some of that warm and fuzzy feeling that is otherwise unknown to programmers in general and to parallel programmers in particular; that feeling, though, is the almost certain yet dangerously wrong belief that your program is MPI bug free.

Comparing Application Traces

You have seen how we compared real and ideal traces (see Figure 5-12). Actually, this is a generic feature you can apply to any two traces. While comparing two unrelated traces might be a bit off topic, comparing two closely related traces may reveal interesting things. For example, you can compare two different runs of the same application, done on different process counts or just having substantially different performance characteristics on the same process count. Looking into the traces side by side will help you spot where they differ. This is how to go about it:

1. Easiest of all, open two trace files you want to compare in one ITAC session when starting up. This is how you can do this:

    ```
    $ traceanalyzer trace1.stf trace2.stf
    ```

2. If you are already in an ITAC session where you have been analyzing a certain trace file, open another file via the global File/Open menu, and then use the File/Compare item.

3. If you want to do this by hand, open the files in any way described above, configure to your liking the charts you want to compare, and then use the global View/Arrange menu item to put them side by side or on top of each other.

For example, if you do any of this for the real and ideal files illustrated in Figure 5-12, you will get the results shown in Figure 5-17.

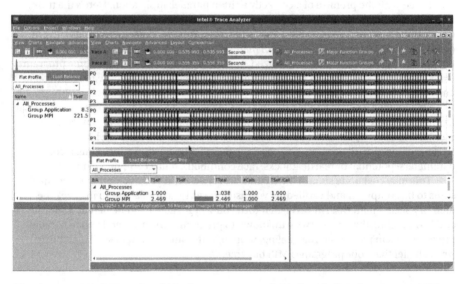

Figure 5-17. *MiniMD real and ideal traces compared side by side (Workstation, 16 MPI processes)*

166

This view confirms the earlier observation that, although there may be up to 2.5 times improvement to haul in the MPI area, the overall effect on the total program's execution time will be marginal. Another interesting view to observe is the Breakdown Mode in the imbalance diagram shown in Figure 5-18 (here we again changed the default colors to roughly match those in the event timeline).

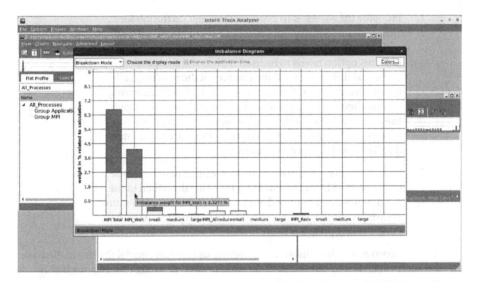

Figure 5-18. *MiniMD trace file in ITAC imbalance diagra breakdown mode (Workstation, 16 MPI processes)*

From this view you can conclude that MPI_Wait is probably the call to investigate as far as pure MPI performance is concerned. The rest of the overhead comes from the load imbalance. If you want to learn more about comparing trace files, follow up with the aforementioned serialization tutorial.

Instrumenting Application Code

Once in a while you may want to know exactly what is happening in the user part of the application, rather than just observe the blue Group Application mentioned in the respective ITAC charts. In this case you can use several features provided by Intel tools to get this information:

1. Probably the easiest is to ask Intel compiler do the job for you. Add the compiler option -tcollect to get all source code functions instrumented to leave a trace in the ITAC trace file. This option needs to be used both at the compilation and at the linkage steps. If the number of the resulting call tracing events is too high, use the -tcollect-filter variety to limit their scope. You may—and probably should—apply these features selectively to those files that interest you most; otherwise, the trace file size may explode. You can find more details in the ITC documentation.[26]

2. If you want complete control and are willing to invest some time, use the ITAC instrumenting interface described in the documentation mentioned above. An instrumentation source code example that comes with the ITAC distribution will be a good starting point here.

You can learn more about these advanced topics and also control the size of the trace file, the latter which is very important if you want to analyze a long running or a highly scalable application, in the *Tutorial: Reducing Trace File Size.*[27]

Correlating MPI and Hardware Events

As a final point before we close the MPI optimization, we give a recommendation on how to correlate the ITAC trace events with the hardware events, including those registered by the Intel VTune Amplifier XE data collection infrastructure.[28] As usual, there is more than one way to do this.

Collecting and Analyzing Hardware Counter Information in ITAC

Believe it or not, you can collect and display a lot of hardware counter information right in the ITAC. Its facilities are not as extensive and automated as those of VTune Amplifier XE; however, they can give you a good first hack at the problem. You can read about this topic in the ITAC documentation. Note that quite a bit of hacking will be required upfront.

Collecting and Analyzing Hardware Counter Information in VTune

If you have no time for hacking, you can choose the normal way. First, you need to launch VTune Amplifier XE. There are, again, several methods to do so:

1. Launch `amplxe-cl` with `mpirun`. For example: Collect 1 result/ rank/node from M nodes – M result directories in total:

   ```
   $ mpirun <machine file> -np <N> ... amplxe-cl -collect <analysis type> ./your_app
   ```

   Assumptions: N>M and at least 1 rank/node.

2. Collect 2 hotspots on the host 'hostname':

   ```
   $ mpirun -host 'hostname' -np 14 ./a.out : \
            -host 'hostname' -np 2 amplxe-cl -r foo -c hotspots
            ./your_app
   ```

3. Launch `mpirun` with `amplxe-cl`. For example: Collect N ranks in one result file on a node (e.g., 'hostname'):

   ```
   $ amplxe-cl -collect <analysis type> ... -- mpirun -host
   'hostname' -np <N> ./your_app
   ```

Limitation: Currently collects only on the `localhost`.

We will cover the rest of this topic in Chapter 6, but you may want to read the *Tutorial: Analyzing MPI Application with Intel Trace Analyzer and Intel VTune Amplifier XE* as well.[29]

Summary

We presented MPI optimization methodology in this chapter in its application to the Intel MPI Library and Intel Trace Analyzer. However, you can easily reuse this procedure with other tools of your choice.

It is (not so) surprising that the literature on MPI optimization in particular is rather scarce. This was one of our primary reasons for writing this book. To get the most out of it, you need to know quite a bit about the MPI programming. There is probably no better way to get started than by reading the classic *Using MPI* by Bill Gropp, Ewing Lusk, and Anthony Skjellum[30] and *Using MPI-2* by William Gropp, Ewing Lusk, and Rajeev Thakur.[31] If you want to learn more about the Intel Xeon Phi platform, you may want to read *Intel Xeon Phi Coprocessor High-Performance Programming* by Jim Jeffers and James Reinders that we mentioned earlier. Ultimately, nothing will replace reading the MPI standard, asking questions in the respective mailing lists, and getting your hands dirty.

We cannot recommend any specific book on the parallel algorithms because they are quite dependent on the domain area you are going to explore. Most likely, you know all the most important publications and periodicals in that area anyway. Just keep an eye on them; algorithms rule this realm.

References

1. MPI Forum, "MPI Documents," www.mpi-forum.org/docs/docs.html.

2. H. Bockhorst and M. Lubin, "Performance Analysis of a Poisson Solver Using Intel VTune Amplifier XE and Intel Trace Analyzer and Collector," to be published in TBD.

3. Intel Corporation, "Intel MPI Benchmarks," http://software.intel.com/en-us/articles/intel-mpi-benchmarks/.

4. Intel Corporation, "Intel(R) Premier Support," www.intel.com/software/products/support.

5. D. Akin, "Akin's Laws of Spacecraft Design," http://spacecraft.ssl.umd.edu/old_site/academics/akins_laws.html.

6. A. Petitet, R. C. Whaley, J. Dongarra, and A. Cleary, "HPL - A Portable Implementation of the High-Performance Linpack Benchmark for Distributed-Memory Computers," www.netlib.org/benchmark/hpl/.

7. Intel Corporation, "Intel Math Kernel Library - LINPACK Download," http://software.intel.com/en-us/articles/intel-math-kernel-library-linpack-download.

8. A. Petitet, R. C. Whaley, J. Dongarra, and A. Cleary, "HPL FAQs," www.netlib.org/benchmark/hpl/faqs.html.

9. "BLAS (Basic Linear Algebra Subprograms)," www.netlib.org/blas/.

10. Sandia National Laboratory, "HPCG - Home," https://software.sandia.gov/hpcg/.

11. "Home of the Mantevo project," http://mantevo.org/.

12. Intel Corporation, "Configuring Intel Trace Collector," https://software.intel.com/de-de/node/508066.

13. Sandia National Laboratory, "LAMMPS Molecular Dynamics Simulator," http://lammps.sandia.gov/.

14. Ohio State University, "OSU Micro-Benchmarks," http://mvapich.cse.ohio-state.edu/benchmarks/.

15. Intel Corporation, "Intel MPI Library - Documentation," https://software.intel.com/en-us/articles/intel-mpi-library-documentation.

16. J. Jeffers and J. Reinders, *Intel Xeon Phi Coprocessor High-Performance Programming* (Waltham, MA: Morgan Kaufman Publ. Inc., 2013).

17. "MiniGhost," www.nersc.gov/users/computational-systems/nersc-8-system-cori/nersc-8-procurement/trinity-nersc-8-rfp/nersc-8-trinity-benchmarks/minighost/.

18. Intel Corporation, "Tutorial: MPI Tuner for Intel MPI Library for Linux OS," https://software.intel.com/en-us/mpi-tuner-tutorial-lin-5.0-pdf.

19. M. Chuvelev, "Collective Algorithm Models," Intel Corporation, Internal technical report, 2013.

20. Intel Corporation, "Tutorial: Detecting and Removing Unnecessary Serialization," https://software.intel.com/en-us/itac_9.0_serialization_pdf.

21. A. Supalov and A. Yalozo, "20 Years of the MPI Standard: Now With a Common Application Binary Interface," *The Parallel Universe* 18, no. 1 (2014): 28–32.

22. M. Brinskiy, A. Supalov, M. Chuvelev, and E. Leksikov, "Mastering Performance Challenges with the New MPI-3 Standard," *The Parallel Universe* 18, no. 1 (2014): 33–40.

23. "PanFS Storage Operating System," www.panasas.com/products/panfs.

24. "Parallel Virtual File System, Version 2," www.pvfs.org/.

25. "Lustre - OpenSFS," http://lustre.opensfs.org/.

26. Intel Corporation, "Intel Trace Analyzer and Collector - Documentation," https://software.intel.com/en-us/articles/intel-trace-analyzer-and-collector-documentation.

27. Intel Corporation, "Tutorial: Reducing Trace File Size," https://software.intel.com/en-us/itac_9.0_reducing_trace_pdf.

28. Intel Corporation, "Intel VTune Amplifier XE 2013," https://software.intel.com/en-us/intel-vtune-amplifier-xe.

29. Intel Corporation, "Tutorial: Analyzing MPI Application with Intel Trace Analyzer and Intel VTune Amplifier XE," https://software.intel.com/en-us/itac_9.0_analyzing_app_pdf.

30. W. Gropp, E. L. Lusk, and A. Skjellum, *Using MPI: Portable Parallel Programming with the Message Passing Interface*, 2nd. ed. (Cambridge, MA: MIT Press, 1999).

31. W. Gropp, E. L. Lusk, and R. Thakur, *Using MPI-2: Advanced Features of the Message Passing Interface* (Cambridge, MA: MIT Press, 1999).

CHAPTER 6

■ ■ ■

Addressing Application Bottlenecks: Shared Memory

The previous chapters talked about the potential bottlenecks in your application and the system it runs on. In this chapter, we will have a close look at how the application code performs on the level of an individual cluster node. It is a fair assumption that there will also be bottlenecks on this level. Removing these bottlenecks will usually translate directly to increased performance, in addition to the optimizations discussed in the previous chapters.

In line with our top-down strategy, we will investigate how to improve your application code on the threading level. On this level, you will find several potential bottlenecks that can dramatically affect the performance of your application code; some of them are hardware related, some of them are related to your algorithm. The bottlenecks we discuss all come down to how the threads of your code interact with the underlying hardware. From the past chapters you already have an understanding of how this hardware works and what the important metrics and optimization goals are.

We will start with an introduction that covers how to apply Intel VTune Amplifier XE and a loop profiler to your application to gain a better understanding of the code's execution profile. The next topic is that of detecting sequential execution and load imbalances. Then, we will investigate how thread synchronization may affect the performance of the application code.

Profiling Your Application

Profiling the code is the first step toward gaining an understanding of what parts of your application are critical. As usual there are several options for performing this profiling and each option provides different insights into your application and the code it executes. Information of particular interest here is how much time the application spends in each part of the code. This analysis is useful because of the two insights it provides:

1. You get a detailed breakdown of the application runtime.

2. It tells you exactly what the points of interest are for code optimizations.

During the optimization work you will focus on the so-called hotspots that contribute most to the application runtime, because improving their performance will be most beneficial to overall runtime.

You have already seen a tool called PowerTOP in Chapter 4 that gives insight into what is currently running on the system. However, it does not show what exactly the running applications are executing. That is what the Linux tool suite perf is for.[1] It contains several tools to record and show performance data. One useful command is perf top, which continuously presents the currently active processes and the function they are currently executing. Figure 6-1 shows how the output of the interactive tool might look for a run of the HPCG benchmark.[2] The first column indicates what percentage of CPU time the function (listed in column 4 of a line) has consumed since the last update of the output. The second column shows in which process or shared library image the function is located. The perf tool also supports the recording of performance data and analyzing it offline with a command-line interface. Have a look at its documentation for a more detailed explanation.

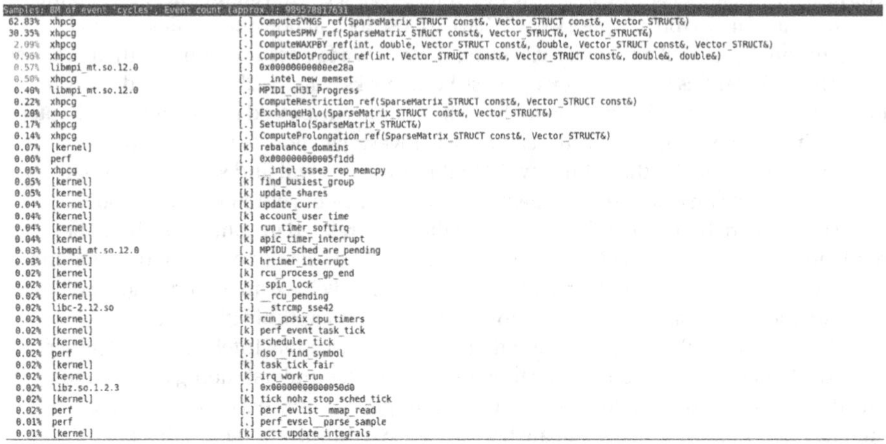

Figure 6-1. *Output of the* perf top *commmand with functions active in the HPCG application*

Although perf is a good start to monitor an application while it is running, most of the performance analysis needs to be done postmortem (i.e., after the application executed and performance data was collected). In this way it is possible to inspect the performance data and focus on a particular performance aspect or code region, without having to run the application all the time. This sets the stage for more visual and more powerful tools like Intel VTune Amplifier XE.

Using VTune Amplifier XE for Hotspots Profiling

Intel VTune Amplifier XE provides a unified graphical user interface (GUI) that supports the collection and analysis of performance data. It helps you configure the data collector and set up the application for a collection run. After the collection, you can then work with the data. VTune Amplifier XE supports both event-based sampling using the processor's built-in performance monitoring units (PMUs) and sampling based on instrumentation of the binary code. In contrast to the Intel Trace Analyzer and Collector (see Chapter 5), the focus of VTune Amplifier XE is on shared-memory and intra-node analysis. The performance data is associated with the source code at all times, so you can easily determine which source line of the application contributed to the performance data.

The most important place to start is with the hotspots analysis to dissect the compute time of the application and relate that information to the application code. This gives a good overview of where the application spends the most compute time. The individual hotspots will be the focus areas of the optimization work to get the biggest bang for the buck. As a side benefit, the hotspots analysis also provides a first insight into how well the code executes on the machine. (We revisit this topic in Chapter 7.)

Hotspots for the HPCG Benchmark

As a first example, let's have a look at the HPCG benchmark. For educational purposes, we pretend that HPCG is an MPI-only code by compiling HPCG without OpenMP. We then try to identify OpenMP candidate loops to add multithreading to the code to make our assumed MPI-only a hybrid MPI/OpenMP code. Of course, in reality the OpenMP directives are already in the code, so we can double-check if we came to same parallelization strategy as the authors of HPCG.

It is a fair assumption that HPC codes are loopy codes that process bulk data in several key loops that will consume most of the compute time. Hence, we need to get a better understanding of the application code by looking at where the code spends time and how this time is spent in the hotspots. We also need to check if the time is spent in loop structures. To do that, we configure an analysis project in the VTune Amplifier XE GUI and run the following command in VTune Amplifier XE using the *Advanced Hotspot* method:

```
$ mpirun -np 48 ./hpcg.x
```

■ **Note**   On most clusters it may not be possible to run the GUI. VTune Amplifier XE also supports data collection and analysis on remote systems and from the command line. If *Remote (SSH)* collection is selected in the project configuration, you can add the hostname and credentials for a remote system. You can also use the *Get Command Line* button in the GUI to get a command line that is ready for cut-and-paste to the cluster console or job script. After the collection has finished, you can copy the resulting data to your local machine for analysis within the GUI. For a command-line analysis, you do not need to create a project. You will see examples of how to use this feature later on in this section. You can find out more about collecting performance data and analyzing it with the command-line interface in the VTune Amplifier XE user's guide.[3]

Running this on our example machine gives us the result shown in Figure 6-2. The code executed for 383 seconds and consumed about 18,330 seconds of CPU time, out of which 10,991 seconds (almost 60 percent) is attributed to execution of a function called `ComputeSYMGS_ref`. Function `ComputeSPMV_ref` contributes another 5,538 seconds (30 percent) to the compute time. That makes up about 90 percent of the total CPU compute time. Thus, these two functions will be of interest when we're looking for optimization opportunities.

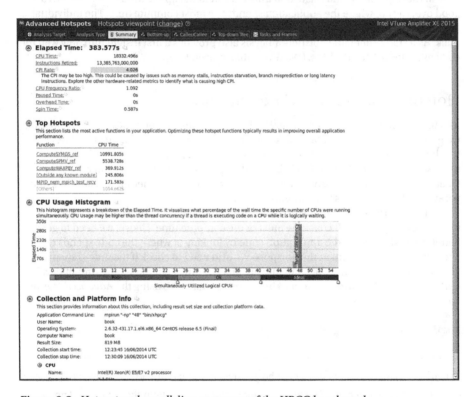

Figure 6-2. *Hotspot and parallelism summary of the HPCG benchmark*

So, the next step is to dig deeper into these functions to find out more about what they do and how they do it. We click on one of the hotspots or the *Bottom-up* button and VTune will show a screen similar to the one in Figure 6-3. Here all relevant functions are shown in more detail, together with their relevant execution time, their containing module (i.e., executable file, shared object, etc.), and the call stack that leads to the invocation of a hotspot. Of course, we will find our two suspect functions listed first and second, as in the Summary screen. As we are interested in finding out more about the hotspot, we change the filter to the *Loops and Functions* mode to let the tool also show hot loops. You can enable this mode by changing the *Loop Mode* filter to *Loops and Functions* in the filter area at the bottom of the GUI.

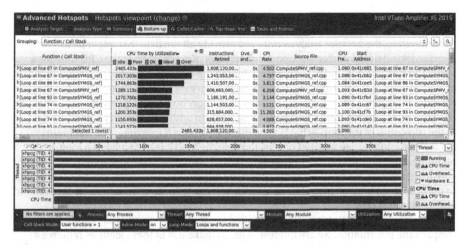

Figure 6-3. *Hotspots (loops and functions) for the HPCG benchmark*

You might be surprised to see that the order of the hotspots now seems to have changed. The functions ComputeSYMGS_ref and ComputeSPMV_ref are now at the tail of the ranking, which can be seen by scrolling down to the bottom of the upper pane of the screen shot in Figure 6-3. The new top hotspots are loops at several locations in these functions. The hottest loop is at line 67 in the function ComputeSPMV_ref and consumes 13 percent of the total compute time. This is a good candidate for parallelization, isn't it? We cannot tell without reading the source code, so we open the source code of the loop by double-clicking the line noting this loop within the VTune Amplifier XE GUI. Listing 6-1 shows the pertinent code of this hotspot.

Listing 6-1. Top Hotspot of the HPCG Benchmark

```
61    for (local_int_t i=0; i< nrow; i++) {
62        double sum = 0.0;
63        const double * const cur_vals = A.matrixValues[i];
64        const local_int_t * const cur_inds = A.mtxIndL[i];
65        const int cur_nnz = A.nonzerosInRow[i];
66
67        for (int j=0; j< cur_nnz; j++)
68            sum += cur_vals[j]*xv[cur_inds[j]];
69        yv[i] = sum;
70    }
```

As you can see, the code consists of two nested loops. VTune Amplifier XE identified the inner loop as the hotspot. Which loop should we select as the target for OpenMP parallelization? In this case, as in many others, the solution will be to parallelize the outer loop. But how do we know how many iterations these loops are executing?

Compiler-Assisted Loop/Function Profiling

Unfortunately, the hotspot analysis does not provide all the data that might be important to make sound decisions for our optimization work. Knowing about the CPU time for a particular hotspot only indicates how much time the code has spent there. It does not tell us how many times a hotspot or parts of it have been executed. For a loop hotspot that we consider for optimization, it will be important to know how many times the loop structure has been encountered from the surrounding code. In addition, we will be interested in the trip count of the loop—that is, how many iterations it executes. The minimum, maximum, and average number of trips through the loop suggest whether a loop might be amenable for certain optimizations, such as parallelization through OpenMP constructs. Hence, we need to complement the hotspots analysis with additional profiling to make sure we have all these bits of information ready to make an informed decision for optimizing the code.

Intel Composer XE ships with a compiler-assisted function and loop profiler that supplies the information we are interested in. To make use of these features requires a recompilation of the code with special command-line flags to augment the compiled code with code to monitor function calls and loop execution at runtime. The profiling can be enabled through the command-line arguments -profile-functions, -profile-loops, and -profile-loops-report. For example, the new command line to compile the HPCG benchmark might start with:

```
$ icc -profile-functions -profile-loops=all -profile-loops-report=2 ...
```

With these settings, the application will record runtime information for functions and loops, including trip counts for all loops. There are several caveats to keep in mind when using this feature, though. First, it only works with single-threaded, single-process applications. Second, it may add considerable overhead to the runtime of the application. The penalty depends on the code structure; many fine-grained functions and loops in the code will add more overhead than fewer large functions and loops. To reduce the overhead, you may try one or more of the command options listed in Table 6-1.

Table 6-1. Additional Command-Line Options for the Compiler-Assisted Profiler

Flag	Effect
-profile-loops=inner	Only profile inner loops
-profile-loops=outer	Only profile outer loops
-profile-loops-report=1	Report execution of loops, but no trip count

The loop profile for the HPCG example is given in Figure 6-4. When we compare Figure 6-4 with the hotspot profile shown in Figure 6-3, we can see that the hotspots and the loop profile do not match. This is no surprise; the loop profile was collected in single-rank mode—that is, with only one MPI process executing. In addition, a loop with a small trip count can exceed loops with large numbers of iterations if the loop body is large and demands a lot of compute time. Nevertheless, the loop profile contains an accurate itemization of the loops and their trip counts.

Loop Profile Viewer: loop_prof_1402913003.xml

File View Filter Help

Function Profile

Function	Function file:line	Time	% Time	Self time ▾	% Self time	Call count	% Time in loops
ComputeSYMGS_ref|SparseMat...	src/ComputeSYMGS_ref.cpp:54	27,933,269,581	49.50	27,923,394,087	49.48	1,148	49.48
SetupHalo|SparseMatrix_STRU...	src/SetupHalo.cpp:50	11,613,407,948	20.58	11,613,407,948	20.58	4	20.58
ComputeSPMV_ref|SparseMatri...	src/ComputeSPMV_ref.cpp:47	9,099,741,780	16.13	9,091,936,369	16.11	687	16.11
GenerateProblem|SparseMatri...	src/GenerateProblem.cpp:52	2,197,073,970	3.89	2,086,456,194	3.70	4	3.69
ComputeWAXPBY_ref|int, doubl...	src/ComputeWAXPBY_ref.cpp:43	1,779,541,059	3.15	1,779,541,059	3.15	528	3.15
ComputeDotProduct_ref|int, Ve...	src/ComputeDotProduct_ref.cp...	1,737,196,352	3.06	1,736,679,655	3.06	535	3.06
ComputeMG_ref|SparseMatrix...	src/ComputeMG_ref.cpp:39	33,197,490,712	58.83	449,905,896	0.80	656	0.00
DeleteMatrix|SparseMatrix_ST...	testing/SparseMatrix.hpp:143	450,761,672	0.80	448,818,110	0.80	4	0.43
ComputeRestriction_ref|Sparse...	src/ComputeRestriction_ref.cpp...	348,976,008	0.62	348,976,008	0.62	492	0.62
TestCG|SparseMatrix_STRUCT...	src/TestCG.cpp:52	2,023,099,785	3.59	340,486,222	0.60	1	0.56
ComputeProlongation_ref|Spar...	src/ComputeProlongation_ref.c...	212,575,338	0.38	212,575,338	0.38	492	0.38
std::_Rb_tree<int, std::pair<int...	/usr/include/c++/4.4.7/bits/stl_t...	108,615,776	0.19	108,615,776	0.19	1,285,245	0.00
CG|SparseMatrix_STRUCT cons...	src/CG.cpp:61	26,762,201,024	47.43	93,009,683	0.16	6	0.13
TestSymmetry|SparseMatrix_S...	src/TestSymmetry.cpp:60	618,013,496	1.10	89,061,748	0.16	1	0.15
main	testing/main.cpp:71	56,429,272,779	100.00	49,225,049	0.09	1	0.06
ExchangeHalo|SparseMatrix_ST...	src/ExchangeHalo.cpp:33	17,680,985	0.03	17,680,985	0.03	1	0.00
std::_Rb_tree<int, std::pair<int...	/usr/include/c++/4.4.7/bits/stl_t...	14,537,301	0.03	14,537,301	0.03	1,285,245	0.00
CG_ref|SparseMatrix_STRUCT c...	src/CG_ref.cpp:60	12,226,623,565	21.67	6,954,069	0.01	1	0.01

Loop Profile

Function	Function file:line	Loop file:line	Time	% Time	Self time ▾	% Self time	Loop entries	Min iterations	Avg iterations	Max iterations
SetupHalo|SparseMatr...	src/SetupHalo.cpp:50	/usr/include/c++/4.4.7/...	9,719,136,801	17.20	9,719,136,801	17.20	33,932,893	10	20	36
ComputeSYMGS_ref|Sp...	src/ComputeSYMGS_re...	src/ComputeSYMGS_re...	8,314,130,001	14.70	8,314,130,001	14.70	420,476,484	1	1	1
ComputeSYMGS_ref|Sp...	src/ComputeSYMGS_re...	src/ComputeSYMGS_re...	13,712,354,623	27.90	6,931,099,819	12.30	1,148	2,197	366,899	1,124,864
ComputeSYMGS_ref|Sp...	src/ComputeSYMGS_re...	src/ComputeSYMGS_re...	6,063,941,712	12.20	6,063,941,712	12.20	420,476,484	1	1	1
ComputeSPMV_ref|Sp...	src/ComputeSPMV_ref...	src/ComputeSYMGS_re...	9,091,299,030	16.10	6,883,162,897	11.90	687	17,576	625,571	1,124,864
ComputeSYMGS_ref|Sp...	src/ComputeSYMGS_re...	src/ComputeSYMGS_re...	12,210,577,056	21.60	4,630,871,911	8.20	1,148	2,197	366,899	1,124,864
ComputeSPMV_ref|Spa...	src/ComputeSPMV_ref...	src/ComputeSPMV_ref...	2,103,764,944	3.70	2,103,764,944	3.70	429,177,808	1	1	1
ComputeWAXPBY_ref|...	src/ComputeWAXPBY_r...	src/ComputeWAXPBY_r...	1,713,922,241	3.00	1,713,922,241	3.00	515	562,432	562,432	562,432
SetupHalo|SparseMatr...	src/SetupHalo.cpp:50	src/SetupHalo.cpp:83	1,451,521,698	2.60	1,451,521,698	2.60	1,285,245	8	26	27
ComputeDotProduct_r...	src/ComputeDotProdu...	src/ComputeDotProdu...	1,221,771,214	2.20	1,221,771,214	2.20	352	562,432	562,432	562,432
GenerateProblem|Spa...	src/GenerateProblem.c...	src/GenerateProblem.c...	996,180,216	1.80	996,180,216	1.80	4	2,197	321,311	1,124,864
ComputeDotProduct_r...	src/ComputeDotProdu...	/usr/include/c++/4.4.7/...	799,972,373	1.40	799,972,373	1.40	1,285,241	1	33	38
ComputeDotProduct_r...	src/ComputeDotProdu...	src/ComputeDotProdu...	503,403,807	0.90	503,403,807	0.90	183	562,432	562,432	562,432
ComputeSYMGS_ref|Sp...	src/ComputeSYMGS_re...	src/ComputeSYMGS_re...	485,199,427	0.90	485,199,427	0.90	51,587,840	2	2	2
SetupHalo|SparseMatr...	src/SetupHalo.cpp:147	src/SetupHalo.cpp:147	10,161,459,134	18.00	442,322,353	0.80	1,285,245	8	26	27
ComputeRestriction_re...	src/ComputeRestrictio...	src/ComputeRestrictio...	348,654,114	0.60	348,654,114	0.60	492	549	13,365	35,132
ComputeSYMGS_ref|Sp...	src/ComputeSYMGS_re...	src/ComputeSYMGS_re...	252,936,613	0.40	252,936,613	0.40	51,587,840	2	2	2
DeleteMatrix|SparseM...	testing/SparseMatrix.h...	testing/SparseMatrix.h...	240,136,075	0.40	240,136,075	0.40	4	2,197	321,311	1,124,864

Figure 6-4. *Function and loop profile for the HPCG benchmark*

With the loop hotspots and the loop profile, we can now make an informed decision about which of the two loops in ComputeSPMV_ref to parallelize. The hotspot analysis told us that the inner loop is the hot loop. However, the loop profile tells us that the loop in line 67 has been encountered 429 million times with a minimum and maximum trip count of 1. It is easy to see that any parallelization would have done a very poor job on this loop. But there is also the highlighted outer loop showing up in the loop profile. It has been encountered 687 times with minimum and maximum trip count of 17,576 and 1.1 million, respectively. Also, the average trip count of about 625,572 iterations tells us that this loop will be an interesting candidate for parallelization. Of course, one still needs to check that there are no loop dependencies that would prevent parallelization. Inspecting the loop body, we can see that this loop can be executed in parallel. Although it is a good idea to check for loop-carried dependencies and data dependencies (Chapter 7) instead of blindly adding OpenMP parallelization pragmas to loops, tools such as Intel Inspector XE[4] or Valgrind[5] can be a great help in detecting and resolving issues introduced by multithreading.

EXERCISE 6-1

Run a hotspot analysis for your application(s) and determine the minimum, maximum, and average trip counts of its loops. Can you find candidates for parallelization?

Sequential Code and Detecting Load Imbalances

In a parallel program, the slowest thread determines the speed of the whole team working in parallel. All the faster threads will have to wait until the slowest straggler thread catches up and finishes its tasks. As a matter of fact, one of the challenges of parallel programming is that of ensuring all threads receive an equal share of the computational load. Please note that by "computational load" we are referring to the total number of cycles spent per thread for the parallel work. For instance, if the loop body takes a different amount of time to execute different iterations, the threads should not receive equal shares of the loop's iterations (for example, through static scheduling). *Sequential* portions of your application can be seen as a special form of load imbalance, as other threads and cores will be idle while the sequential code is executing in the master thread of the application.

The hotspots analysis for a particular parallel region of code in your application is a useful tool for detecting such load imbalances. VTune Amplifier XE indicates such problems through various elements in the analysis GUI. First, the tabular view (or *grid*) at the top contains, in column "User Time by Utilization," a color code to visualize the quality of parallel execution relative to the number of cores in the system. Red indicates that the hotspot was not using the machine properly and exposes too low an average degree of parallelism. Yellow stands for medium, whereas green suggests an ideal parallel execution. These color codes should not be taken as the only source of information, though; red or yellow hotspots always need closer investigation. Although load imbalances typically show up as a lower degree of parallelism, the red and yellow color codes can also be indicating too low a number of threads executing in parallel, owing to locks, lower number of threads requested, or sequential regions in the hotspots. In case you deliberately execute the application with a lower target thread count (for example, only the physical cores of a system with Intel Hyper-Threading Technology enabled), you can manually adjust the intervals for green, yellow, and red in the Summary tab of the VTune Amplifier XE GUI.

The second GUI element that uses color coding as a visual guide to performance data is the timeline view in the bottom part of the GUI. VTune Amplifier XE shows a horizontal bar for each of the threads in the application and provides insights into their behavior over time. A non-active thread is marked as light green, but once it consumes cycles its color turns to brown. The red color signals overhead, such as time spent waiting for a lock to be released or threads waiting to join a barrier. A load imbalance can easily be detected by looking at when the threads start and stop executing instructions compared to other threads of an OpenMP region, which are indicated by brackets at the top of the thread timeline.

Figure 6-5 shows the performance data and timeline that we collected for a run of the MiniFE application. We used the following command line to produce the performance data on a single node (eight MPI ranks with six OpenMP threads each):

```
$ export OMP_NUM_THREADS=6
$ mpirun -np 8 amplxe-cl -collect hotspots --result-dir miniFE-8x6 -- \
    miniFE.x -nx=500
```

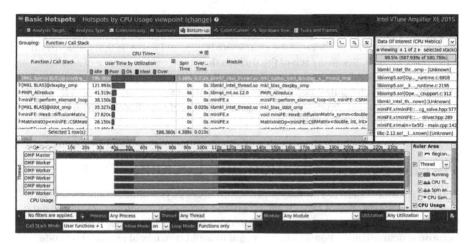

Figure 6-5. *Hotspot profile of the miniFE application to determine potential load imbalances*

Using this command line to collect performance data, VTune Amplifier XE produced eight different results databases (miniFE-8x6.0 to miniFE-8x6.7), each of which contains the performance data for one of the eight MPI ranks. Figure 6-5 only shows the performance data for the first MPI rank. The other seven MPI ranks expose the same performance characteristics, and thus we can restrict ourselves to the one MPI rank in this case. For other applications, it will be required to check all MPI ranks and their performance data individually to make sure there are no outliers in the runtime profile.

Let us have a look at the timeline view at the bottom of Figure 6-5. The timeline shows several threads active over time. There are some particular areas of interest. First, we can observe that only one thread is executing for about 40 seconds before multithreading kicks in. We can also spot a second sequential part ranging for about 56 seconds in total, from 54 seconds to 110 seconds in the timeline. Zooming in and filtering the timeline, we can find out that the code is doing a matrix initialization in the first 40 seconds of its execution. About one-third of the compute time in this part is also attributed to an MPI_Allreduce operation. A similar issue leads to the sequential part that begins at 54 seconds of the execution. While this is not a true load imbalance in the code, because OpenMP is not active in these parts of the application, its exposure is similar to a load imbalance. From a timeline perspective, a load imbalance will look similar to what we see in Figure 6-5. In our example, finding a parallelization scheme to also parallelize the sequential fractions may boost application performance, owing to the amount of time spend in these parts of the application.

The general approach to solving a load imbalance is to first try to modify the loop scheduling of the code in question. Typically, OpenMP implementations prefer static scheduling that assigns equally large numbers of loop iterations to individual worker threads. While it is a good solution for loops with equal compute time per iteration, any unbalanced loop will cause problems. OpenMP defines several loop scheduling types that you can use to resolve the load imbalance. Although switching to fully dynamic schedules such as dynamic or guided appears to be a good idea, these scheduling

181

schemes tend to increase contention between many OpenMP threads, because a shared variable that maintains the work distribution. Static scheduling can still be used despite the load imbalance it introduces if the chunk size is adjusted down so that round-robin scheduling kicks in. Because each of the threads then receives a sequence of smaller blocks, there is a good chance that, on average, all the threads will receive compute-intensive and less compute-intensive loop chunks. At the same time, it ensures that each thread can compute all iterations it has to process, without synchronizing with the other threads through a shared variable.

Thread Synchronization and Locking

Thread synchronization is a double-edged sword. It keeps your data structures safe in that it allows you to control concurrent access and avoid race conditions on shared data; but if synchronization is introduced into the code, then parallelism may naturally suffer because synchronization constructs are meant to avoid concurrent execution of code regions. As a matter of fact, there will always be a tradeoff between limiting the degree of parallelism by introducing synchronization and choosing data structures and algorithms that need less synchronization for better parallelization.

In Table 5-8, you saw the performance of the MiniMD application on a workstation equipped with two Xeon processors. The data was for an execution that used Intel MPI on a single system to create several processes for execution. The version of MiniMD that we used to produce Table 5-8 also supported OpenMP-parallel execution instead of only MPI. So, a valid question is: Why did we use a message-passing library if there is shared memory available and if we could use multithreading instead? Let's hold that thought for a minute and just repeat the same benchmark, but now with OpenMP multithreading.

Figure 6-6 shows a speedup chart that compares the multiprocess MPI run with the multithread execution on the same machine. While the single-process and single-thread configuration exhibits the same performance behavior, there is a large gap between the MPI and the OpenMP versions. The OpenMP code is almost two times slower in all cases in comparison with the MPI version. In principle, an n-body algorithm should nicely scale with the number of cores, as shown by the MPI version. There is undoubtedly something going on in the OpenMP version of the code. Let's use VTune Amplifier XE to find out.

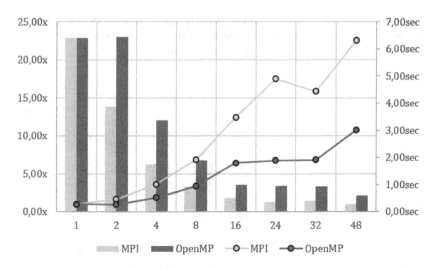

Figure 6-6. *Speedup graph (lines) and absolute runtime (bars) for the MiniMD benchmark*

We have executed the application with the following sequence of commands:

```
$ source /opt/intel/vtune_amplifier_xe/amplxe-vars.sh
$ amplxe-cl -collect advanced-hotspots -r omp -- \
    ./miniMD_intel --num_threads 24
$ amplxe-cl -collect advanced-hotspots -r mpi -- \
    mpirun -np 24 ./miniMD_intel
```

These commands instruct VTune Amplifier XE to collect two profiles:

1. One process with 24 OpenMP threads

2. Twenty-four MPI ranks with one thread each

The collected profiles are named omp and mpi, respectively, through the --result-dir command line option of the collector.

The profiles are fundamentally different in what they represent from a data collection perspective. For the omp profile, VTune Amplifier XE monitored the performance events while MiniMD executed and created a performance database for just a single process with 24 threads. In the case of the mpi profile, the collector recognized that multiple MPI processes were spawned by the mpirun command. The performance database thus contains performance data from all 24 MPI ranks in a single profile.

Figure 6-7 shows the hotspots profiles of both executions. MPI is shown at the top, OpenMP at the bottom. As you can see from the hotspots profile, for MPI the hotspot is the ForceLJ::compute_halfneigh function, whereas for OpenMP it is a function called __kmp_test_then_add_real64. Functions that have a prefix __kmp in their name are compiler-internal functions used to implement OpenMP in Intel Composer XE.

In typical applications these functions show up in the hotspots profile from time to time and sometimes, as in this case, they are the culprit. To find out, we need to take a closer look at what the __kmp_test_then_add_real64 function does.

Grouping: Function / Call Stack									
Function / Call Stack	CPU Time▾	★	Instructions Retired	Ove.. and...	CPI Rate	Source File	CPU Fre...	Sl Ad
▷ __kmp_test_then_add_real64		39.1%	23,325,300,000	0s	1.376		1.109	0x8
▷ __kmp_wait_sleep		23.0%	15,776,100,000	6.320s	1.199	kmp_runtime.c	1.111	0x5
▷ ForceLJ::compute_halfneigh_threaded<(int)		17.7%	14,247,900,000	0s	1.000	force_lj.cpp	1.087	0x4
▷ __kmp_x86_pause		5.6%	8,243,100,000	1.547s	0.554		1.095	0x8
▷ Neighbor::build		4.6%	5,861,700,000	0s	0.642	neighbor.cpp	1.110	0x4
▷ [Outside any known module]		1.8%	1,185,300,000	0s	1.223		1.065	0
▷ Integrate::initialIntegrate		1.4%	521,100,000	0s	2.155	integrate.cpp	1.052	0x4
▷ __kmpc_atomic_float8_sub		1.3%	999,000,000	0s	1.103	kmp_atomic.c	1.152	0x3
▷ [Import thunk __kmpc_atomic_float8_sub]		1.0%	1,004,400,000	0s	0.804		1.128	0x4
Selected 1 row(s):		39.1%	23,325,300,000	0s	1.376		1.109	

Grouping: Function / Call Stack								
Function / Call Stack	CPU Time▾	★	Instructions Retired	Ove.. and...	CPI Rate	Source File	CPU Fre..
▷ ForceLJ::compute_halfneigh<(int)0, (int)1>		54.5%	28,247,400,000	0s	0.638	force_lj.cpp	1.048
▷ MPID_nem_mpich_blocking_recv		17.4%	6,779,700,000	0s	0.850	mpid_nem_inline.h	1.048
▷ Neighbor::build		10.8%	5,702,400,000	0s	0.636	neighbor.cpp	1.070
▷ [Outside any known module]		7.1%	726,300,000	0s	3.112		1.014
▷ ForceLJ::compute_halfneigh<(int)1, (int)1>		1.8%	928,800,000	0s	0.637	force_lj.cpp	1.041
▷ MPIDI_CH3_iStartMsgv		1.1%	5,400,000	0s	66.500	ch3_istartmsgv.c	1.014
▷ __I_MPI__intel_ssse3_rep_memcpy		1.0%	189,000,000	0s	1.700		0.986
▷ Atom::unpack_reverse		0.8%	378,000,000	0s	0.707	atom.cpp	1.078
▷ Integrate::initialIntegrate		0.7%	583,200,000	0s	0.569	integrate.cpp	1.469
Selected 1 row(s):		54.5%	28,247,400,000	0s	0.638		1.048

Figure 6-7. *Hotspots profiles for the MPI version (top) and OpenMP version (bottom) of MiniMD*

Let's have a closer look at it by double-clicking its line in the tabular view. This takes us to the assembly code of the function, because runtime libraries shipped with Intel Composer XE usually do not ship with full debugging symbols and source code, for obvious reasons. If you inspect the machine code, you will find that its main operation consuming a lot of time is a machine instruction lock cmpxchg. This instruction is an atomic compare-and-exchange operation, which is frequently used to implement an atomic add operation.

Functions like __kmp_test_then_add_real64 and similar ones that implement OpenMP locks are hints that the code issues too many fine-grained atomic instructions. In case of MiniMD, the culprit is an atomic directive that protects the force update and that causes slowdown compared to the MPI version. It is also responsible for the limited scalability of the OpenMP version because it quickly becomes a bottleneck for an increased number of threads.

EXERCISE 6-2

Browse through the MiniMD code and try to find the OpenMP atomic constructs that cause the overhead in the OpenMP version. Can you find similar synchronization constructs in your application?

How such a synchronization issue can be resolved depends on the type of application, its data structures, and the algorithms used. For the MiniMD application, the synchronization is required because the effect of force on one atom also has an effect on the source of the force. According to Newton's third law, this effect is exactly the reverse force: if atom A is affected by a positive amount, then atom B, the source of the force, will be affected by a negative amount. The MPI version exploits this physical law to compute the force on atom A and then simply updates atom B without recomputing the force from scratch. This roughly cuts the computation required by 50 percent. Because of this optimization, multithreading becomes a bit more complex. For OpenMP, the atoms are distributed across the OpenMP threads. But as the computation for one atom requires an update of the forces for a second atom, synchronization must be added to avoid a race between the threads owning the atom. MiniMD already offers such a mode that can be enabled by setting the command-line option --half_neigh 0. Figure 6-8 compares the two modes of MiniMD. As you can see, performance and scalability are greatly improved by avoiding the excess synchronization.

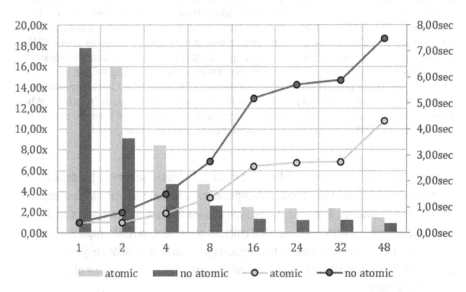

Figure 6-8. *Comparision of MiniMD with and without OpenMP* atomic *construct*

Another source of overhead are traditional locks, such as omp_lock_t or critical regions (#pragma omp critical in C/C++ or !$omp critical in Fortran). Whereas they share the property of mutual exclusion with their atomic instruction counterpart, they are typically more expensive and are widely used to protect code fragments and data structures that are more complex than simple updates of memory locations. VTune Amplifier XE offers a specialized analysis for problems that stem from these locks and helps to more easily pinpoint them in the code and their behavior at runtime. The analysis is called *Locks and Waits* and it specifically monitors the most commonly used

APIs to implement user-space locks. For each lock operation in the code, the analyzer helps browse through the participating threads (lock owner and waiting threads), the lock object involved, and the respective source code locations where the lock was acquired and released.

Dealing with Memory Locality and NUMA Effects

With the algorithmic improvements to obtain higher degrees of parallelism, we can now investigate how best to execute the parallel code on today's hardware. If you recall the features of the platform architecture that were described in Chapter 2, you will remember that a compute node typically contains several sockets with locally attached memory (NUMA), last level cache, and the compute cores with their private L1 and L2 caches. Because of the different bandwidth characteristics of local memory and remote memory, the placement of data and computation (i.e., threads and processes) becomes an important optimization target. It is key to keep data and computation on the same NUMA region to ensure lowest latency and highest memory bandwidth for the data accesses performed.

You may recall that each virtual page of the virtual memory associated with a process is backed up by a physical page that resides on one of the memory modules in one NUMA region. The Linux kernel uses a default strategy called *first touch* to allocate the physical pages. When an application allocates memory (for example, by calling malloc in C/C++), it receives a pointer to the allocated memory. However, the Linux kernel does not yet create any new physical pages unless the memory is accessed, or "touched." When a thread first touches the data by reading from it or writing into it, the physical page is allocated in the NUMA region that belongs to the core running that thread.

■ **Note**   The numactl command introduced in Chapter 2 can also change the default allocation strategy of the Linux kernel. The argument --localalloc enables the standard Linux allocation strategy. With --preferred you can ask to place physical pages on a specific NUMA region, whereas --membind enforces placement on NUMA regions. Finally, the --interleave option interleaves the physical pages on several NUMA regions in a round-robin fashion. You can find additional details about this in the man page of the numactl command.

In a real application, this may severely penalize performance. If data is frequently accessed from a thread that runs on a different socket than the one that it ran on during allocation, the application will suffer from the lower bandwidth and higher latency of the remote data access. Figure 6-9 shows the achieved bandwidth of the STREAM Triad benchmark on our example machine. For the black line ("local memory") in the chart, we have executed the benchmark on socket 0 and used numactl to force memory allocation to the local memory:

```
$ (for i in `seq 1 12`; do OMP_NUM_THREADS=$i numactl --cpunodebind
    0 --membind 0 ./stream;
done) | grep "Triad:" | awk '{print $2}'
```

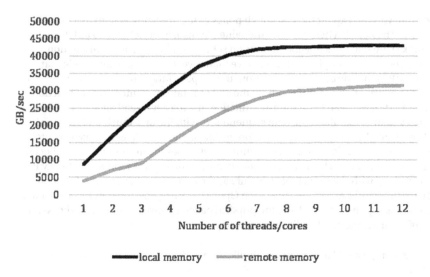

Figure 6-9. Bandwidth as measured by the STREAM Triad benchmark

The gray line shows the bandwidth we have obtained by forcing memory allocation to the second NUMA region, while keeping the threads on the first socket:

```
$ (for i in `seq 1 12`; do OMP_NUM_THREADS=$i numactl --cpunodebind
  0 --membind 1 ./stream;
done) | grep "Triad:" | awk '{print $2}'
```

It is easy to see how much available memory bandwidth we lost by choosing a wrong placement for data and computation. It is key to tie data and computation together on the same NUMA region whenever possible. This will greatly improve application performance. If the application is too complex to improve its NUMA awareness, you can still investigate if interleaved page allocation or switching off the NUMA mode in the BIOS improves overall performance. With these settings, the memory allocations are then distributed across the whole machine and thus all accesses are going equally to local and remote memory, on average.

If you wish to optimize the application and improve its NUMA awareness, then there are several ways to accomplish this mission. First, there are ways to bind threads and processes to individual NUMA regions so that they stay close to their data. We used the numactl command earlier to do this, but Linux offers several other APIs (for instance, sched_setaffinity) or tools (for example, taskset) to control process and threads in a machine-dependent manner. You may also recall the I_MPI_PIN environment variable and its friends (see Chapter 5) that enable a more convenient way of controlling process placement for MPI applications. Of course, typical OpenMP implementations also provide similar environment variables. (We will revisit this topic later in this chapter, when we look at hybrid MPI/OpenMP applications.)

Second, you can exploit the first-touch policy of the operating system in a threaded application. The key idea here is to use the same parallelization scheme to initialize data and to make sure that the same parallelization scheme is also used for computation. Listing 6-2 shows an example of a (very) naïve matrix-vector multiplication code that uses OpenMP for multithreading. Apart from the compute function, which computes the result of the matrix-matrix multiplication, the code contains two initialization functions (init and init_numa_aware). In the init function, the master thread allocates all data structures and then initializes the data sequentially. With the first-touch policy of the Linux kernel, all physical pages will therefore reside on the NUMA region that executed the master thread. The init_numa_aware function still uses the master thread to allocate the data through malloc. However, the code then runs the initialization in an OpenMP parallel for loop with the same loop schedule as the accesses in the compute function happen for the A and c arrays. Because each OpenMP thread now touches the same data for A and c it is supposed to work on, the physical pages are distributed across the NUMA regions of the machine and locality is improved.

Listing 6-2. Simplistic Matrix-vector Multiplication with NUMA-aware Memory Allocation

```
void init() {
    A = (double*) malloc(sizeof(*A) * n * n);
    b = (double*) malloc(sizeof(*b) * n);
    c = (double*) malloc(sizeof(*c) * n);
    for (int i = 0; i < n; i++)
        for (int j = 0; j < n; j++)
            A[i*n+j] = ((double) rand())/((double) RAND_MAX);

    for (int i = 0; i < n; i++) {
        b[i] = ((double) rand())/((double) RAND_MAX);
        c[i] = 0.0;
    }
}

void init_numa_aware() {
    A = (double*) malloc(sizeof(*A) * n * n);
    b = (double*) malloc(sizeof(*b) * n);
    c = (double*) malloc(sizeof(*c) * n);
#pragma omp parallel
    {
#pragma omp for
        for (int i = 0; i < n; i++)
            for (int j = 0; j < n; j++)
                A[i*n+j] = ((double) rand())/((double) RAND_MAX);
```

```
#pragma omp for
        for (int i = 0; i < n; i++) {
            b[i] = ((double) rand())/((double) RAND_MAX);
            c[i] = 0.0;
        }
    }
}

void compute() {
#pragma omp parallel for
    for(int i = 0; i < n; i++)
        for(int j = 0; j < n; j++)
            c[i] += A[i*n+j] * b[j];
}
```

The array b is a special case in this example. If you consider the compute function, you will see that b is read equally from all threads. So at first glance it does not seem to make a real difference if we used a NUMA-aware allocation or just allocate it in a single NUMA region. Unless the matrix size becomes unreasonably large, it will likely be that b will fit in the last-level cache of the individual sockets, so that no NUMA effects can be measured.

Of course, all this only happens if the working size of the application requires allocation of several physical pages so that they can be distributed across the different NUMA regions. The data also needs to be large enough so that the caches are not effective and that out-of-cache data accesses happen. For a perfectly cache-optimized code, the effect of this optimization may be low or even negligible. If threads frequently access a large, shared, but read-only data structure (like b) that does not fit the LLC of the sockets, then distributing it across several NUMA regions will still likely benefit performance. In this case, distributing the data helps avoid overloading a single NUMA region with memory accesses from other NUMA regions.

The effect of parallel data allocation in Listing 6-2 can be visualized nicely with the STREAM Triad benchmark. Figure 6-10 summarizes different thread placements and the effect of NUMA-aware allocation on memory bandwidth. The compact (gray solid and dashed line) in the chart indicates that the OpenMP runtime was instructed to first fill a socket with threads before placing threads on the second socket. "Scatter" (black solid and dashed line) distributes the threads in round-robin fashion. (We will have a closer look at these distribution schemes in the next section).

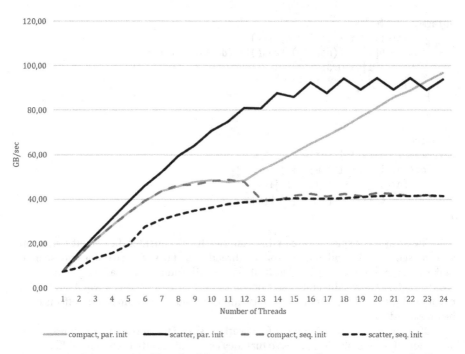

Figure 6-10. *STREAM Triad bandwidth with NUMA-aware allocation across multiple NUMA regions*

What you can observe from Figure 6-10 is that NUMA awareness always provides best results, as it fully exploits the capabilities of the memory subsystem. If threads are kept close to each other (`compact`), adding the second NUMA region contributes additional memory bandwidth, which is expected. For the `scatter` distribution, the memory bandwidth of the two NUMA regions of the system contributes to the aggregate memory bandwidth when at least two threads are executing. However, memory bandwidth will be up to a factor of two less if memory is allocated in only one NUMA region.

Unfortunately, NUMA-aware data allocation is not possible in all cases. One peculiar example is MPI applications that employ OpenMP threads. In many cases, these applications use the `MPI_THREAD_FUNNELED` or `MPI_THREAD_SERIALIZED` modes in which only one thread performs the MPI operations. If messages are received into a newly allocated buffer, then the first-touch policy automatically allocates the backing store of the buffer on a single NUMA region in which the communicating thread was executing. If you wish to run OpenMP threads across multiple NUMA regions and still maintain NUMA awareness, things tend to become complex and require a lot of thought and fine-tuning. Depending on how long the data will be live in the buffer and how many accesses the threads will make, it might be beneficial to either make a multithreaded copy of the buffer so that the accessing threads also perform the first touch, or use the Linux kernel's interface for page migration to move the physical pages into the right NUMA domain. However, these will be costly operations that need to be amortized by enough data accesses. Plus, implementing the migration strategies adds a lot of boilerplate code to the application. The easiest way of solve this is to use one MPI rank per NUMA region and restrict OpenMP threading to that region only. In this case, there are no changes required to the application code, but you will need to properly bind threads and processes to the NUMA regions and their corresponding cores.

Thread and Process Pinning

Besides the aforementioned need to properly place processes and threads to get a better data locality in NUMA systems, thread and process pinning also offer other benefits that may lead to performance improvements.

As shown in Figure 6-10, putting threads or processes far apart in the system (scatter)—that is, on different sockets of the machine—can improve the aggregated memory bandwidth. As each socket has its own memory subsystem, the threads on different sockets do not compete for the same memory channels and thus receive more memory bandwidth in total. The same applies to the total amount of last-level cache (LLC) available to the application.

On the other hand, scattered distribution has some disadvantages. If threads communicate a lot by reading and writing to variables and data structures shared between them, then communication across the QPI link can easily become a bottleneck. The same applies to synchronization constructs such as barriers, locks, and atomic operations. Synchronization constructs are much more efficient if the participating threads are on the same socket. This is because the memory operations involved in implementing the synchronization are much faster when running from the same shared (last-level) cache instead of involving communication over the QPI links of the system. While synchronization is a good reason to keep threads as close as possible, it conflicts with the above benefits of spreading the threads across the system. In general, one can only hope to find a good tradeoff between the conflicting benefits and to approximate the ideal placement configuration.

Controlling OpenMP Thread Placement

Intel Composer XE, and its implementation of OpenMP, offers two ways to control thread placement in an application:

1. KMP_AFFINITY environment variable

2. OMP_PROC_BIND interface of the OpenMP 4.0 API

For a long time, before the OpenMP API version 4.0 was released, KMP_AFFINITY was the standard way of controlling thread placement for the Intel implementation of OpenMP. Through this environment variable, you can control thread placement on several levels ranging from abstract placement policies to a fine-grained mapping of OpenMP threads to sockets, cores, and hyper-threads. The settings of KMP_AFFINITY are effective for the whole application process—that is, if the process spawns multiple parallel regions, the same settings pertain for all parallel regions. KMP_AFFINITY also supports only one level of parallelism, but no nested OpenMP parallel regions.

Listing 6-3 shows the effect of different values for the KMP_AFFINITY variable on the thread placement. It shows how 18 threads are mapped to the cores of our two-socket example machine. For the compact placement, all 18 threads will be assigned to the first socket. The scatter strategy assigns the threads to the sockets of the machine in a round-robin fashion; even thread IDs are assigned to the first socket, threads with odd ID execute on the second socket. We can check this allocation by adding the verbose modifier to the KMP_AFFINITY environment variable, which requests to print information about the machine structure and how the threads are assigned to the (logical) cores of the system (Listing 6-3). To make sense of the different IDs and the underlying machine structure, you may use the cpuinfo tool introduced in Chapter 5.

Listing 6-3. OpenMP Thread Pinning with Additional Information Printed for Each OpenMP Thread

```
$ OMP_NUM_THREADS=18 KMP_AFFINITY=granularity=thread,compact,verbose \
    ./my_app
OMP: Info #204: KMP_AFFINITY: decoding x2APIC ids.
OMP: Info #202: KMP_AFFINITY: Affinity capable, using global cpuid leaf 11
info
OMP: Info #154: KMP_AFFINITY: Initial OS proc set respected: {0,1,2,3,4,5,6,
7,8,9,10,11,12,13,14,15,16,17,18,19,20,21,22,23,24,25,26,27,28,29,30,31,32,3
3,34,35,36,37,38,39,40,41,42,43,44,45,46,47}
OMP: Info #156: KMP_AFFINITY: 48 available OS procs
OMP: Info #157: KMP_AFFINITY: Uniform topology
OMP: Info #179: KMP_AFFINITY: 2 packages x 12 cores/pkg x 2 threads/core (24
total cores)
OMP: Info #206: KMP_AFFINITY: OS proc to physical thread map:
OMP: Info #171: KMP_AFFINITY: OS proc 0 maps to package 0 core 0 thread 0
OMP: Info #171: KMP_AFFINITY: OS proc 24 maps to package 0 core 0 thread 1
[...]
OMP: Info #144: KMP_AFFINITY: Threads may migrate across 1 innermost levels
of machine
OMP: Info #242: KMP_AFFINITY: pid 85939 thread 0 bound to OS proc set {0}
OMP: Info #242: KMP_AFFINITY: pid 85939 thread 1 bound to OS proc set {24}
OMP: Info #242: KMP_AFFINITY: pid 85939 thread 2 bound to OS proc set {1}
OMP: Info #242: KMP_AFFINITY: pid 85939 thread 3 bound to OS proc set {25}
OMP: Info #242: KMP_AFFINITY: pid 85939 thread 4 bound to OS proc set {2}
OMP: Info #242: KMP_AFFINITY: pid 85939 thread 5 bound to OS proc set {26}
OMP: Info #242: KMP_AFFINITY: pid 85939 thread 6 bound to OS proc set {3}
OMP: Info #242: KMP_AFFINITY: pid 85939 thread 7 bound to OS proc set {27}
OMP: Info #242: KMP_AFFINITY: pid 85939 thread 8 bound to OS proc set {4}
OMP: Info #242: KMP_AFFINITY: pid 85939 thread 9 bound to OS proc set {28}
OMP: Info #242: KMP_AFFINITY: pid 85939 thread 10 bound to OS proc set {5}
OMP: Info #242: KMP_AFFINITY: pid 85939 thread 11 bound to OS proc set {29}
OMP: Info #242: KMP_AFFINITY: pid 85939 thread 12 bound to OS proc set {6}
OMP: Info #242: KMP_AFFINITY: pid 85939 thread 13 bound to OS proc set {30}
OMP: Info #242: KMP_AFFINITY: pid 85939 thread 14 bound to OS proc set {7}
OMP: Info #242: KMP_AFFINITY: pid 85939 thread 16 bound to OS proc set {8}
```

```
OMP: Info #242: KMP_AFFINITY: pid 85939 thread 15 bound to OS proc set {31}
OMP: Info #242: KMP_AFFINITY: pid 85939 thread 17 bound to OS proc set {32}
[...]

$ OMP_NUM_THREADS=18 KMP_AFFINITY=granularity=thread,scatter,verbose \
   ./my_app
OMP: Info #204: KMP_AFFINITY: decoding x2APIC ids.
OMP: Info #202: KMP_AFFINITY: Affinity capable, using global cpuid leaf 11
info
OMP: Info #154: KMP_AFFINITY: Initial OS proc set respected: {0,1,2,3,4,5,6,
7,8,9,10,11,12,13,14,15,16,17,18,19,20,21,22,23,24,25,26,27,28,29,30,31,32,3
3,34,35,36,37,38,39,40,41,42,43,44,45,46,47}
OMP: Info #156: KMP_AFFINITY: 48 available OS procs
OMP: Info #157: KMP_AFFINITY: Uniform topology
OMP: Info #179: KMP_AFFINITY: 2 packages x 12 cores/pkg x 2 threads/core (24
total cores)
OMP: Info #206: KMP_AFFINITY: OS proc to physical thread map:
OMP: Info #171: KMP_AFFINITY: OS proc 0 maps to package 0 core 0 thread 0
OMP: Info #171: KMP_AFFINITY: OS proc 24 maps to package 0 core 0 thread 1
OMP: Info #171: KMP_AFFINITY: OS proc 1 maps to package 0 core 1 thread 0
OMP: Info #171: KMP_AFFINITY: OS proc 25 maps to package 0 core 1 thread 1
OMP: Info #171: KMP_AFFINITY: OS proc 2 maps to package 0 core 2 thread 0
OMP: Info #171: KMP_AFFINITY: OS proc 26 maps to package 0 core 2 thread 1
OMP: Info #171: KMP_AFFINITY: OS proc 3 maps to package 0 core 3 thread 0
[...]
OMP: Info #242: KMP_AFFINITY: pid 85979 thread 0 bound to OS proc set {0}
OMP: Info #242: KMP_AFFINITY: pid 85979 thread 1 bound to OS proc set {12}
OMP: Info #242: KMP_AFFINITY: pid 85979 thread 2 bound to OS proc set {1}
OMP: Info #242: KMP_AFFINITY: pid 85979 thread 3 bound to OS proc set {13}
OMP: Info #242: KMP_AFFINITY: pid 85979 thread 4 bound to OS proc set {2}
OMP: Info #242: KMP_AFFINITY: pid 85979 thread 5 bound to OS proc set {14}
OMP: Info #242: KMP_AFFINITY: pid 85979 thread 6 bound to OS proc set {3}
OMP: Info #242: KMP_AFFINITY: pid 85979 thread 7 bound to OS proc set {15}
OMP: Info #242: KMP_AFFINITY: pid 85979 thread 8 bound to OS proc set {4}
OMP: Info #242: KMP_AFFINITY: pid 85979 thread 9 bound to OS proc set {16}
OMP: Info #242: KMP_AFFINITY: pid 85979 thread 10 bound to OS proc set {5}
OMP: Info #242: KMP_AFFINITY: pid 85979 thread 11 bound to OS proc set {17}
OMP: Info #242: KMP_AFFINITY: pid 85979 thread 12 bound to OS proc set {6}
OMP: Info #242: KMP_AFFINITY: pid 85979 thread 13 bound to OS proc set {18}
OMP: Info #242: KMP_AFFINITY: pid 85979 thread 14 bound to OS proc set {7}
OMP: Info #242: KMP_AFFINITY: pid 85979 thread 16 bound to OS proc set {8}
OMP: Info #242: KMP_AFFINITY: pid 85979 thread 15 bound to OS proc set {19}
OMP: Info #242: KMP_AFFINITY: pid 85979 thread 17 bound to OS proc set {20}
[...]
```

If you carefully inspect the printout of Listing 6-3, it appears that the OpenMP runtime system has assigned the threads in a way that we did not expect in the first place. The compact policy assigned multiple OpenMP threads to the same physical core (e.g., thread 0 and 1 to cores 0 and 24, respectively), whereas for scatter, it assigned different physical cores. Due to SMT, each physical core appears as two logical cores that may execute threads. With compact, we have requested from the OpenMP runtime to fill one socket first, before utilizing the second socket. The most compact thread placement is to put thread 0 to logical core 0 and use logical core 24 for thread 1, and so on. Thinking of a compact placement, this might not be what we have intended to do; you might have expected something along the line of placing 12 threads on the first socket and deploy the remaining six threads on the other socket.

The syntax for KMP_AFFINITY provides modifiers to further control its behavior. We already silently used granularity in Listing 6-3. You can use it to tell the Intel OpenMP implementation whether an OpenMP thread is to be assigned to a single logical core (granularity=thread) or to the hardware threads of a physical core (granularity=core). Once you have played a bit with these two settings, you will see that neither will deploy the 18 threads of our example to two sockets. The solution is to use compact,1 as the policy. The effect is shown in Listing 6-4, in which 12 threads have been deployed to the first socket, and the remaining six threads have been assigned to the second socket. The documentation of Intel Composer XE[6] can give you more information on what compact,1 means and what other affinity settings you can use.

Listing 6-4. Compact KMP_AFFINITY Policy Across Two Sockets of the Example Machine

```
$ OMP_NUM_THREADS=18 KMP_AFFINITY=granularity=thread,compact,1,verbose ./
my_app
[...]
OMP: Info #242: KMP_AFFINITY: pid 86271 thread 0 bound to OS proc set {0}
OMP: Info #242: KMP_AFFINITY: pid 86271 thread 1 bound to OS proc set {1}
OMP: Info #242: KMP_AFFINITY: pid 86271 thread 3 bound to OS proc set {3}
OMP: Info #242: KMP_AFFINITY: pid 86271 thread 2 bound to OS proc set {2}
OMP: Info #242: KMP_AFFINITY: pid 86271 thread 4 bound to OS proc set {4}
OMP: Info #242: KMP_AFFINITY: pid 86271 thread 5 bound to OS proc set {5}
OMP: Info #242: KMP_AFFINITY: pid 86271 thread 6 bound to OS proc set {6}
OMP: Info #242: KMP_AFFINITY: pid 86271 thread 7 bound to OS proc set {7}
OMP: Info #242: KMP_AFFINITY: pid 86271 thread 8 bound to OS proc set {8}
OMP: Info #242: KMP_AFFINITY: pid 86271 thread 9 bound to OS proc set {9}
OMP: Info #242: KMP_AFFINITY: pid 86271 thread 10 bound to OS proc set {10}
OMP: Info #242: KMP_AFFINITY: pid 86271 thread 11 bound to OS proc set {11}
OMP: Info #242: KMP_AFFINITY: pid 86271 thread 12 bound to OS proc set {12}
OMP: Info #242: KMP_AFFINITY: pid 86271 thread 13 bound to OS proc set {13}
OMP: Info #242: KMP_AFFINITY: pid 86271 thread 14 bound to OS proc set {14}
OMP: Info #242: KMP_AFFINITY: pid 86271 thread 16 bound to OS proc set {16}
OMP: Info #242: KMP_AFFINITY: pid 86271 thread 15 bound to OS proc set {15}
OMP: Info #242: KMP_AFFINITY: pid 86271 thread 17 bound to OS proc set {17}
```

With version 4.0 of the OpenMP API specification, OpenMP now defines a common way to deal with thread placement in OpenMP applications. In OpenMP terms, a *place* denotes an entity that is capable of executing an OpenMP thread and is described as an unordered list of numerical IDs that match the processing elements of the underlying hardware. For Intel processors, these IDs are the core IDs as they appear in the operating system (e.g., as reported in /proc/cpuinfo or by KMP_AFFINITY=verbose). A *place list* contains an ordered list of places and is defined through the OMP_PLACES environment variable. The place list can also contain abstract names for places, such as threads (logical cores), cores (physical cores), or sockets (the sockets in the machine).

OpenMP also defines three placement policies with respect to an existing place list:

- master: Assign all threads of a team to the same place as the master thread of the team.

- close: Assign OpenMP threads to places such that they are close to their parent thread.

- spread: Sparsely distribute the OpenMP threads in the place list, dividing the place list into sublists.

In contrast to KMP_AFFINITY, the OpenMP placement policies can be used on a per-region basis by using the proc_bind clause at a parallel construct in the OpenMP code. It also supports nested parallelism through a list of policies separated by commas for the OMP_PROC_BIND variable. For each nesting level, one can specify a particular policy that becomes active, once a parallel region on that level starts executing. This is especially useful for applications that either use nested parallelism or that need to modify the thread placement on a per-region basis.

Listing 6-5 contains a few examples of different thread placements using OMP_PLACES and OMP_PROC_BIND. The first example has the same effect as the compact placement in Listing 6-4, whereas the second example assigns the threads in a similar fashion as the scatter policy of KMP_AFFINITY.

Listing 6-5. Examples for Using OMP_PLACES and OMP_PROC_BIND

```
$ OMP_NUM_THREADS=18 OMP_PROC_BIND=close OMP_PLACES=threads \
    KMP_AFFINITY=verbose ./my_app
[...]
OMP: Info #242: KMP_AFFINITY: pid 86565 thread 0 bound to OS proc set {0}
OMP: Info #242: OMP_PROC_BIND: pid 86565 thread 3 bound to OS proc set {25}
OMP: Info #242: OMP_PROC_BIND: pid 86565 thread 14 bound to OS proc set {7}
OMP: Info #242: OMP_PROC_BIND: pid 86565 thread 16 bound to OS proc set {8}
OMP: Info #242: OMP_PROC_BIND: pid 86565 thread 8 bound to OS proc set {4}
OMP: Info #242: OMP_PROC_BIND: pid 86565 thread 12 bound to OS proc set {6}
OMP: Info #242: OMP_PROC_BIND: pid 86565 thread 11 bound to OS proc set {29}
OMP: Info #242: OMP_PROC_BIND: pid 86565 thread 7 bound to OS proc set {27}
OMP: Info #242: OMP_PROC_BIND: pid 86565 thread 4 bound to OS proc set {2}
OMP: Info #242: OMP_PROC_BIND: pid 86565 thread 10 bound to OS proc set {5}
OMP: Info #242: OMP_PROC_BIND: pid 86565 thread 5 bound to OS proc set {26}
OMP: Info #242: OMP_PROC_BIND: pid 86565 thread 6 bound to OS proc set {3}
OMP: Info #242: OMP_PROC_BIND: pid 86565 thread 13 bound to OS proc set {30}
OMP: Info #242: OMP_PROC_BIND: pid 86565 thread 9 bound to OS proc set {28}
OMP: Info #242: OMP_PROC_BIND: pid 86565 thread 1 bound to OS proc set {24}
OMP: Info #242: OMP_PROC_BIND: pid 86565 thread 17 bound to OS proc set {32}
```

```
OMP: Info #242: OMP_PROC_BIND: pid 86565 thread 15 bound to OS proc set {31}
OMP: Info #242: OMP_PROC_BIND: pid 86565 thread 2 bound to OS proc set {1}
[...]

$ OMP_NUM_THREADS=18 OMP_PROC_BIND=spread OMP_PLACES=cores \
    KMP_AFFINITY=verbose ./my_app
[...]
OMP: Info #242: KMP_AFFINITY: pid 86690 thread 0 bound to OS proc set {0,24}
OMP: Info #242: OMP_PROC_BIND: pid 86668 thread 1 bound to OS proc set {2,26}
OMP: Info #242: OMP_PROC_BIND: pid 86668 thread 2 bound to OS proc set {3,27}
OMP: Info #242: OMP_PROC_BIND: pid 86668 thread 3 bound to OS proc set {4,28}
OMP: Info #242: OMP_PROC_BIND: pid 86668 thread 4 bound to OS proc set {6,30}
OMP: Info #242: OMP_PROC_BIND: pid 86668 thread 5 bound to OS proc set {7,31}
OMP: Info #242: OMP_PROC_BIND: pid 86668 thread 6 bound to OS proc set {8,32}
OMP: Info #242: OMP_PROC_BIND: pid 86668 thread 7 bound to OS proc set {10,34}
OMP: Info #242: OMP_PROC_BIND: pid 86668 thread 8 bound to OS proc set {11,35}
OMP: Info #242: OMP_PROC_BIND: pid 86668 thread 9 bound to OS proc set {12,36}
OMP: Info #242: OMP_PROC_BIND: pid 86668 thread 10 bound to OS proc set {14,38}
OMP: Info #242: OMP_PROC_BIND: pid 86668 thread 11 bound to OS proc set {15,39}
OMP: Info #242: OMP_PROC_BIND: pid 86668 thread 12 bound to OS proc set {16,40}
OMP: Info #242: OMP_PROC_BIND: pid 86668 thread 13 bound to OS proc set {18,42}
OMP: Info #242: OMP_PROC_BIND: pid 86668 thread 14 bound to OS proc set {19,43}
OMP: Info #242: OMP_PROC_BIND: pid 86668 thread 15 bound to OS proc set {20,44}
OMP: Info #242: OMP_PROC_BIND: pid 86668 thread 16 bound to OS proc set {22,46}
OMP: Info #242: OMP_PROC_BIND: pid 86668 thread 17 bound to OS proc set {23,47}
[...]
```

For more information on how to use KMP_AFFINITY and the OpenMP interface for threaded applications, see the user's guide of Intel Composer XE. For more advanced usage scenarios, the documentation also contains useful information on how programmers can use special runtime functions that allow for specific control of all aspects of thread pinning.

EXERCISE 6-3

Use different settings for KMP_AFFINITY and OMP_PROC_BIND, and conduct performance runs with these settings. What are the best settings for your application?

Thread Placement in Hybrid Applications

Process and thread placement may also lead to performance improvements for MPI/OpenMP hybrid applications. Depending on how many MPI ranks you are running per node, you may need to consider thread placement and find the ideal placement, similarly to what we have discussed for purely threaded applications.

If you configure the application to run only a single MPI rank per node, so that the remaining cores of the node are used to execute OpenMP threads, you'll need to place the threads appropriately to avoid NUMA issues and to make sure that the operating system keeps the threads where their data has been allocated.

If the application runs with one or more MPI ranks per socket, thread placement will be less of an issue. If the MPI rank is bound to a certain socket (the default for Intel MPI), the threads of each MPI process are automatically confined to execute on the same set of cores (or socket) that are available for their parent process (see Listing 6-6). Since now the MPI ranks' threads cannot move away from their executing socket, the NUMA issue is automatically solved. Data allocation and computation will always be performed on the same NUMA region. Pinning threads to specific cores might still lead to improvements, since it effectively avoids cache invalidations of the L1 and L2 caches that may happen owing to the threads' wandering around on different cores of the same socket.

In Listing 6-6, we instruct both the Intel MPI Library and the Intel OpenMP runtime to print their respective process and thread placements for MiniMD on a single node with two MPI ranks. As you can see, the Intel MPI Library automatically deploys one MPI rank per socket and restricts execution of the OpenMP threads to the cores of each socket. We can use this as a starting point and apply what we saw earlier in this section. Adding the appropriate KMP_AFFINITY settings, we can now make sure that each OpenMP thread is pinned to the same core during execution (shown in Listing 6-7).

Listing 6-6. Default Process and Thread Placement for an MPI/OpenMP Hybrid Application

```
$ I_MPI_DEBUG=4 KMP_AFFINITY=verbose mpirun "-prepend-rank  -np 2 \
   ./miniMD_intel --num_threads 12
[0] [0] MPI startup(): Single-threaded optimized library
[0] [0] MPI startup(): shm data transfer mode
[1] [1] MPI startup(): shm data transfer mode
[0] [0] MPI startup(): Rank    Pid       Node name  Pin cpu
[0] [0] MPI startup(): 0       87096     book       {0,1,2,3,4,5,6,7,8,9,
10,11,24,25,26,27,28,29,30,31,32,33,34,35}
[0] [0] MPI startup(): 1       87097     book       {12,13,14,15,16,17,18,19,
20,21,22,23,36,37,38,39,40,41,42,43,44,45,46,47}
[...]
[0] OMP: Info #242: KMP_AFFINITY: pid 87135 thread 0 bound to OS proc set
{0,1,2,3,4,5,6,7,8,9,10,11,24,25,26,27,28,29,30,31,32,33,34,35}
[0] OMP: Info #242: KMP_AFFINITY: pid 87135 thread 1 bound to OS proc set
{0,1,2,3,4,5,6,7,8,9,10,11,24,25,26,27,28,29,30,31,32,33,34,35}
[0] OMP: Info #242: KMP_AFFINITY: pid 87135 thread 3 bound to OS proc set
{0,1,2,3,4,5,6,7,8,9,10,11,24,25,26,27,28,29,30,31,32,33,34,35}
[0] OMP: Info #242: KMP_AFFINITY: pid 87135 thread 2 bound to OS proc set
{0,1,2,3,4,5,6,7,8,9,10,11,24,25,26,27,28,29,30,31,32,33,34,35}
[0] OMP: Info #242: KMP_AFFINITY: pid 87135 thread 4 bound to OS proc set
{0,1,2,3,4,5,6,7,8,9,10,11,24,25,26,27,28,29,30,31,32,33,34,35}
[0] OMP: Info #242: KMP_AFFINITY: pid 87135 thread 5 bound to OS proc set
{0,1,2,3,4,5,6,7,8,9,10,11,24,25,26,27,28,29,30,31,32,33,34,35}
```

```
[0] OMP: Info #242: KMP_AFFINITY: pid 87135 thread 6 bound to OS proc set
{0,1,2,3,4,5,6,7,8,9,10,11,24,25,26,27,28,29,30,31,32,33,34,35}
[0] OMP: Info #242: KMP_AFFINITY: pid 87135 thread 8 bound to OS proc set
{0,1,2,3,4,5,6,7,8,9,10,11,24,25,26,27,28,29,30,31,32,33,34,35}
[0] OMP: Info #242: KMP_AFFINITY: pid 87135 thread 7 bound to OS proc set
{0,1,2,3,4,5,6,7,8,9,10,11,24,25,26,27,28,29,30,31,32,33,34,35}
[0] OMP: Info #242: KMP_AFFINITY: pid 87135 thread 9 bound to OS proc set
{0,1,2,3,4,5,6,7,8,9,10,11,24,25,26,27,28,29,30,31,32,33,34,35}
[0] OMP: Info #242: KMP_AFFINITY: pid 87135 thread 10 bound to OS proc set
{0,1,2,3,4,5,6,7,8,9,10,11,24,25,26,27,28,29,30,31,32,33,34,35}
[0] OMP: Info #242: KMP_AFFINITY: pid 87135 thread 11 bound to OS proc set
{0,1,2,3,4,5,6,7,8,9,10,11,24,25,26,27,28,29,30,31,32,33,34,35}
[1] OMP: Info #242: KMP_AFFINITY: pid 87136 thread 0 bound to OS proc set
{12,13,14,15,16,17,18,19,20,21,22,23,36,37,38,39,40,41,42,43,44,45,46,47}
[1] OMP: Info #242: KMP_AFFINITY: pid 87136 thread 1 bound to OS proc set
{12,13,14,15,16,17,18,19,20,21,22,23,36,37,38,39,40,41,42,43,44,45,46,47}
[1] OMP: Info #242: KMP_AFFINITY: pid 87136 thread 2 bound to OS proc set
{12,13,14,15,16,17,18,19,20,21,22,23,36,37,38,39,40,41,42,43,44,45,46,47}
[1] OMP: Info #242: KMP_AFFINITY: pid 87136 thread 3 bound to OS proc set
{12,13,14,15,16,17,18,19,20,21,22,23,36,37,38,39,40,41,42,43,44,45,46,47}
[1] OMP: Info #242: KMP_AFFINITY: pid 87136 thread 4 bound to OS proc set
{12,13,14,15,16,17,18,19,20,21,22,23,36,37,38,39,40,41,42,43,44,45,46,47}
[1] OMP: Info #242: KMP_AFFINITY: pid 87136 thread 5 bound to OS proc set
{12,13,14,15,16,17,18,19,20,21,22,23,36,37,38,39,40,41,42,43,44,45,46,47}
[1] OMP: Info #242: KMP_AFFINITY: pid 87136 thread 6 bound to OS proc set
{12,13,14,15,16,17,18,19,20,21,22,23,36,37,38,39,40,41,42,43,44,45,46,47}
[1] OMP: Info #242: KMP_AFFINITY: pid 87136 thread 7 bound to OS proc set
{12,13,14,15,16,17,18,19,20,21,22,23,36,37,38,39,40,41,42,43,44,45,46,47}
[1] OMP: Info #242: KMP_AFFINITY: pid 87136 thread 8 bound to OS proc set
{12,13,14,15,16,17,18,19,20,21,22,23,36,37,38,39,40,41,42,43,44,45,46,47}
[1] OMP: Info #242: KMP_AFFINITY: pid 87136 thread 9 bound to OS proc set
{12,13,14,15,16,17,18,19,20,21,22,23,36,37,38,39,40,41,42,43,44,45,46,47}
[1] OMP: Info #242: KMP_AFFINITY: pid 87136 thread 10 bound to OS proc set
{12,13,14,15,16,17,18,19,20,21,22,23,36,37,38,39,40,41,42,43,44,45,46,47}
[1] OMP: Info #242: KMP_AFFINITY: pid 87136 thread 11 bound to OS proc set
{12,13,14,15,16,17,18,19,20,21,22,23,36,37,38,39,40,41,42,43,44,45,46,47}
[...]
```

Listing 6-7. Hybrid MPI/OpenMP Application with Thread-to-Core Pinning

```
$ I_MPI_DEBUG=4 KMP_AFFINITY=granularity=thread,compact,1,verbose \
    mpirun -prepend-rank -np 2
    ./miniMD_intel --num_threads 12
[0] [0] MPI startup(): Single-threaded optimized library
[0] [0] MPI startup(): shm data transfer mode
[1] [1] MPI startup(): shm data transfer mode
[0] [0] MPI startup(): Rank    Pid      Node name  Pin cpu
```

```
[0] [0] MPI startup(): 0        87377     book
{0,1,2,3,4,5,6,7,8,9,10,11,24,25,26,27,28,29,30,31,32,33,34,35}
[0] [0] MPI startup(): 1        87378     book
{12,13,14,15,16,17,18,19,20,21,22,23,36,37,38,39,40,41,42,43,44,45,46,47}
[...]
[0] OMP: Info #242: KMP_AFFINITY: pid 87377 thread 0 bound to OS proc set {0}
[0] OMP: Info #242: KMP_AFFINITY: pid 87377 thread 1 bound to OS proc set {1}
[0] OMP: Info #242: KMP_AFFINITY: pid 87377 thread 2 bound to OS proc set {2}
[0] OMP: Info #242: KMP_AFFINITY: pid 87377 thread 3 bound to OS proc set {3}
[0] OMP: Info #242: KMP_AFFINITY: pid 87377 thread 4 bound to OS proc set {4}
[0] OMP: Info #242: KMP_AFFINITY: pid 87377 thread 5 bound to OS proc set {5}
[0] OMP: Info #242: KMP_AFFINITY: pid 87377 thread 6 bound to OS proc set {6}
[0] OMP: Info #242: KMP_AFFINITY: pid 87377 thread 7 bound to OS proc set {7}
[0] OMP: Info #242: KMP_AFFINITY: pid 87377 thread 8 bound to OS proc set {8}
[0] OMP: Info #242: KMP_AFFINITY: pid 87377 thread 9 bound to OS proc set {9}
[0] OMP: Info #242: KMP_AFFINITY: pid 87377 thread 10 bound to OS proc set {10}
[0] OMP: Info #242: KMP_AFFINITY: pid 87377 thread 11 bound to OS proc set {11}
[1] OMP: Info #242: KMP_AFFINITY: pid 87378 thread 0 bound to OS proc set {12}
[1] OMP: Info #242: KMP_AFFINITY: pid 87378 thread 1 bound to OS proc set {13}
[1] OMP: Info #242: KMP_AFFINITY: pid 87378 thread 2 bound to OS proc set {14}
[1] OMP: Info #242: KMP_AFFINITY: pid 87378 thread 3 bound to OS proc set {15}
[1] OMP: Info #242: KMP_AFFINITY: pid 87378 thread 4 bound to OS proc set {16}
[1] OMP: Info #242: KMP_AFFINITY: pid 87378 thread 5 bound to OS proc set {17}
[1] OMP: Info #242: KMP_AFFINITY: pid 87378 thread 6 bound to OS proc set {18}
[1] OMP: Info #242: KMP_AFFINITY: pid 87378 thread 7 bound to OS proc set {19}
[1] OMP: Info #242: KMP_AFFINITY: pid 87378 thread 8 bound to OS proc set {20}
[1] OMP: Info #242: KMP_AFFINITY: pid 87378 thread 9 bound to OS proc set {21}
[1] OMP: Info #242: KMP_AFFINITY: pid 87378 thread 10 bound to OS proc set {22}
[1] OMP: Info #242: KMP_AFFINITY: pid 87378 thread 11 bound to OS proc set {23}
[...]
```

Summary

This chapter was all about optimizations on the threading level of the application to achieve better performance on a single node.

If your application is using only MPI to exchange messages on the process level and you are thinking about multithreading, this chapter showed how you can create a hotspot and loop profile to get a better understanding of the application behavior. This is your foundation for making informed decisions about where to apply OpenMP (or other threading models) to your code to move it to a hybrid MPI/OpenMP solution.

The hotspot profile is the tool for getting to know about optimization and parallelization candidates. The hotspots are always the optimization candidates that you will investigate closely and in depth so that you can find bottlenecks in these parts of your code. We have presented some of the most common application bottlenecks, such as sequential and load imbalanced parts of code, excessive thread synchronization, and issues introduced by the NUMA.

References

1. "Perf: Linux profiling with performance counters,"
   https://perf.wiki.kernel.org/index.php/Main_Page.

2. J. Dongarra and M. A. Heroux, *Toward a New Metric for Ranking High Performance Computing Systems* (Albuquerque, NM: Sandia National Laboratories, 2013).

3. *Intel VTune Amplifier XE User's Guide* (Santa Clara, CA: Intel Corporation, 2014).

4. "Intel® Inspector XE 2015,"
   https://software.intel.com/intel-inspector-xe.

5. Valgrind Developers, "Valgrind," http://valgrind.org/.

6. *User and Reference Guide for the Intel C++ Compiler 15.0* (Santa Clara, CA: Intel Corporation, 2014).

■ ■ ■

## CHAPTER 7

Addressing Application Bottlenecks: Microarchitecture

Microarchitectural performance tuning is one of the most difficult parts of the performance tuning process. In contrast to other tuning activities, it is not immediately clear what the bottlenecks are. Usually, discovering them requires studying processor manuals, which provide the details of the execution flow. Furthermore, a certain understanding of assembly language is needed to reflect the findings back onto the original source code. Each processor model will also have its own microarchitectural characteristics that have to be considered when writing efficient software.

In this chapter, we outline some of the general design principles of modern processors that will allow you to understand the do's and don'ts of diagnosing bottlenecks and to exploit tools to extract the required information that will allow you to tune software on the microarchitectural level.

Overview of a Modern Processor Pipeline

Let's discuss the most important features of a current CPU core in these beginning few pages. Features that you will find in most cores are pipelining, out-of-order and superscalar execution, data-parallel (SIMD) execution, and branch prediction. We will associate these features with the Intel Xeon E5-2600 series processor (code name Sandy Bridge).

To begin, let's briefly define some important terms that we will use extensively in this chapter:

- *Register:* A small, but very fast storage directly connected to the processor core. Since registers must be able to hold memory addresses, they need to be as big as the address space. A 64-bit architecture has 64-bit registers. And there might be additional, larger registers that we will deal with later.

- *Assembly language*: The one-to-one translation of the machine instructions that the CPU is able to understand. On a Linux system, you can see the assembly language for an object file with the objdump tool. For example,

```
$ objdump -M intel intel-mnemonic -d <object file or executable>
```

The output will look like

```
48 89 c1    mov    rcx,rax
```

where the numbers on the left are the actual numerical codes of the machine language and the right hand side is the translation into an assembly language instruction, consisting of human-readable mnemonics and its arguments. In this example, the translation into English would be "move the contents of register rax to the register rcx." Machine language and assembly language can be thought of as *bijective*. A compiler is not required; instead, a "translator" is used, called an *assembler*. The system-supplied assembler on a Linux system is called "as." (If you are interested in the details of assembly language programming, there are good books available, such as Sivara P. Dandamudi's.[1] We also recommend the Intel processor manuals.[2])

- *Instruction*: A machine language command having none, one, or more arguments. One line of assembly language as described above corresponds to a single machine command. The instructions valid for a given processor are defined in the *instruction set architecture* (ISA). The ISA that 64-bit Intel processors understand is often dubbed *x86_64* with various downward-compatible extensions; that is, a processor being able to execute Advanced Vector Extensions (AVX) can also execute Streaming SIMD extensions (SSE), but not vice versa.

- *Micro-operation (uop)*: Instructions translated into micro-operations in the decoder. This is done in order to formally keep the ISA as is and still be able to change the underlying functionality of a processor. It allows programs written for one ISA to execute on two fundamentally different processor architectures. In the case of Intel processors, this is the Intel64 ISA. The micro-operations are not disclosed, nor are they directly programmable.

Pipelined Execution

Pipelines are the computer-science version of an industrial assembly line, and they are the overarching design principle of a modern CPU core. Thus, all techniques introduced here need to be seen in light of this concept. In a pipeline, throughput performance is gained by exploiting parallelism in the execution of a stream of instructions. *Pipeline stages* are each executing specialized tasks.

A classic pipeline model used by Tanenbaum[3] looks like this:

- *Instruction fetch* (IF): Loads the instruction indicated by the *instruction pointer*. The instruction pointer is a CPU register containing the memory address of the next instruction to be executed.

- *Instruction decode* (ID): The processor parses the instruction and associates it with the functionality to be executed.

- *Load operands* (LO): Data from the argument(s) are loaded. In general this is data thought to be contained in a CPU register, but it might also be a memory address.

- *Execution* (EX): The instruction is executed. In the case of an arithmetic instruction, the actual computation will be done.

- *Write-back results* (WB): The computed result is committed to the specified destination, usually a register.

In a non-pipelined approach, each of these steps needs to be completed before another instruction can be fetched. While one of these stages is active, the other ones is idle, which renders most of the processor's capacity unutilized. In a pipeline approach, however, each pipeline stage is active at the same time, leading to a throughput of one instruction per clock cycle (assuming that completion of a stage requires one clock cycle). If you assume that there is no dependence between individual instructions, you can fetch the third instruction while the second one is being decoded; you can load the operands for the first one at the same time, and so on. In this way, no pipeline stage is ever idle, as shown in Figure 7-1.

No pipeline

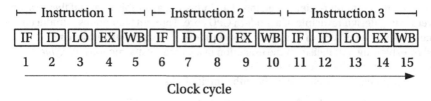

Pipeline

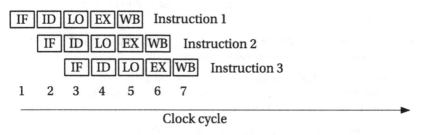

Figure 7-1. *Comparison of pipelined vs. non-pipelined execution of instructions*

In a pipeline, although the latency of the individual instruction (the time during which the instruction is individually executed) does not change, the overall throughput increases dramatically.

Let's estimate the time it takes to execute a number of instructions $N_{instructions}$ in N_{stages} stages, where we assume each stage takes the same time T_{stages} to complete:

$$T_{no\text{-}pipeline} = N_{instructions} \, N_{stages} \, T_{stage}$$

$$T_{pipeline} = N_{stages} \, T_{stage} + (N_{instructions} - 1) \, T_{stage}.$$

The ideal speedup is

$$S = T_{no\text{-}pipeline} / T_{pipeline} = N_{stages},$$

assuming an infinite number of instructions. This estimation is highly idealized. If, for some reason, one stage of the pipeline fails to complete in time, the whole pipeline will come to a halt—that's what we call a *pipeline stall*. Without claiming completeness, some common reasons for pipeline stalls are as follows.

Data Conflicts

Data conflicts arise from the parallel execution of instructions within a pipeline when the results of one instruction are an input argument to another instruction. Data conflicts play an important role when we speak about vectorization, and we will come back to them when we deal with this topic later in the chapter.

We can distinguish three important types of data conflict:

1. *Read after write (RAW) or flow dependence*: A variable must
    be read after it was written previously. The use of the updated
    value cannot be started until the update is completed.
    Example in C:

    ```
    var1=5;
    var2=var1+2;
    ```

    Clearly, the first line needs to complete before the second can
    be executed, since otherwise the variable var1 might contain
    an arbitrary value.

2. *Write after read (WAR) or anti-dependence*: This is just the
    opposite of RAW: a variable must be written after it has been
    read previously. Example in C:

    ```
    var2=var1+2;
    var1=5;
    ```

    The second line must be prohibited from committing the
    value 5 to var1 before the first completes.

3. *Write after write (WAW)*: This is a situation where the same
    variable is written by two different values in very close
    proximity. Example in C:

    ```
    var1=1;
    <other instructions>
    var1=2;
    ```

The WAW case is not a problem in a simple in-order pipeline. However, in the
context of out-of-order and superscalar execution discussed later, this conflict is possible
when the order of instructions can be changed and instructions might even be executed
concurrently.

Control Conflicts

The instruction flow often reaches a point where a decision needs to be made about
which further instructions will be executed. Such points are unmistakably indicated by
explicit conditional constructs (e.g., if-statements) in the source code. Other language
constructs require decisions to be made, as well. A common example is loops where a
counter variable is compared with the upper limit of the loop. If the upper limit is not
reached, the instruction pointer will be set to the beginning of the loop body and the next
iteration is executed. If the upper limit is reached, the execution will continue with the
next instruction after the loop body.

Consider a loop summing up all numbers below 100:

```
for(i=0;i<100;i++)
    s=s+i;
```

In assembly language, this is translated into a comparison and a conditional jump:

```
mov eax, 0x0       # set the counter variable to zero
loop1:             # a marker, translated into a position by the assembler
    add ebx, eax   # this is the loop body
    inc eax        # increment the loop counter
    cmp eax, 0x64  # compare if we have reached the upper limit
    jle <loop1>    # if the comparison yields less or equal, jump to loop1
...
```

With the result of the comparison not yet being available, the pipeline cannot reliably execute the jump and the pipeline will stall until the comparison has written-back its results. A control conflict can partly be resolved by branch prediction, as discussed later.

Structural Conflicts

A structural conflict appears when more hardware functionality is required than is available in a section of the instruction flow. If you have only, say, four registers and two instructions, each uses two registers to copy data; if these two instructions are executing in the pipeline, an instruction that requires one of the registers will have to wait until the resources are freed up.

Out-of-order vs. In-order Execution

In the previous section we considered pipelines and how they improve performance when issued instructions are independent and do not show any conflicts. One problem a pipeline does not solve is the following. Consider an instruction, inst1, which shows a true dependence and will have to wait until some result of a number of previous calculations becomes available. The next instruction, inst2, might have all its dependences satisfied but cannot execute because the order of instructions needs to be guaranteed for the instruction flow to deliver consistent results. We call this *in-order execution*. However, if we could keep track of the order of instructions and reorder them again before the results become apparent when we commit them to the register in the WB (write-back) stage, we could allow inst2 to bypass inst1 and be executed while inst1 is waiting.

This idea is implemented in *out-of-order execution* pipelines. We do not go into detail on how this is exactly implemented, as those details are of no importance here, but there is a considerable amount of literature covering this subject.[4,5] What is important, though, are the additional two stages this strategy introduces to the pipeline. First, we need one stage to check the instruction flow for data dependences, record the order, and issue the instruction into execution. We call this stage the *dispatch* or *reservation station*. Then, we need a pipeline stage that reorders the instructions after execution and commits the results to registers in the original execution order. We call this stage *retirement*. On Intel architectures, the out-of-order engine is the part that works on micro-operations (uops).

Superscalar Pipelines

With out-of-order execution in place, there is a straightforward way to increase performance: instead of executing out-of-order in a single pipeline, you could execute the micro-instructions in parallel, in two or more independent pipelines, because their execution is independent from the beginning (see Figure 7-2). The retirement buffer will then take care of the proper ordering across all pipelines after the execution. The level of parallelism that can be achieved in this approach is, of course, limited by the inherent parallelism in the flow of instructions.

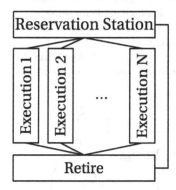

Figure 7-2. *Parallel execution in a superscalar out-of-order pipeline*

SIMD Execution

In practice, we often apply the same instructions to each element of a large dataset. This gives rise to an additional level of parallelism to be exploited. The potential speedup is proportional to the number of data elements we can process in parallel. In hardware, this is implemented by making registers available that are as wide as the number of elements that we want to treat in parallel, which is a significant hardware investment limiting the vector length.

Current Intel CPUs support three types of vector extensions: multimedia extensions (MMX, 64 bit), various versions of Stream SIMD extensions (SSE, 128 bit), and advanced vector extensions (AVX, 256 bit). Chapter 2 discussed the benefits of SIMD execution in detail; see especially Figures 2-2 through 2-8 for AVX.

Speculative Execution: Branch Prediction

A limiting factor for the performance of a pipeline is the presence of branches. Branches appear when the execution can continue at another position in the instruction flow. There are two types of branches: conditional and unconditional. *Conditional* branches implement decisions taken at runtime, such as "if" and "while." *Unconditional* branches are created for subroutines, functions, and function pointer calls.

When a conditional branch appears in the instruction flow, the pipeline stalls at this position until the condition has been calculated and the next instruction can be fetched, which can mean a big hit to performance. To alleviate this problem, the processor could predict the target of the branch and continue feeding the pipeline with instructions from this point in the code. For this purpose, the processor has a *branch target buffer* that stores the last branch target taken from this point in the code, along with information about the success of the last predictions.

A very simple implementation of a branch prediction would be to predict the last observed behavior; that is, we predict "branch taken" if we took it the last time and "not taken" if we didn't take it. This is easy to store in a single bit associated with the position of the branch in the code. Figure 7-3 shows a more advanced branch predictor using two bits. If a branch is taken, the predictor will enter the state 11 "predict taken." While the prediction is true, it will stay in this state. If the prediction is once false, it will not immediately predict "not taken" but, rather, go to state 10, but still "predict taken." Only if the prediction is wrong a second time will the state change to "00" and "predict not taken."

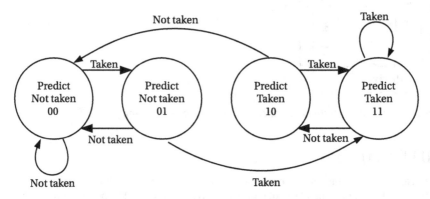

Figure 7-3. *A 2-bit branch predictor (see description in text)*

These branch prediction schemes are called *dynamic predictions*. The branch predictor compares the current position in the code with information it already has stored for this particular branch. At the first encounter of a particular branch, this solution will not work because there is no information available in the branch target buffer. For this instance, the branch predictor has a default behavior, called the *static prediction*. The rules for static branch prediction are as follows:

- A forward conditional branch (an if-statement) is predicted *not to be taken*

- A backward conditional branch (a loop) is predicted *to be taken*

- An unconditional branch (a call to or return from a subroutine) is predicted *to be taken*

Branch predictors can have a very high hit rate, but at one point a prediction will fail. If you consider a loop, the prediction will be wrong when the loop counter has reached the limit. In this case, the processor speculatively executes the wrong code path and the pipeline will be cleared (called a *pipeline flush*). The computation is then restarted at the point before the prediction, using the now-known correct branch target. A pipeline flush can have a serious performance impact. The minimum impact is the time it takes to refill the pipeline—which is, at best, the number of pipeline stages.

Memory Subsystem

A problem in the last decade of CPU design was the growing divergence in performance of memory and CPU. While the CPU follows the principle of Moore's Law and doubles the number of components (translating directly into performance) each 18 months, memory performance (that is, the number of bytes delivered per second) grows much slower. To have the data readily available when needed by the execution units, fast but small and expensive storage is directly built into the CPU, called a *cache*. The idea of a cache was inspired by the temporal principle of locality: data that you have used once you will likely use again in the near future. The cache memory, then, stores intermediate copies of data that actually reside in the main memory. Often, more than one cache is present, which is then called a *cache hierarchy*.

Three different cache implementations are used:

- *Direct-mapped cache*: Each memory address can be stored only in a specific cache line. If a memory address is loaded in a cache line that is already occupied, the previous content of this line is evicted. This approach allows for a much leaner logic to determine a hit and has relatively low access latency. The hit ratios are lower than with the fully associative cache, but this technique is cheaper.

- *Fully associative cache*: The memory address of the data within the cache is stored alongside. To find where a memory location has been stored in the cache requires a compare operation across the memory addresses stored for each line. Fully associative caches have high hit rates but relatively long access latencies. Also, they require a larger chip space to incorporate the extensive hit logic and are therefore more expensive.

- *Set associative cache*: This is a compromise between the two aforementioned alternatives. The set associative cache divides the cache into a number of sets (say eight). A cache line is placed into a given set, based on its memory address. Searching within a set, then, is internally fully associative. While cost and chip space stay reasonable, this technique offers a high hit ratio.

Current product lines of Intel processor cores feature 32 Kbyte instruction and data Level 1 (L1) caches and a 256 Kbyte unified Level 2 cache (L2), both eight-way set associative. (Cache latencies and bandwidth have been discussed in Chapter 2.)

Even if we cache data entries for fast access by the execution units, many programs stream data through the processor, which exceeds the cache capacity. The cache then becomes useless because you will not find the entry you loaded in the past, as it was already evicted. The cache also adds latency to the loading of such streaming data into

209

the processor. In modern CPU design, this problem is attacked by preloading data in the caches that is likely to be used next, so that it is readily available. This technique is called *prefetching* and is extensively used in the Sandy Bridge architecture, which has four different hardware prefetchers.[6]

Putting It All Together: A Final Look at the Sandy Bridge Pipeline

Let's now relate the architecture design principles discussed to the block diagram of the Sandy Bridge microarchitecture, as shown in Figure 7-4, and follow an instruction from fetching to retirement. Instructions stored in main memory come in through the 32 KB L1 instruction cache (ICache) at a rate of 16 bytes per cycle and are decoded (there is actually a pre-decode stage) into microinstructions. Up to four instructions can be decoded in one cycle. Instructions that have already been decoded are stored into a uop cache that can hold up to 1536 uops. Then, resources (for example registers) are allocated whereby unnecessary structural conflicts are resolved through register renaming. The scheduler can queue up to 56 uops and distribute up to six uops to the execution ports, depending on the requested functionality by the instruction. Instructions are dispatched out-of-order and a reorder buffer is used to keep track of the original sequence. Upon completion of an instruction, execution results are committed in the right sequence and the instructions retire, up to four per cycle.

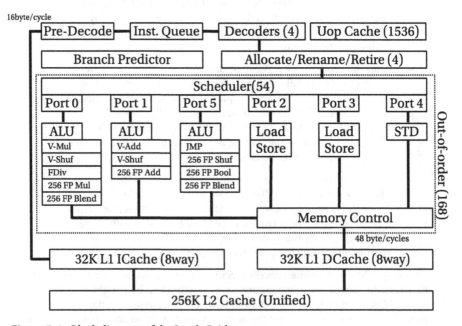

Figure 7-4. *Block diagram of the Sandy Bridge core*

A Top-down Method for Categorizing the Pipeline Performance

The Sandy Bridge pipeline is designed to deliver maximum performance. The target of all software microarchitectural optimization is to keep the pipeline running and avoid pipeline stalls. But how do you actually know what good performance is and what is not? How can you determine where in the pipeline the problems appear? In this section, we introduce an easy scheme to categorize optimization opportunities and determine where the pipeline stalls.

The Sandy Bridge core pipeline, as shown in Figure 7-4, is certainly very complicated with a lot of interacting units. We could look at each unit individually, which gets confusing and is hard to remember; instead, we will consider the broader picture.

Let us start with the most basic performance metric first. The CPI rate (cycles per instruction) is a measure of how well the code has been executing in the pipeline. Because of the super-scalar properties of the core architecture, multiple instructions can be executed at the same time. For a current Intel Core or Intel Xeon processor, the limit is four instructions, which corresponds to a CPI rate of 0.25; on average, only a quarter of a cycle is spent on an instruction if four of them are executed and retired. Applications with a CPI rate of 0.25 to 0.7 are considered to be efficient. A CPI rate above the threshold of 1.0 usually indicates that a performance problem might exist and that further analysis should be performed. The CPI rate specifies how *many* instructions are executed per cycle (it is not a good metric to discuss the usefulness of these instructions!). If you don't reach a good CPI value, the pipeline is not retiring as many instructions as possible and is stalling at some point; see the diagram shown in Figure 7-4.

It is useful to subdivide the Sandy Bridge pipeline into two parts: front end and back end. We define these two parts as follows:

- *Front end*: fetching of the instruction, the decoding, the branch prediction, and the uops queue

- *Back end*: renaming, scheduling, and execution (the out-of-order engine)

The front end is responsible for decoding instructions and delivering micro-operations; the back end has to execute and retire them. If the front end can't deliver, the back end will starve. If the back end can't take more uops, the front end will stall. In either of these two cases, no uops will be issued from front to back end.

If no uops can be issued, we again have two cases: either we can allocate resources in the back end (registers, ports) or we cannot. If resources are free but no uops are issued, we call such a code *front-end bound*. If no resources are free (the execution units are busy), we call it *back-end bound*. This might happen because the code is either core bound (waiting for computation to complete) or memory bound (waiting for memory operations to complete).

If uops can be issued into the pipeline, the next question we need to ask is: Do the uops actually retire? If the uops do retire, we have the desired outcome. If they do not, they must have vanished from the pipeline although they were issued; they must have been cleared due to bad speculation. Figure 7-5 outlines the decision tree for this categorization.

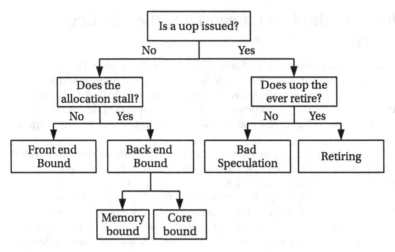

Figure 7-5. *Hierarchical top-down analysis method (Source: Intel 64 and IA-32 Architectures Optimization Reference Manual)*

Ideally we would like to see all compute cycles spent in the retired category, although this doesn't mean there is no room for improvement. As for the other categories, let's discuss some common reasons they will appear:

- *Front-end bound*: This is caused by misses in the instruction cache (ICache) or the instruction translation lookaside buffer (ITLB), owing to a large code, excessive inlining or loop unrolling. Also, inefficiencies in the decoder, such as length-changing prefixes,[7] can be the reason. (See inlining in later sections "Dealing with Branching" and "Basic Usage and Optimization.")

- *Back-end memory bound*: The cache misses at all levels—irregular data access, streaming data access, large datasets, cache conflicts, and unaligned data. (See the later section "Optimizing for Vectorization.")

- *Back-end core bound*: There are long latency instructions (divide), chains of dependent instructions, and code that is not vectorizing. (See the later section "Optimizing for Vectorization.")

- *Bad speculation*: There is wrong prediction of branches and resulting pipeline flushes and short loops. (See the later section "Dealing with Branching.")

Intel Composer XE Usage for Microarchitecture Optimizations

Before we go into details about particular optimization problems, let's review some basic usage of the compiler.

Basic Compiler Usage and Optimization

The first important choice to make is to specify the architecture and ISA extension you want to compile for. If you do not specify anything, the default will be SSE3, which is the one available on all 64-bit platforms. In most cases, you will have a more feature-rich and higher performance set of instructions available on more recent CPUs. The compiler switch -x<arch> will compile only for the architecture specified in <arch> and downward compatible, succeeding Intel platforms. We use -xAVX in this chapter because we want to address this instruction set. Please refer to the compiler manual for all options. If you compile on the platform you will be running on, it is easiest to use -xHOST, which will detect and apply the correct architecture automatically.

If you need to have a binary for an alternative architecture, by all means there is a workaround. By specifying -ax instead of -x, you tell the compiler to create a binary for multiple architectures that is auto-dispatching—that is, using the code path that is best for the architecture that the software is currently running on. For example, the compiler command

```
$ icc -axAVX,SSE4.1 <source file>
```

will create a binary that can execute on all Intel CPUs supporting SSE4.1, but it will still run the highest performing code path on the Sandy Bridge and Ivy Bridge processors.

The next basic choice is the optimization level. There are four optimization levels, which can be controlled with the -On switch, where n is between 0 and 3. The -O0 switch turns off optimization completely. The -O1 optimizes for speed, but doesn't increase the code size. The default optimization level is -O2, which optimizes for speed, but increases code size through unrolling and inlining. The -O3 performs similar optimizations as -O2, but is more aggressive. When using -O3, you'll find that increased inlining and loop unrolling can sometimes lead to slower code because of front-end stalls. It is worth playing with this switch and measuring performance before deciding on the final level to use.

Using Optimization and Vectorization Reports to Read the Compiler's Mind

Compiler reports are an essential tool for understanding whether a particular optimization has been done by the compiler. This information is difficult to obtain otherwise, and even advanced performance-monitoring tools like VTune Amplifier XE will not provide it, hence it is worth spending some time on it here. Note that the reporting features of the compiler changed with Intel Composer XE 2015—some of the functionality described here might not be valid for older versions.

Intel Composer XE 2015 can provide extensive optimization reports in six levels, from 0 (no optimization report) to 5 (maximum). Although the level 5 report provides the most insight, it generates a lot of information for large codes.

The reports contain information for a total of nine phases, if applicable:

- *LOOP*: High-level loop optimization
- *PAR*: Auto-parallelization
- *VEC*: Vectorization
- *OPENMP*: OpenMP thread parallelization
- *OFFLOAD*: Offloading to the Intel Xeon Phi co-processor
- *IPO*: Inter-procedural optimization
- *PGO*: Profile-guided optimization
- *CG*: Code generation
- *TCOLLECT*: Trace collection in MPI parallelized programs

For the scope of this chapter, three of these phases are the most interesting: LOOP, VEC, and IPO. For this first example, consider a program implementing a square matrix-matrix multiplication and inspect the optimization report produced by the compiler. The function for doing the computation is shown in Listing 7-1.

Listing 7-1. Square Matrix Multiplication in C/C++

```
void squaregemm(int size, double* a, double* b, double* c){
    for(int i=0;i<size;i++){
        for(int j=0;j<size;j++){
            for(int k=0;k<size;k++){
                c[i*size+j]+=a[i*size+k]*b[k*size+j];
            }
        }
    }
}
```

Let's look at the optimization report of the compiler generated with -opt-report5. First, there is a report header summarizing the setting for IPO, inlining, and the inlined functions. After this header information, the optimization report for the code starts, usually with the main routine:

```
Begin optimization report for: main

Report from: Interprocedural optimizations [ipo]

INLINE REPORT: (main) [1/2=50.0%]
  -> printf(EXTERN)
  -> rand(EXTERN)
  -> INLINE: squaregemm(int, double*, double*, double*)() (isz = 57)
     (sz = 68 (33+35))
```

```
-> operator new[](unsigned long)(EXTERN)
-> operator new[](unsigned long)(EXTERN)
-> operator new[](unsigned long)(EXTERN)
```

The function squaregemm that we have defined is inlined; all other functions (not shown in Listing 7-1) for which no code could be found are marked extern, such as rand() or printf(). The numbers behind the inlined function summarize the increase of the code size. In this case, the size of the calling function plus the called function is 68 = 33 + 35, whereas the size of the inlined function is only 57, owing to further optimizations.

The next interesting point is the optimization report for the squaregemm function:

```
...
Begin optimization report for: squaregemm(int, double*, double*, double*)

Report from: Interprocedural optimizations [ipo]

INLINE REPORT: (squaregemm(int, double*, double*, double*)) [2/2=100.0%]
...
```

The function squaregemm was inlined.

```
...
Report from: Loop nest, Vector & Auto-parallelization optimizations
[loop, vec, par]

LOOP BEGIN at main1.cpp(5,3)
   remark #25448: Loopnest Interchanged : ( 1 2 3 ) --> ( 1 3 2 )
...
```

The compiler has changed the order of the loops form i,j,k to i,k,j to provide better conditions for vectorization.

```
...
remark #15145: vectorization support: unroll factor set to 4
...
```

The last line indicates the compiler has unrolled the loop by four iterations. Checking the assembly output of objdump -d, we indeed find a vectorized version of the loop that is fourfold unrolled (four AVX vector multiplies and four AVX vector adds):

```
401070:    c5 fd 59 da            vmulpd %ymm2,%ymm0,%ymm3
401074:    c5 fd 59 fe            vmulpd %ymm6,%ymm0,%ymm7
401078:    c4 41 7d 59 da         vmulpd %ymm10,%ymm0,%ymm11
40107d:    c4 41 7d 59 fe         vmulpd %ymm14,%ymm0,%ymm15
401082:    c4 c1 65 58 24 d4      vaddpd (%r12,%rdx,8),%ymm3,%ymm4
401088:    c4 41 45 58 44 d4 20   vaddpd 0x20(%r12,%rdx,8),%ymm7,%ymm8
40108f:    c4 41 25 58 64 d4 40   vaddpd 0x40(%r12,%rdx,8),%ymm11,%ymm12
401096:    c4 c1 05 58 4c d4 60   vaddpd 0x60(%r12,%rdx,8),%ymm15,%ymm1
```

So you should now have an idea of what type of information the report creates. We have deliberately left out quite a number of lines so as to keep this readable. The original report for this very short program with a single function call is about 200 lines at report level 5. Very often this is too much detail, as you might be interested in only one function in a file or in a particular phase of the report. In this case, you can specify a filter—for instance, for a function:

```
-opt-report-filter="squaredgemm"
```

Or you can indicate a phase—for instance, vectorization:

```
-opt-report-phase=vec
```

The phase must be one of CG, IPO, LOOP, OFFLOAD, OPENMP, PAR, PGO, TCOLLECT, VEC, or all, as described earlier.

Optimizing for Vectorization

SIMD vectorization is one of the main sources of performance for Intel CPUs. There are many ways to support vectorization:

- *Automatic vectorization:* Expressing code in a way the compiler can easily recognize vectorizable code

- *User-assisted vectorization:* Indicating vectorization opportunities to the compiler, or even forcing the compiler into vectorization via annotation by compiler pragmas

- *Language extensions:* Expressing vectorization explicitly in a high-level language

We will put a strong focus on loop vectorization, since this is the most common, but it's not the only source of vectorization.

■ **Note**　This section addresses the front-end/back-end categories of the top-down method for the pipeline performance.

The AVX Instruction Set

The Sandy Bridge architecture introduced a set of new instructions operating on 256-bit vector registers (see also the section "Process More Data with SIMD Parallelism" in Chapter 2), called Advanced Vector Extensions (AVX). AVX supersedes the 128-bit SSE instruction set extension introduced in the Pentium processor line and doubles the floating-point performance of the CPU.

AVX instructions can operate on sixteen 256-bit vector registers ymm0-ymm15. In contrast to its predecessor SSE, which only allowed two arguments for each instruction, AVX introduces a three-argument instruction format:

```
<instruction> <destination>, <source1>, <source2>
```

This allows for non-destructive operations (none of the sources are altered) and avoids frequent save operations necessary to preserve the contents of a vector register, as well as reduces register pressure (the shortage of registers). Examples of AVX functionality for 256-bit vectors include the following (see illustrations of some vector functions in Figure 7-6):

- Loading and storing of aligned and unaligned data. The operations may be masked, so that a load ranging into an unallocated memory range does not cause a fault.

- Broadcasting of a memory element in all elements of a vector.

- Elementary arithmetic operations of addition, subtraction, multiplication, and division, as well as addsub (alternating addition/subtraction), (inverse) square root, and reciprocal.

- Comparison, minimum, maximum, and rounding.

- Permutation of elements within a lane and permutation of lanes.

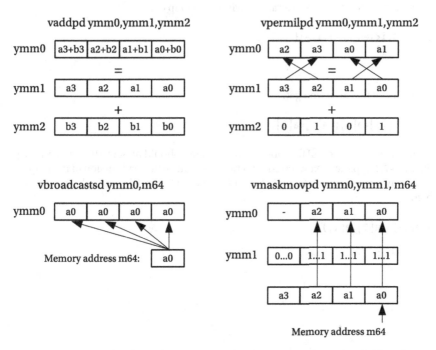

Figure 7-6. *Examples of AVX functionality: simple vector addition (top left), in-lane permutation (top right), broadcasting (bottom left), and mask loading (bottom right)*

We will consider the direct programming of AVX later, in the section "Understanding AVX: Intrinsic Programming."

Why Doesn't My Code Vectorize in the First Place?

Before going into actual optimizations for vectorization, let's briefly look at reasons why the compiler can't vectorize your code. The root cause are actual or assumed data dependences that are not resolvable at compile time.

Data Dependences

In regard to pipeline conflicts, we covered data dependences that prevent instructions from being executed in parallel in a pipelined, out-of-order, or superscalar fashion. As this pertains to the pipeline, where arbitrary instructions might act on the same data at different times, it applies even more so to vectors. Here, only a single instruction is executed on multiple, possibly dependent data elements at exactly the same time. In this sense, vector dependences are more controllable and more easily solved.

Recall the data conflicts discussed earlier: flow dependence (read after write, or RAW), anti-dependence (write after read, or WAR), and output dependence (write after write, or WAW). It is important to realize how dependences affect vectorization. Let's look at a simple example. When a variable is written in one iteration and read in a subsequent one, we have a RAW dependence, as we can see within the loop code:

```
for(int i=0;i<length-1;i++){
    a[i+1]=a[i];
}
```

If you unroll this loop, you get:

```
a[1]=a[0]; a[2]=a[1]; a[3]=a[2]; ...
```

After correct execution of the loop, all the elements should be set to the value in a[0] (see Figure 7-7, left panel). Now, consider a two-element vectorized version of the loop. At one time, two successive values will be loaded from the array (the parentheses indicate the vector):

```
(a[1],a[2])=(a[0],a[1]);
```

```
for(int i=0;i<length-1;i++){
    a[i+1]=a[i]
}
```

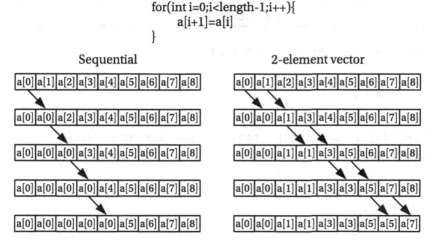

Figure 7-7. *Flow (RAW) data dependence-analysis of a shift-copy loop executed sequentially and with a two-element vector*

The second value is already wrong, according to the original algorithm. In the next iteration, you get:

(a[3],a[4])=(a[2],a[3])

a[2] has already been changed to a[1] in the previous iteration and the corresponding values are loaded. Carrying this on, you get, as the final result:

a[0],a[1],a[1],a[3],a[3],a[5] ...

This is obviously wrong according to the original algorithm (see Figure 7-7, right panel). Clearly, the compiler must prevent this loop from being vectorized. Very often, however, the compiler assumes an unproven vector dependence, although you will know better that this will never occur; we will treat this case extensively later.

EXERCISE 7-1

Try the example discussed in the preceding text:

```
for(int i=0;i<length-1;i++){
    a[i+1]=a[i];
}
```

You can enforce vectorization by placing a pragma simd (to be explained below) before the loop.

```
#pragma simd
for(int i=0;i<length-1;i++){
    a[i+1]=a[i];
}
```

Can you confirm the results? For which shifts i+1, i+2,... do you get correct results? For which do you get wrong results?

Data Aliasing

Another, related reason why code does not vectorize is *aliasing*. Under aliasing, we understand the fact that two variables (pointers or references) are associated with the same memory region. Consider a simple copy function:

```
void mycopy(double* a, double* b, int length){
    for(int i=0;i<length-1;i++){
        a[i]=b[i];
    }
}
```

In principle, the compiler should be able to vectorize this easily. But wait—can the compiler be sure that the arrays a and b do not overlap? It cannot. And C/C++ explicitly allows for this situation! Call the above function from the main function like this:

```
int main(void){
    int length=100;
    int copylength=50;
    double* a;
    double* b;
    double* data = (double*) malloc(sizeof(double)*length);
    a=&data[1];
    b=&data[0];
    mycopy(a,b,copylength);
}
```

You will get the same situation as with the earlier code showing an explicit vector dependence. Consequently, the compiler must assume that there is a dependence.

Array Notations

The array notation (AN) introduced with Intel Cilk Plus is an Intel-specific language extension of C/C++ that allows for direct expression of data-level parallelism (in contrast to loops, which have the abovementioned problems). AN relieves the compiler of the dependence and aliasing analysis to a degree and provides an easy way to a correct, performing code.

AN introduces an array section notation that allows the specification of particular elements, compact or regularly strided:

```
<array base>[<lower bound>:<length>[:<stride>]]
```

The syntax resembles the Fortran syntax, but Fortran programmers beware: the semantic requires start:length and not start:end!

Examples for the array section notation are:

```
a[:]        // the whole array
a[0:10]     // elements 0 through 9
a[0:5:2]    // elements 0,2,4,6,8
```

Based on this notation, operators will now act element-wise:

```
c[0:10]=a[0:10]*b[0:10];    // element-wise multiplication of 10 elements
a[0:10]++;                  // increments all elements
m[0:10]=a[0:10]<b[0:10];    // m[i] will contain 1 if a[i]<b[i], 0 otherwise
```

It is also possible to use AN with fields of higher dimension:

```
a[0:10][0:10]=b[10:10][10:10];
```

Or even with totally different ranks:

```
a[0:10][0:10]=b[10:10][2][10:10];
```

The only requirement is that the number of ranks and rank sizes must match. AN provides reducer intrinsics to exercise all-element reductions. The following expression,

```
_sec_reduce_add(a[:]);
```

will return the sum of all elements. Of course, this can also be used with more complex expression as arguments, so that,

```
_sec_reduce_add(a[:]*b[:]);
```

will return the inner vector product.

Let's look at an example using AN. A problem often encountered in scientific codes is partial differential equations. Consider a 1D acoustic wave equation,

$$\frac{\partial^2}{\partial t^2}\varphi(x,t)=c^2\frac{\partial^2}{\partial x^2}\varphi(x,t),$$

where x and t are continuous variables. This translates into a second-order finite difference equation as,

$$\frac{\varphi_x^{t+1}+\varphi_x^{t-1}-2\varphi_x^t}{(\Delta t)^2}=c^2\frac{\varphi_{x+1}^t+\varphi_{x-1}^t-2\varphi_x^t}{(\Delta x)^2},$$

where x and t are now discrete space and time indices with distances Δx and Δt. We want to know the strength of the field at the time $t+1$ at position x. Solving the above equation for the field element φ_{x+1}^t yields:

$$\varphi_x^{t+1}=c^2\frac{(\Delta t)^2}{(\Delta x)^2}(\varphi_{x+1}^t+\varphi_{x-1}^t-2\varphi_x^t)-\varphi_x^{t-1}-2\varphi_x^t.$$

In C/C++, this maybe expressed as:

```
for(int i=0;i<iterations;i++){        // number of time steps
   for(int n=1;n<size-1;n++){         // iterate over the space dimension
      f_next[n]= prefac*(f_curr[n-1]+f_curr[n+1]
         -2.0*f_curr[n])-f_prev[n]+2.0*f_curr[n];
   }
   tmp=f_prev;
   f_prev=f_curr; // in the iteration, the next field becomes the current
   f_curr=f_next; // ... and the current become the previous
   f_next=tmp;    // The old previous we will be used to store the new next
}
```

The same example in AN would look like this:

```
for(int i=0;i<iterations;i++){
   f_next[1:size-2]=prefac*(f_curr[0:size-2]+f_curr[2:size-2]
      -2.0*f_curr[1:size-2])-f_prev[1:size-2]+2.0*f_curr[1:size-2];
   tmp=f_prev;
   f_prev=f_curr;
   f_curr=f_next;
   f_next=tmp;
}
```

Although the compiler might vectorize this simple example even in straight C/C++, more complex problems—for example, a three-dimensional wave equation of a finite difference equation solved to a higher order—might not or not fully vectorize. With AN, the vector code becomes explicit.

Vectorization Directives

Pragmas are an annotation technique you already learned about in the context of OpenMP. They allow you to hint information to the compiler, for which other means of expressing it in C/C++ or Fortran are not available.

A pragma is treated by the compiler like a comment or an unknown preprocessor directive if it doesn't know it; in the end, it does ignore it. Consequently, the resulting code maintains its portability for compilers that don't support a certain feature, but it has the desired effect if the compiler *does* understand the meaning of the pragma.

ivdep

The #pragma ivdep tells the compiler that assumed vector dependences in the following loop body are to be ignored. Note that proven vector dependences are not affected. The pragma has no further arguments. The #pragma ivdep is available in most compilers, though its implementation might differ.

vector

The #pragma vector is similar in its effect as #pragma ivdep in the sense that it will ignore assumed dependences but not proven ones, but it has additional optional clauses:

> *always*: This overrides the heuristics on efficiency, alignment, and stride.

> *aligned/unaligned*: This tells the compiler to use aligned or unaligned data movement for memory references.

> *temporal/nontemporal*: This tells the compiler to use streaming stores in case of nontemporal, or to avoid those in case of temporal. Streaming stores write directly into memory bypassing the cache, which saves an ubiquitous read for ownership (RFO) that is required to modify the data in the cache. The nontemporal clause can take a comma-separated list of variables that should be stored nontemporal.

simd

The #pragma simd is the most powerful of the three vectorization pragmas. So, #pragma simd tells the compiler to ignore any heuristics and dependence, proven or not; you will be fully responsible for making sure the result is correct. #pragma simd is a powerful construct that can be extended by more arguments/subclauses, some similar in spirit to the OpenMP parallel for pragma discussed earlier. We discuss them briefly here:

- *vectorlength(arg1)*: Tells the compiler to use the specified vector length. arg<n> must be a power of 2. Ideally, the vector length is the maximum vector length supported by the underlying hardware, such as 2 for SSE2 double vectors or 4 for AVX double vectors. For example:

```
#pragma simd vectorlength(2)
for(int i=0;i<L;i++)
    a[i]=b[i]*c[i];
```

- *vectorlengthfor(datatype)*: Tells the compiler to choose the appropriate vector length for the architecture and data type compiled for—for example, vectorlengthfor(double) will result in a vector length of 2 for SSE2 and 4 for AVX. The benefit is that you will get the optimal vector length independent of the architecture chosen by the -x compiler switch. For example:

```
#pragma simd vectorlengthfor(double)
for(int i=0;i<L;i++)
    a[i]=b[i]*c[i];
```

The following clauses of pragma simd resemble the interface used in the OpenMP data-sharing clauses and maybe thought of in the same manner—just that a vector lane would correspond to a thread:

- *private(var1 [,var2,...])*: With this clause the compiler will assume that the scalar variable var1 can take different values in each loop iteration (see also the OpenMP private clause). The initial (at start of the loop) and final (after the loop) values are undefined, so make sure you set the value in the loop and after the loop completion. For example:

```
#pragma simd private(c)
for(int i=0;i<L;i++){
    c=i;
    a[i]=c*b[i];
}
```

- *firstprivate(var1[,var2...]):* The variable is considered to be private, and on entry the compiler will set the value of the private variable var1 to its value outside the loop.

- *lastprivate(var1[,var2...]):* The variable is considered to be private, and on exit the compiler will maintain the value of the variable var1 achieved in the last iteration of the loop.

- *reduction(op:var):* This performs a reduction operation of the variable var with the operator op. The value of this clause becomes immediately obvious by looking at an example:

```
#pragma simd reduction(+:c)
for(int i=0;i<L;i++){
    c+=a[i];
}
```

Here, each SIMD element performs a + reduction (accumulates all the values) in the variable c, but in the end all values of all SIMD elements are summed up to give the correct result of the sum of all elements of the array a.

- *(no)assert*: This causes the compiler to generate an error if the vectorization fails. The default is noassert and will generate a warning.

You will notice the close similarity between #pragma simd and the OpenMP construct #pragma omp for, which was discussed in Chapter 6.

Understanding AVX: Intrinsic Programming

We have touched on the AVX instructions a couple of times in this chapter. AVX is the most important performance improvement in the Sandy Bridge architecture, but we have described it only briefly up to this point. Here, we want to go into somewhat more detail by programming with AVX explicitly by using intrinsics. This is more for educational purposes than for practical use. Intrinsics are supposed to be the last resort when vectorization cannot be facilitated otherwise.

What Are Intrinsics?

Intrinsics are functions that the compiler recognizes and treats in special way. In our case, they are functions and types that can directly deal with vectors of a given length, hence they also directly address a particular architecture independent of what is used with the -x<architecture> switch. In most cases, intrinsics directly translate into machine instructions. In some cases, they are more complex and involve a couple of instructions.

Intrinsics mostly operate on and return vector types. For AVX, those are 256-bit vectors and the types are as follows:

> Eight 32-bit integer elements or four 64-bit integer elements: `__m256i`

> Eight single precision elements: `__m256`

> Four double precision elements: `__m256d`

We will focus here on the double-precision types for the sake of brevity; everything we present applies to single-precision types in a similar fashion. A listing of all intrinsics can be found in the "Intel Intrinsics Guide."[8]

The 256-bit floating-point intrinsic function for AVX starts with a `_mm256_`, then a meaningful description of the functionality—say, add–and then two letters, encoding packed (p) or scalar (s), as well as single (s) or double (d) precision. *Packed and scalar* in this context means to execute the operation on all elements of the vector, or only on the first element (see Figure 7-8).

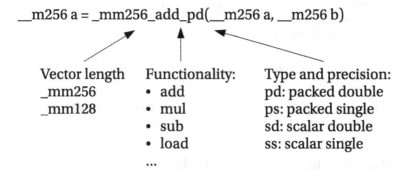

Figure 7-8. AVX intrinsics encoding scheme

An example of an intrinsic function is:

```
c=_mm256_add_pd(a,b);
```

This will add the elements of the vectors a and b and write the results into the elements of c. The a, b, and c are of type `__m256d`. See also Figure 7-6.

Intrinsics are only available for C/C++ and can be used in the source code freely. All AVX intrinsics are listed in the file `immintrin.h` that you will find in the include directory of Intel Composer XE 2015. There are hundreds of intrinsics; we will restrict discussion to the most important ones.

First Steps: Loading and Storing

The first thing we want to do is get data into a vector and back into main memory. There two ways of loading, aligned and unaligned:

- `__m256d a = _mm256_load_pd(double* memptr)`: Loads the four packed double precision numbers contained in the 256 bit starting at `memptr`. And `memptr` must be 32 byte aligned.

- `__m256d a = _mm256_loadu_pd(double* memptr)`: Loads the four packed double precision numbers contained in the 256 bit starting at `memptr`. And `memptr` does not need to be 32 byte aligned.

Notice that we now have the information in a vector register exclusively; there is no association with the memory anymore. We may now freely modify the data without having to deal with memory transactions other than use more register than the architecture can supply; the information will spill over to the cache. When we are done with the data modification in the registers, we want to write them back into memory. That's as easy as loading:

- `void _mm256_store_pd(double* memptr, __m256 a )`: Stores the four packed double precision numbers contained in the register a into the 256 bit starting at `memptr`. And `memptr` must be 32 byte aligned.

- `void _mm256_storeu_pd(double* memptr, __m256 a )`: Stores the four packed double precision numbers contained in the register a into the 256 bit starting at `memptr`. And `memptr` doesn't need to be 32 byte aligned.

A simple example program summarizing this would be:

```
void foo(double* d){
    __mm256d a;
    a=_mm256_loadu_pd(d);
    ...
    // do something meaningful
    ...
    _mm256_storeu_pd(d,a);
}
```

Sometimes you want to have one value in all of the vector elements. This is called *broadcasting*:

- `__m256 a _mm256_broadcast_sd(double* memptr)`: Copies the double precision value contained in the 64 bit following `memptr` into all the four elements of a vector register. No alignment is required.

Arithmetic

Now that we can load data into registers, we can start computing something. The four basic arithmetic instructions are as follows:

- `__m256 c = _mm256_add_pd(__m256 a, __m256 b)`: Adds the four elements in the registers a and b element wise and puts the result into c.

- `__m256 c = _mm256_sub_pd(__m256 a, __m256 b)`: Subtracts the four elements in the register b from a element wise and puts the result into c.

- `__m256 c = _mm256_mul_pd(__m256 a, __m256 b)`: Multiplies the four elements in the registers a and b element wise and puts the result into c.

- `__m256 c = _mm256_div_pd(__m256 a, __m256 b)`: Divides the four elements in the registers a by b element wise and puts the result into c.

These four are already sufficient to do some important computation. Very often multiplication of very small matrices is required—for instance, of 4x4 matrices in a scenario covering three-dimensional space and time. (We will revisit this example in this chapter.) There are highly optimized libraries providing the BLAS[9] (basic linear algebra subroutines) functionality, such as matrix-matrix multiplication. Those libraries, such as Intel MKL, are powerful and feature rich. We might require less functionality. Say, we don't need the multiplicative factors in the DGEMM (double general matrix-matrix subroutine), just straight multiplication of the matrices. In this case, a special matrix-matrix multiplication like the following would do the trick:

```
#include <immintrin.h>
void dmm_4_4_4(double* a, double* b, double* c){
  int i;
  __m256d xa0;
  __m256d xa1;
  __m256d xa2;
  __m256d xa3;
  __m256d xb0;
  __m256d xb1;
  __m256d xb2;
  __m256d xb3;
  __m256d xc0;
  xb0 = _mm256_loadu_pd(&b[0]);
  xb1 = _mm256_loadu_pd(&b[4]);
  xb2 = _mm256_loadu_pd(&b[8]);
  xb3 = _mm256_loadu_pd(&b[12]);
```

```
for(i=0;i<4;i+=1){
  xc0 = _mm256_loadu_pd(&c[i*4]);
  xa0=_mm256_broadcast_sd(&a[i*4]);
  xa1=_mm256_broadcast_sd(&a[i*4+1]);
  xa2=_mm256_broadcast_sd(&a[i*4+2]);
  xa3=_mm256_broadcast_sd(&a[i*4+3]);
  xc0=_mm256_add_pd(_mm256_mul_pd(xa0,xb0),xc0);
  xc0=_mm256_add_pd(_mm256_mul_pd(xa1,xb1),xc0);
  xc0=_mm256_add_pd(_mm256_mul_pd(xa2,xb2),xc0);
  xc0=_mm256_add_pd(_mm256_mul_pd(xa3,xb3),xc0);
  _mm256_storeu_pd(&c[i*4],xc0);
  }
}
```

EXERCISE 7-2

Measure the performance of the preceding routine versus MKL's DGEMM or a manual C implementation, such as:

```
void dmm_4_4_4_c(double* a, double* b, double* c){
  for(int i=0;i<4;i++){
    for(int j=0;j<4;j++){
      for(int l=0;l<4;l++){
        c[i*4+j]+=a[i*4+l]*b[l*4+j];
      }
    }
  }
}
```

The number of floating-point operations in a matrix-matrix multiplication are $2 \times M \times N \times K = 2 \times 4 \times 4 \times 4 = 128$, in this case. You will have to measure many million matrix multiplications are necessary to get some reasonable runtime. How does the performance compare? How far can you tune the performance of the C version by using pragmas and loop unrolling?

Data Rearrangement

Of course, those few intrinsics are not all there are; in few cases do we get data presented so readily usable, as with a matrix multiplication. More frequently, data needs to be rearranged in one vector or between different vectors. The intrinsics functions specialized in data rearrangement often are difficult to configure, as you will see. Still, these intrinsics have high importance because this is exactly what the compiler has the biggest problems with. We provide some examples for configurations that are useful, but we don't claim completeness:

- `__m256 b = _mm256_permute_pd(__m256d a, int m)`: Permutes the elements within each lane according to the bits in m from left to right. If the bit is 0, take the first element; if the bit is 1, take the second.

Let's look at the functionality with an example: Consider a vector containing the values a0-a3: `(a3,a2,a1,a0)`. Then, `_mm256_permute_pd` allows you to move the elements of the vector within each lane (remember—a lane is half the vector); see Table 7-1 for examples.

Table 7-1. *Control Integer m and Result Vector for _mm256_permute_pd*

int m	Result vector b	Description
1010b=10	(a3,a2,a1,a0)	Identity
0000b=0	(a2,a2,a0,a0)	Copy the first element of each lane into both elements of a lane
1111b=15	(a3,a3,a1,a1)	Copy the second element of each lane into both elements of a lane
0101b=5	(a2,a3,a0,a1)	Swap the elements of each lane

You can form all 16 variations, of course.

Next, we want to exchange data between whole lanes:

- `__m256d c = _mm256_permute2f128_pd(__m256d a, __m256d b, int m)`: The integer value controlling this operation is somewhat more complicated, and we refer to the documentation for exact functionality. In Table 7-2 we show some functionality for different control integers.

Table 7-2. *Control Integer m and Result Vector for _mm256_permute2f128_pd*

int m	Result vector c	Description
00010000b=48	(a3,a2,a1,a0)	Identity c=a
00110010b=50	(b3,b2,b1,b0)	Identity c=b
00000001b=1	(a1,a0,a3,a2)	Swap the two lanes of the first source a
00100011b=35	(b1,b0,b3,b2)	Swap the two lanes of the second source b
00000011b=3	(a1,a0,b3,b2)	The first lane of a and the second lane of b

Last, we want to look at blending:

- `__m256d c = _mm256_blend_pd(__m256d a, __m256d b, const int m)`: Copies the elements of a and b into c according to the bits in m. If the bit position n is 0, take the element from the first source (a); if it is 1, take it from the second source (b). Examples for blending can be found in Table 7-3.

Table 7-3. *Control Integer m and Results Vector for _mm256_blend_pd*

int m	Result vector c	Description
0101b=5	(a3,b2,a1,b0)	Copy the first and third from the second source, the second and fourth element from the first source
1010b=10	(b3,a2,b1,a0)	Copy the first and third from the first source, the second and fourth element from the second source
0000b=0	(a3,a2,a1,a0)	Copy all elements from the first source
1111b=15	(b3,b2,b1,b0)	Copy all elements from the second source

Let's see what we can do with all this. Consider a cyclic rotation of a vector by one element (see also Figure 7-9):

$$(a3,a2,a1,a0) \rightarrow (a0,a3,a2,a1)$$

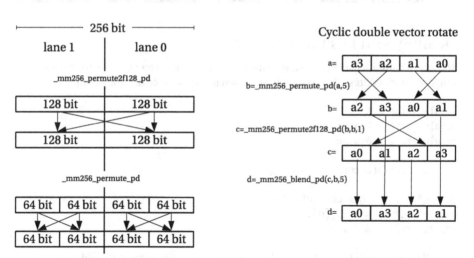

Figure 7-9. *Right panel: The lane concept of AVX. Left panel: The construction of a cycle rotate of a double vector with in-lane and cross-lane permutes*

Here is the recipe:

1. Swap the elements of each lane of a into a new vector:

   b=_mm256_permute_pd(a,5);

2. Swap the two lanes of the vector b:

   c=_mm256_permute2f128_pd(b,b,1);

3. Blend the vectors b and c, taking the first and third elements of the second source and the second third elements of the first source:

   d=_mm256_blend_pd(c,b,5);

4. The vector d now contains the cyclically rotated elements of a.

This concludes our short introduction to intrinsic programming. You are encouraged to have a look at the "Intel Intrinsics Guide,"[10] which contains a description of all intrinsics and they can be filtered by architecture and scope.

EXERCISE 7-3

Create a version of the cyclic rotate that shifts by two and three elements.

Dealing with Disambiguation

Aliasing in computer sciences refers to the existence of more than one reference to a single memory address. This is easy to see when it comes to scalars; for example:

```
double value = 5;
double* ref1 = &value;
double* ref2 = &value;
```

For arrays, it becomes more complex:

```
double* array = new double[200];
double* ref1 = & array[0];
double* ref2 = & array[50];
```

Of course, ref1[50] and ref2[0] are referring to the same memory address:

```
for(int i=0;i<50;i++){
   ref1[i+m]=2*ref2[i];
}
```

If we assume m to be known at compile time, we can easily observe what the compiler is doing. For 0<=m<=50, the above code is vectorizable. For m=51, we obviously have a RAW dependence and the vectorization fails. If m is not known at compile time, the compiler will assume both a RAW and WAR dependence.

In practice, you will often encounter exactly these situations, in which the compiler has to make conservative assumptions to guarantee the correct execution of the program. In most cases, this is related to a function signature, like:

```
void foo(double* a, double* b){ ... }
```

The compiler has to assume that a and b reference the same memory location. It will therefore suspect that there might be a dependence. In most cases, we will know that the assumed vector dependence can never happen and so we must have ways to hint to the compiler that it should not interfere. The following are various methods that can be used to allow the compiler to vectorize our code.

- *Compiler switches*: The switch -no-ansi-alias disables the use of ANSI aliasing rules and allows the compiler to optimize more aggressively. Notice that this is the default. The opposite is -ansi-alias, which will enforce the ANSI aliasing rules. A more aggressive version is -fno-alias, where no aliasing is assumed altogether. Both compiler switches are effective for the whole file that is currently compiled; you want to be careful applying those switches when more than the function under consideration is contained in the file.

- *The restrict keyword*: A more comfortable and precise way to instruct the compiler to ignore assumed dependences is to use the *restrict* keyword defined in the C99 standard. Placed right in front of the variable, it indicates that this pointer is not referencing data referenced by other pointers. For example:

```
foo(double* restrict a, double* restrict b, int length){
    for(int i=0;i<length;i++){
        a[i]=b[i]+1;
    }
}
```

  The restrict keyword is preferred over use of the compiler switches because it only affects the pointers explicitly declared this way.

- *Directives*: If you want to be even more specific, you can indicate where a particular dependence should be ignored. As shown above, you can force the compiler into ignoring assumed dependences by #pragma ivdep, and even stronger by #pragma simd, as discussed earlier.

Dealing with Branches

Branches are points in the instruction flow that set the instruction pointer to other than the next instruction, either static or dynamic, based on previously done comparison. Branches are a necessary evil in structured programming; function calls lead to branches if not inlined, loops will check their limits, and we have true conditional branches from "if-else" statements in the code. As outlined earlier in the discussion of the pipeline, branches pose a considerable problem for the CPU because the condition on which a branch is taken first needs to be evaluated before the instruction flow can continue at another point. CPUs deal with this by predicting the target of the branch based on previous encounters with this address in the code. Frequent wrong predictions can have a severe impact on performance.

■ **Note**   This section addresses the bad speculation category in the of the top-down method for pipeline performance.

__builtin_expect

If you observe bad speculation at a particular conditional branch, and you have a good estimation of what the expected value should be, it is quite easy to let the compiler know about it explicitly by using the build-in function, __builtin_expect. The syntax is quite straightforward: instead of writing the condition in the argument of the if-statement, you write if(__builtin_expect(condition,expectation)), where expectation is either 0 for false or 1 for true. For example:

```
if(__builtin_expect(x<0,1)){
    somefunction(x);
} else {
    someotherfunction(x);
}
```

Profile-Guided Optimization

If you don't have a good clue as to which conditions to put first into if-statements, then *profile-guided optimization* (PGO) might help. The virtue of this technique is that it gives you a way to exactly check for such cases such as wrongly predicted conditions and to correct them without impacting the source code. PGO is a three-step process:

1. Create an instrumented binary with the compiler option -prof-gen.

2. Run this binary with one or more representative workloads. This will create profile files containing the desired information.

3. Compile once more with the compiler option -prof-use.

Profile-guided optimization can produce considerable performance improvements for code not matching the default assumption of the compiler regarding, for example, branch behavior or loop iteration count.

Pragmas for Unrolling Loops and Inlining

Loops and calls to subroutines and functions can be another source of frequent branching. One way to reduce the number of branches caused by loops and calls is to use pragmas to unroll the loops and inline function and the subroutine calls.

unroll/nounroll

The #pragma unroll allows you to control the unroll factor of loops. Unrolling a loop can speed up the loop execution considerably, because the loop condition doesn't need to be checked as often and additional optimizations might become possible in the unrolled code. Loop unrolling does increase the code size, the pressure on the instruction cache, the decode unit, and the registers.

The #pragma unroll can take an additional argument indicating the unroll factor. For example:

```
#pragma unroll(2)
for(int i=0;i<size;i++){
    a[i]=b[i]*c[i]
}
```

This will give you a loop transformation similar to this:

```
// unrolled loop
for(int i=0;i<size-(size%2);i+=2){
    a[i]=b[i]*c[i];
    a[i+1]=b[i+1]*c[i+1];
}
// remainder loop - deals with remaining iteration
// for sizes not divisible by 2
for(int i=size-(size%2);size;i++){
    a[i]=b[i]*c[i];
}
```

The #pragma nounroll will prohibit the unrolling of a particular loop.

EXERCISE 7-4

Write a program with a simple loop, such as the above one, for a different loop length. Compile it with -xAVX -opt-report5. Do you get unrolling? Try placing a #pragma unroll in front of the loop; can you change the unrolling behavior of the compiler for this loop? Have a look at the earlier discussion on optimization reports.

---

unroll_and_jam/nounroll_and_jam

The #pragma unroll_and_jam does perform a nested loop transformation, where the outer loop is unrolled and the resulting inner loops are then united. Consider our squaregemm function used in the earlier optimization reports example. If you put a #pragma unroll_and_jam in front of the middle loop,

```
void squaregemm(int size, double* a, double* b, double* c){
  for(int i=0;i<size;i++){
#pragma unroll_and_jam(2)
    for(int j=0;j<size;j++){
      for(int k=0;k<size;k++){
        c[i*size+j]+=a[i*size+k]*b[k*size+j];
      }
    }
  }
}
```

the resulting code will be equivalent to:

```
void squaregemm(int size, double* a, double* b, double* c){
  for(int i=0;i<size;i++){
#pragma unroll_and_jam(2)
    for(int j=0;j<size;j+=2){
      for(int k=0;k<size;k++){
        c[i*size+j]+=a[i*size+k]*b[k*size+j];
        c[i*size+j+1]+=a[i*size+k+1]*b[k*size+j+1];
      }
    }
  }
}
```

Plus, you have additional remainder loops from the unrolling.

inline, noinline, forceinline

The Intel compiler has a large set of settings to influence inline behavior. If there are particular functions you want to see inlined, you can, of course, change the general settings for the compilation of a source file, but this a shotgun approach that will try to inline all the functions in the file. A more surgical approach is to specify exactly where you want the inlining and where to avoid it when unnecessary.

The #pragma inline will instruct the compiler to inline the function after the pragma if possible within the heuristic. You can override the heuristics by using #pragma forceinline, which will definitely inline when possible. If you want to inline functions recursively, that is, inlining functions in the inline functions and so on, you augment the behavior by adding the recursive clause—for instance, #pragma forceinline recursive.

Specialized Routines: How to Exploit the Branch Prediction for Maximal Performance

Many programs are capable of dealing with a lot of different circumstances and boundary conditions. For instance, your program might be able to deal with polynomial interpolation to a degree of the nth order. If you program such versatile software, you generally leave the parameter controlling the order of the polynomial free, but in one single run or over a longer time in the execution, you use only a single case—say eighth order. In such a circumstance, the branch prediction might do magic for you! If a branch fails, it might fail once or maybe twice, but not more often. If the condition stays constant, no further misprediction will occur until the program finishes or until another polynomial order is valid over a longer period of time.

Consider a case where you have a highly specialized routine for, say, a 4th-, 8th-, and 16th-order polynomial, since this is what you are mostly using. The general case can be treated, but it is much less well performing. In this case, a simple switch will do the trick for you:

```
void myswitchedpolynomial(n,...){
    switch(order){
        case 4:
            polynomial_4(...);
        case 8:
            polynomial_8(...);
        case:16
            polynomial_16(...);
        default:
            polynomial_n(n, ...);
    }
}
```

Although this seems like a brute-force method, it can be a powerful technique, especially if you have a limited set of choices. The number of specialized routines can still be high, and can go into the thousands. In each individual routine, you can now program a particular case explicitly, which will help the compiler produce better code.

When Optimization Leads to Wrong Results

Aggressive optimization is a necessity if you want to achieve the highest level of performance. Under special circumstances, aggressive optimization can lead to problematic or even erratic behavior. In this case, you need to decrease the optimization level with the command-line switch, which will affect the methods of the whole file that's compiled. Again, pragmas allow you to control the behavior of the compiler more specifically.

The #pragma optimize off disables the optimization for code after the pragma until its counterpart, #pragma optimize on, is found. This is a huge step, as optimization is totally switched [7]off. More often, it will suffice to change the optimization level—say, to the basic -01—to guarantee the correct behavior.

The #pragma intel optimization_level 1 applies -O1 to the following function. Notice the intel clause; this is to distinguish the use from GNU compiler's use of the same pragma, which switches the optimization level for all code after the pragma.

Analyzing Pipeline Performance with Intel VTune Amplifier XE

We have discussed the Sandy Bridge pipeline and have given potential reasons why it can stall in the front end or back end, or owing to bad speculation. We also have discussed potential remedies for each of these problems by means of the compiler. In this section, we analyze the pipeline using VTune to obtain information about pipeline performance, and we apply the solutions learned to overcome stalls in particular sections of the pipeline. We covered VTune Amlifier XE earlier in this book when we discussed share memory parallelization problems. Here, we look at one analysis type in detail: general exploration. General exploration gives us exactly the front-end/back-end analysis discussed earlier.

To have a simple example demonstrating a VTune Amplifier XE analysis, we use the 4×4 matrix multiplication introduced earlier in this chapter. But here, for all N matrices C_i we want to perform M matrix-matrix multiplications,

$$C_i = C_i + \sum_{m=1}^{M} A_{i,m} B_{i,m},$$

where the indices indicate full matrices, not elements.

The example is loosely based on the problem of small matrix-matrix multiplication in the DBCSR method of CP2K.[11] We will only consider square matrices:

```
int main(void){
  int msize=4;              // the matrix side length
  int msize2=msize*msize;   // the number of elements in each matrix
  int nmatrices=100000;     // how many c-matrices are there
  int nab=100;              // how many a and b matrix multiplication
                            // per c-matrix
  double** b = (double**) _mm_malloc(sizeof(double*)*nmatrices,32);
  double** a = (double**) _mm_malloc(sizeof(double*)*nmatrices,32);
  double*  c = (double*)  _mm_malloc(sizeof(double)*nmatrices*msize2,32);

  // allocate matrices
  for(int i=0;i<nmatrices*msize2;i++){
    c[i]=((double) rand())/((double) RAND_MAX);
  }
  for(int i=0;i<nmatrices;i++){
    b[i] = (double*) _mm_malloc(sizeof(double)*msize2*nab,32);
    a[i] = (double*) _mm_malloc(sizeof(double)*msize2*nab,32);
  }
```

```
// init matrices
for(int i=0;i<nmatrices;i++){
  for(int n=0;n<nab*msize2;n++){
    b[i][n]=((double) rand())/((double) RAND_MAX);
    a[i][n]=((double) rand())/((double) RAND_MAX);
  }
}


// do a couple of iterations in order to have a reasonable runtime
for(int l=0;l<10;l++){
  // for all matrices C perform ...
  for(int i=0;i<nmatrices;i++){
    int cpos=msize*i;
    // ... a number of A-B matrix multiplications
    for (int n=0;n<nab;n++)
      {
        #pragma inline      // inline the method
        mymatrixmethod(4,&a[i][n], &b[i][n], &c[cpos]);
      }
  }
}
}
```

Using a Standard Library Method

The basic linear algebra system (BLAS)[12] is a standard library specializing in linear algebra operations, such as matrix multiplications. The subroutine applicable here is the double precision general matrix-matrix multiplication DGEMM, which computes:

$$C = \beta C + \alpha AB.$$

We will first use Intel MKL's DGEMM method to perform the matrix-matrix multiplication:

```
void mymatrixmethod(int m, double* a, double* b, double* c){
        cblas_dgemm(CblasRowMajor, CblasNoTrans, CblasNoTrans,
                m, m, m,1.0, a,m, b,m, 1.0,c,m);
}
```

DGEMM is too powerful a method, since we are asking for a lot fewer features than it has to offer (it can also transpose the matrices and multiply with scalar factors, all of which we don't need here).

Figure 7-10 shows the output of a basic hotspot analysis done with VTune Amplifier XE. As expected, we have the majority of time in the DGEMM method, with some fraction coming from the initialization (functions main and rand).

⊘ **Elapsed Time: 15.381s**

Total Thread Count:	1
Overhead Time:	0s
Spin Time:	0s
CPU Time:	15.360s
Paused Time:	0s

⊘ **Top Hotspots**

This section lists the most active functions in your application. Optimizing these hotspot functions typically results in improving overall application performance.

Function	CPU Time
cblas_dgemm	11.320s
main	1.830s
rand	1.550s
malloc	0.350s
[MKL BLAS]@xdgemm	0.270s
[Others]	0.040s

Figure 7-10. *Summary output of basic hotspot analysis*

If we do the math on the number of floating-point operations (Flops) performed, we get 100 A-B-matrix multiplications for 1,000,000 C matrices with 2×4×4×4 Flops each and a total of 12.80 GFlops. We need 11.32s for this, hence we get 12.80/11.32=1.13 GFlops. This is not too impressive because a Sandy Bridge core at 2.7 GHz can deliver 21.6 GFlops!

Let's look at the next level of details for the same run. Figure 7-11 shows the summary page of a general exploration analysis performed with VTune Amplifier XE for the same binary. Actually, the results seem not that bad; the pipeline execution is quite good with a CPI of 0.503 (about 2 instructions retired per cycle). Bad speculation is at a low ratio. There is some divider activity, which VTune points out. A division is a very expensive operation. This is caused by the initialization of the matrices, where we normalize our random numbers to be between 0.0 and1.0; we can easily get rid of this by setting:

```
double randnorm = 1.0/((double) RAND_MAX);
```

and replacing division by multiplication; for instance:

```
for(int i=0;i<nmatrices*msize2;i++){
    c[i]=((double) rand())*randnorm;
}
```

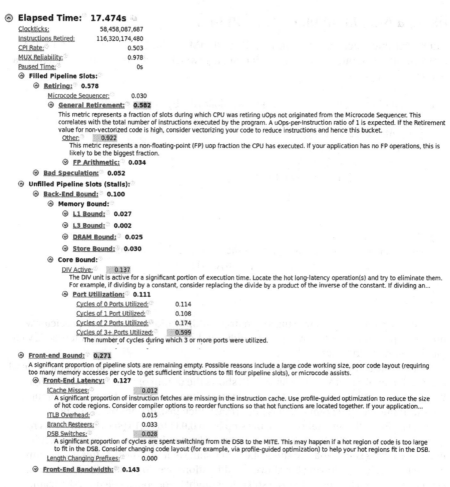

Figure 7-11. *Summary output of a general exploration analysis in VTune*

Similarly, for the initialization of a and b. More severe seems to be the low floating-point utilization of 0.034. This goes hand in hand with our observation of low GFLOP rates. In the next section, we will make a first attempt to tackle this.

Using a Manual Implementation in C

Our real problem here seems to be that the DGEMM routine is a total overkill for a 4×4 matrix multiplication. We could make it more lightweight and spell out the mathematical operations explicitly:

```
void mymatrixmethod(int m, double* a, double* b, double* c){
  if(m==4){
    for(int i=0;i<4;i++){
      for(int j=0;j<4;j++){
        for(int l=0;l<4;l++){
          c[i*4+j]+=a[i*4+l]*b[l*4+j];
        }
      }
    }
  } else {
    cblas_dgemm(CblasRowMajor, CblasNoTrans, CblasNoTrans,
          m, m, m,1.0, a,m, b,m, 1.0,c,m);
  }
}
```

Since we are exclusively using 4x4 matrix multiplications, the branch predictor will not cause pipeline flushes, owing to the additional if statement; still, the method is valid for all square matrix sizes.

Let's now create a new binary with the code changes lined out and rerun the general exploration analysis of VTune. Figure 7-12 shows the output of VTune. What a big leap. We improved from 17.474s to 6.166s in execution time. We dropped in the CPI, though, but this reinforces the point that it is important which instructions we retire, not how many. The FP arithmetic ratio took a big step from 0.034 to 0.213 (see output). This result is going in the right direction. Now let's estimate the floating-point performance. A basic hotspot analysis shows that we spend 4.04s in main; we'll assume that this is all compute, for the time being. Following the above considerations, we do 12.80 GFLOP/4.04s = 3.17 GFLOP/s. That's a lot better, but is it still not enough! If you look at Figure 7-12 again, you will see that all the FP arithmetic is spend in "FP scalar." The code doesn't vectorize properly. Now, let's use the compiler directives to help the compiler vectorize the code.

⊙ **Elapsed Time: 6.166s**

Clockticks: 20,392,030,588
Instructions Retired: 37,218,055,827
CPI Rate: 0.548
MUX Reliability: 0.997
Paused Time: 0s

⊝ **Filled Pipeline Slots:**

⊙ **Retiring: 0.639**

Microcode Sequencer: 0.018

⊝ **General Retirement: 0.628**

This metric represents a fraction of slots during which CPU was retiring uOps not originated from the Microcode Sequencer. This correlates with the total number of instructions executed by the program. A uOps-per-Instruction ratio of 1 is expected. If the Retirement value for non-vectorized code is high, consider vectorizing your code to reduce instructions and hence this bucket.

Other: 0.760

This metric represents a non-floating-point (FP) uop fraction the CPU has executed. If your application has no FP operations, this is likely to be the biggest fraction.

⊙ **FP Arithmetic: 0.213**

This metric represents an overall arithmetic floating-point (FP) uops fraction the CPU has executed.

FP x87: 0.000

FP Scalar: 0.213

This metric represents an arithmetic floating-point (FP) scalar uops fraction the CPU has executed. Analyze metric values to identify why vector code is not generated, which is typically caused by the selected algorithm or missing/wrong compiler...

FP Vector: 0.000

⊙ **Bad Speculation: 0.011**

⊙ **Unfilled Pipeline Slots (Stalls):**

⊙ **Back-End Bound: 0.255**

Identify slots where no uOps are delivered due to a lack of required resources for accepting more uOps in the back-end of the pipeline. Back-end metrics describe a portion of the pipeline where the out-of-order scheduler dispatches ready uOps into their respective execution units, and, once completed, these uOps get retired according to program order. Stalls due to data-cache misses or stalls due to the overloaded divider unit are examples of back-end bound issues.

⊙ **Memory Bound:**

⊙ **L1 Bound: 0.026**

⊙ **L3 Bound: 0.000**

⊙ **DRAM Bound: 0.030**

Memory Bandwidth: 0.004

Memory Latency: 0.143

This metric shows how often CPU could be stalled due to the latency of the main memory (DRAM). Consider optimizing data layout or using Software Prefetches (through the compiler).

Local DRAM: 0.023

Remote DRAM: 0.000

Remote Cache: 0.000

Figure 7-12. Summary page of general exploration analysis after changing to an explicit c expression

Vectorization with Directives

We found that we increased our performance significantly with a highly specialized method, but there was no vectorization present and hence the pressure was increasing on the back end. Let's now try to ease the pressure by mandating vectorization:

```
void mymatrixmethod(int m, double* a, double* b, double* c){
    if(m==4){
        for(int i=0;i<4;i++){
#pragma simd
            for(int j=0;j<4;j++){
#pragma unroll(4)
                for(int l=0;l<4;l++){
                    c[i*4+j]+=a[i*4+l]*b[l*4+j];
                }
            }
        }
```

```
  } else {
      cblas_dgemm(CblasRowMajor, CblasNoTrans, CblasNoTrans,
                  m, m, m, 1.0, a, m, b, m, 1.0, c, m);
  }
}
```

Here, we unrolled the inner loop four times and vectorized the outer loop.

Figure 7-13 shows the result of a general exploration analysis. We got even better results, but—no surprise—the "FP arithmetic" literally vanished because now everything is executed in vectors. Compared to memory operations, there is comparatively little time spent in computing. The pressure is now almost fully on the memory subsystem, so our execution functions perfectly.

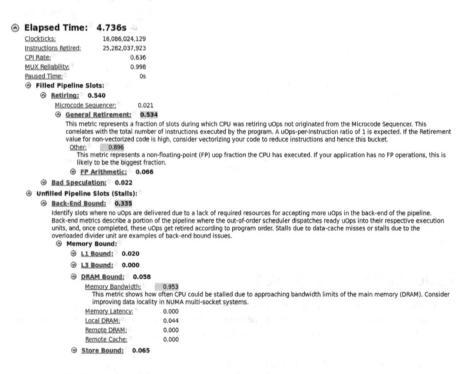

Figure 7-13. *General exploration summary after enforcing vectorization*

EXERCISE 7-5

Try to insert the intrinsics method for a 4x4 matrix multiplication developed earlier in this chapter into our sample problem. Can you get better than the result achieved with the compiler only?

Summary

We presented a brief account of the microarchitecture of modern Intel processors, plus discussed how to detect microarchitectural issues and how to solve them, ranging from hinting the compiler via directives to programming brute-force solutions using intrinsics.

As for microarchitectural design, the scope of this chapter is certainly too tight to look much deeper. Many good textbooks are available, such as the standards by Hennessy and Patterson[13] or Tanenbaum.[14] Hager and Wellein[15] focus particularly on tuning and performance aspects. Intel's software developer manual[16] and its optimization reference manual[17] are always good, if extensive, reads.

Innovative usage employing the techniques presented here can be found in the open-source space, particularly in software that has confined hotspots, such as quantum chromodynamics, molecular dynamics, or quantum chemistry applications, such as CP2K[18] or Gromacs.[19]

References

1. S. P. Dandamudi, *Introduction to Assembly Language Programming* (Springer, 2005).

2. Intel, "Intel 64 and IA-32 Architectures Software Developer Manuals," 2014, www.intel.com/products/processor/manuals.

3. A. S. Tanenbaum, Structured Computer Organization, 5th ed. (Pearson, 2006).

4. Ibid.

5. J. L. Hennessy and D. A. Patterson, *Computer Architecture* (Morgan Kaufmann, 2007).

6. "Intel 64 and IA-32 Architectures Software Developer Manual."

7. Intel, "Intel 64 and IA-32 Architectures Optimization Reference Manual," 2014, www.intel.com/products/processor/manuals.

8. "Intel Intrisics Guide," https://software.intel.com/sites/landingpage/IntrinsicsGuide.

9. "BLAS (Basic Linear Algebra Subprograms)," http://www.netlib.org/blas.

10. "Intel Intrinsics Guide"

11. J. Hutter, M. Krack, T. Laino, and J. VandeVondele, "CP2K Open Source Molecular Dynamics," www.cp2k.org.

12. "BLAS (Basic Linear Algebra Subprograms)"

13. Hennessy and Patterson, *Computer Architecture*.

14. Tanenbaum, *Structured Computer Organization.*

15. G. Hager and G. Wellein, *Introduction to High Performance Computing for Scientists and Engineers* (CRC Press, 2011).

16. "Intel 64 and IA-32 Architectures Software Developer Manual."

17. "Intel 64 and IA-32 Archtectures Optimization Reference Manual."

18. Hutter et al., "CP2K Open Source Molecular Dynamics."

19. E. Lindahl, D. van der Spoel, and B. Hess, "Gromacs," www. Gromacs.org.

CHAPTER 8

■ ■ ■

Application Design Considerations

In Chapters 5 to 7 we reviewed the methods, tools, and techniques for application tuning, explained by using examples of HPC applications and benchmarks. The whole process followed the top-down software optimization framework explained in Chapter 3. The general approach to the tuning process is based on a quantitative analysis of execution resources required by an application and how these match the capabilities of the platform the application is run on. The blueprint analysis of platform capabilities and system-level tuning considerations were provided in Chapter 4, based on several system architecture metrics discussed in Chapter 2.

In this final chapter we would like to generalize the approach to application performance analysis, and offer a different and higher level view of application and system bottlenecks. The higher level view is needed to see potentially new, undiscovered performance limitations caused by invisible details inside the internal implementations of software, firmware, and hardware components.

Abstraction and Generalization of the Platform Architecture

Middleware and software architectures play a big role in HPC and in other application areas. Today, almost nobody interacts with the hardware directly. Instead, the interaction of the programmer and the hardware is facilitated via an application programming interface (API). If you think that programming in assembly language today is direct interaction with hardware, we have to disappoint you; it is not. The instruction stream is decoded into sequences of special microcode operations that in the end serve as the commands to the execution units.

Software abstractions are an unavoidable part of modern applications design, and in this part of the book we will look at the software architecture from the point of view of abstraction and the consequences of using one set of abstractions over others. Selection of some abstractions may result in performance penalties because of the added translation steps; for others, the impact may be hidden by efficient pipelining (such as happens with microcode translation inside processors) and causes almost no visible overhead.

247

Types of Abstractions

An abstraction is a technique used to separate conceptualized ideas from specific instances and implementations of those at hand. These conceptualizations are used to hide the internal complexity of the hardware, allow portability of software, and increase the productivity of development via better reuse of components. Abstractions that are implemented in software, middleware, or firmware also allow for fixing hardware bugs with software that results in a reduced time to market for very complex systems, such as supercomputers. We believe it is generally good to have the right level of abstraction. Abstractions today are generally an unavoidable thing: we have to use different kinds of APIs because an interaction with the raw hardware is (almost) impossible. During performance optimization work, any performance overhead must be quantified to judge whether there is need to consider a lower level of abstraction that could gain more performance and increase efficiency.

Abstractions apply to both control flow and data structures. *Control abstraction* hides the order in which the individual statements, instructions, or function calls of a program are executed. The *data abstraction* allows us to use high-level types, classes, and complex structures without the need to know the details about how they are stored in a computer memory or disk, or are transferred over the network. One can regard the notion of an object in object-oriented programming as an attempt to combine abstractions of data and code, and to deal with instances of objects through their specific properties and methods. Object-oriented programming is sometimes a convenient approach that improves code modularity, reuses software components, and increases productivity of development and support of the application.

Some examples of control flow abstractions that a typical developer in high-performance computing will face include the following:

- *Decoding of processor instruction set into microcode.* These are specific for a microarchitecture implementation of different processors. The details of the mapping between processor instructions and microcode operations are discussed in Chapter 7. The mapping is not a simple one-to-one or one-to-many relation. With technologies like macro fusion,[1] the number of internal micro-operations may end up smaller than the number of incoming instructions. This abstraction allows processor designers to preserve a common instruction set architecture (ISA) across different implementations and to extend the ISA while preserving backwards compatibility. The decoding of processor instructions into micro-operations is a pipeline process, and it usually does not cause performance penalties in HPC codes.

- *Virtual machine, involving just-in-time compilation* (JIT, widely used, for example, in Java or in the Microsoft Common Language Runtime [CLR] virtual machines) or *dynamic translation* (such as in scripting or interpreted languages, such as Python or Perl). Here, compilation is done during execution of a program, rather than prior to execution. With JIT, the program can be stored in a higher level compressed byte-code that is usually a portable representation, and a virtual machine translates it into processor instructions on the fly. JIT implementations can be sufficiently fast for use even in HPC applications, and we have seen large HPC apps written in Java and Python. And, by the way, the number of such applications grows.

- *Programming languages.* These control abstraction. They offer notions such as functions, looping, conditional execution, and so on, to make it easier and more productive to write programs. Higher level languages, such as Fortran or C, often *require compilation of programs* to translate code into a stream of processor-specific instructions to achieve high performance. Unlike instruction decoding or just-in-time compilation, this happens ahead of time before the program executes. The approach ensures that overheads related to compilation of the program code to machine instructions are not impacting application execution.

- *Library of routines and modules.* Most programming languages support extensions of programs with subprograms, modules, or libraries of routines. This enables modular architecture of final programs for faster development, better test coverage, and greater portability. Several well-known libraries provide de-facto standard sets of routines for many HPC programs, such as basic linear algebra subprograms (BLAS),[2] linear algebra package (LAPACK),[3] and the FFTW[4] software library for computing discrete Fourier transforms (DFTs). These libraries not only hide the complexity of underlying algorithms but also enable vendors of hardware to provide highly tuned implementations for best performance on their computer architectures. For example, Intel Math Kernel Library (MKL), included in Intel Parallel Studio XE, provides optimized linear algebra (BLAS, LAPACK, sparse solvers, and ScaLAPACK for clusters), multidimensional (up to 7D) fast Fourier transformations and FFTW interfaces, vector math (including trigonometric, hyperbolic, exponential, logarithmic, power, root, and rounding) routines, random number generators (such as congruent, recursive, Wichman-Hill, Mersenne twister, Sobol sequences, etc.), statistics (quantiles, min/max, variance-covariance, etc.), and data fitting (spline, interpolation, cell search) routines for the latest Intel microprocessors.

- *API calls.* Any kind of API calls provided by the operating system (OS) hide the complexity of an interaction between operating system tasks and the hardware-supported context of execution exposed by the processors. Examples of these include calls from OS to the basic input/output subsystem (BIOS) abstracting the implementation of the underlying hardware platform or a threading API that creates, controls, and coordinates the threads of execution within the application.

- *Operating system.* This, and specifically its *scheduler*, makes every program believe that it runs continuously on the system without any interruptions. In fact, the OS scheduler does interrupt execution, and even puts execution of a program on hold to give other programs access to the processor resources.

- *Full system virtualization.* This includes using virtual machine monitors (VMM), such as Xen, KVM, VMWare, or others. VMMs usually abstract the entire platform so that every operating system believes it is the only one running on a system, while, in fact, VMMs are doing both control and data abstraction among all the different OS versions currently executing on a platform.

Data abstraction allows handling of data bits in meaningful ways. For example, data abstraction can be found behind:

- Datatypes

- Virtual memory

The notion of a *datatype* enforces a clear separation between the abstract properties of a data type and the concrete details of its implementation in hardware. The abstract properties of datatype are visible to client code and can be as simple as an integer datatype or as complex as a hash-table or a class. While the specific implementation (i.e., the way the bytes are stored in computer memory) is kept entirely private, the internal implementation of storing data in memory can differ from machine to machine (e.g., little-endian vs. big-endian storage), and can change over time to incorporate efficiency improvements. A specific example, relevant for high-performance computing, is the representation of *real numbers using floating-point datatypes,* which are limited in length.

As the length of processor registers is limited, it is not possible to equally represent all possible floating-point numbers in digital hardware. The number of possible representations is very large, and different encodings of the floating-point numbers in the fixed-length register will have significantly different numerical qualities of the computations, causing problems for application developers and users comparing results. IEEE 754-1985 was an industry standard for representing (and processing) floating-point numbers in computers, officially adopted in 1985 and superseded in 2008 by IEEE 754-2008. IEEE 754 characterizes numbers in binary, providing definitions of precision, as well as defining representations for positive and negative infinity, a "negative zero," exceptions to handle invalid results like division by zero, special values called NaNs (Not-a-Number) for representing those exceptions, denormalized numbers, and rounding modes.

Virtual memory abstraction is made by OS's virtual memory manager with help of hardware. This abstraction makes every 64-bit program believe it has 2^{64} bytes (or 16 exabytes) of byte-addressable memory to use, while in fact the amount of physical memory available to be shared by multiple programs on a system is much lower: tens or, at best, hundreds of gigabytes. Virtual memory offers a significant reduction of complexity in writing software, and makes it run on a wide range of machines. However, the mechanisms implementing virtual memory involve translation from virtual address to physical address may require a high-cost process called *page walk* to happen and use of a lot of memory-management hardware inside the processor (e.g., translation lookaside buffers, or TLBs). This page walk process and the entire virtual to physical memory translation are invisible to the application. However, it has its hidden cost, which may be seen as a performance cost associated with the loading of page tables. Some measurements (such as one reported by Linus Torvalds)[5] provide an estimate of over 1000 processor cycles required for handling a page fault in the Linux operating system on modern processors.

Levels of Abstraction and Complexities

As we said previously, abstraction is an important notion in computer science, and it is used throughout many instances in computer and software engineering. In practice, software development abstractions are used to reduce duplication of information in a program. The basic mechanism of control abstraction is a function or subroutine; and the ones for data abstraction include various forms of type polymorphism. The more advanced mechanisms that combine data and control abstractions include abstract data types, such as classes, polytypism, and so on. These are the abstractions the software developer usually deals with.

In essence, the approach of abstraction is to deal with the problem at a higher level by focusing on the essential details, ignoring specifics and implementation at the lower level, and to reuse lower level implementations following the "DRY principle" ("Don't repeat yourself"). This approach leads to layered architectures across the entire computer engineering discipline. The examples of layered architectures include Intel QuickPath Interconnect (QPI) protocol,[6] OSI model for computer network protocols,[7] the OpenGL library,[8] and the byte stream input/output (I/O) model used in most modern operating systems. Historically, in computer architecture the computer platform is represented as constituting five abstraction levels: hardware, firmware, assembler, operating system, and processes.[9] Recent developments in virtualization support add more layers to the stack. While those additional layers of abstraction are necessary to achieve higher productivity, the increase in stack depth may impact application performance.

Raw Hardware vs. Virtualized Hardware in the Cloud

One specific abstraction method that became widely used in enterprise and cloud computing, and is being greatly debated in relation to HPC applications, is full hardware virtualization. Hardware virtualization, or platform virtualization, is a method in which a virtual machine acts like a real computer for an operating system. Software executed on these virtual machines is separated from the underlying hardware resources and hides specific implementation details. Different levels of hardware virtualization use techniques like emulation, binary translation, and dynamic code generation. The virtual machines are created and managed by *hypervisor* or *virtual machine monitor* (VMM), which can be (and most often are) implemented in software, but may also be a firmware or even a hardware implementation.

The virtualization techniques have their roots in mainframe computers, and have been available in mainframes and RISC servers for a long time. Hardware assistance and support for hypervisor, introduced in x86 servers in 2005, has started a growth of interest and usage of virtualization in the x86 world. Hardware assistance helped reduce performance overhead considerably and removed a need for binary patching of the operating system kernel. The active development of several commercial (like ones by VMWare, Parallels, etc.) and open-source (Xen, KVM, etc.) hypervisors helped establish hardware virtualization as a base technology for enterprise data center and cloud computing applications. It promoted the development of such popular directions these days as software-defined storage (SDS) and software-defined networks (SDN), and finally brought the concept of the software-defined data center (SDDC) that extends virtualization concepts such as abstraction, pooling, and automation to all of the data center's resources and services to achieve IT as a service.

A complete system virtualization brings certain operational advantages, such as simplified provisioning (through a higher level of integration of application software with the operating system environment) to provide a stable software image to applications (and handling of emulation of newer or obsolete hardware at VMM level) that would be beneficial in making legacy software work on modern hardware without software modifications. For enterprise and cloud applications, virtualization offers additional value, as a hypervisor allows for the implementation of several reliability techniques (virtual machine migration from one machine to another, system-level memory snapshotting, etc.) and utilization improvements via consolidation—i.e., putting several underutilized virtual machines on one physical server).

However, hardware virtualization has not progressed at the same pace within the HPC user community. Though the main quoted reason for not adopting hardware virtualization is performance overhead caused by hypervisor, it is probably the most debatable one. There are studies showing that the overhead is rather small for certain workloads, and running jobs using a pay-per-use model can be more cost-effective versus buying and managing your own cluster.[10] We tend to believe there are other reasons; for example, that the values of virtualization recognized by enterprise and cloud application customers are not compelling for HPC users. Consolidation is almost of no use (though it is possible to implement it using popular HPC batch job schedulers), and live migration and snapshotting are not more scalable than checkpointing techniques used in HPC. However, the cost reduction of virtualized hardware, predominantly hosted by large cloud providers, in some sense already generates demand exploration of high-performance computing applications in the hosted cloud services.

This trend will drive a need for optimization of HPC applications (which are tightly coupled, distributed memory applications) for execution in the hosted virtualized environments, and we see a great need for the tools and techniques to evolve to efficiently carry out this job.

Questions about Application Design

Abstractions are unavoidable. There are some abstractions we can choose (such as your own application architecture, programming language, and so on, or whether to run it under a virtualized or "bare-metal" operating system), while most others we have to live with (such as instruction decoding inside modern processors, or operating system virtual memory management). In any case, each abstraction layer will add a stage to a pipeline of queues for data flow and will complicate the control path, which may, or may not, become a bottleneck for the application performance. As the complexity of application increases, a necessity grows as well to characterize the bottlenecks imposed by abstractions involved and quantify their impact on your application.

As it is not feasible to write a cookbook or produce a fully comprehensive set of recommendations to avoid any potential performance problem with an application, we would rather offer a different approach. While developing a new application or analyzing existing code, you will need to understand the available options, or the unavoidable limitations. Practically, there are tradeoffs between application performance and productivity and between maintainability and quality of the resulting program. It is important to consider several questions during your application or system design and optimization work so as to drive proper decision making in regard to programming and execution environments, and related middleware. These questions, when answered or addressed, will improve your knowledge about the application. At the same time, this approach allows development of structured understanding of the tradeoffs necessary to achieve those desired characteristics.

Designing for Performance and Scaling

HPC is about scalability of applications and the ability to solve large problems by using parallel computers. So, achieving high performance by enabling scalability is a key differentiation of an HPC approach. We dedicate a lot of material in Chapters 6 and 7 to methods for achieving great single-node and single-threaded performance, but we also spent significant time in Chapter 5 discussing how to achieve great parallel efficiency of MPI applications.

The main tools for high performance and scalable design are Amdahl's Law and Gustafson's observation that we both discussed in Chapter 2. They have to be kept in mind when asking questions related to application scaling. For instance:

- What is the minimum share of time the application is running serially (non-parallel)? We assigned f to that share of time in the Amdahl's Law formula.

- How does the share of time taken by the serial part change when more computing nodes or threads are added? In other words, consider whether f is a constant or it depends on the number of processors p used.

Practical answers to these two questions are a sufficient start toward understanding the scaling limits for applications. Let us consider an example of running an application on 64 processors. If, in the specific implementation, approximately 10 percent of the time is serial execution (i.e., $f = 0.1$), then the maximum theoretical performance improvement (speedup) over a single processor will be limited to 8.76. Usually, some amount of serial execution is unavoidable, but the cumulative contribution to the application runtime should not exceed some fraction of a percent to allow efficient use of large parallel machines.

Some of the most prominent sources of serialization in high-performance computing applications, which can be somehow addressed by the application developer, are:

- *Disk and network input/output:* Though there may be parallel storage hardware, people tend to forget that widely used APIs are serial and synchronous. The local disk I/O takes significant amounts of time, and you could consider using the POSIX asynchronous I/O API (see, for example, an article by M. Tim Jones)[11] instead of traditional synchronous blocking system calls.

- *Explicit barriers and serial sections:* In the parallel patterns, such as MPI_Barrier, these are called inside MPI programs, or OpenMP barrier or single directives. There are certainly necessary cases to have synchronizations between parallel sections of code, but the manual serialization has to be used with care.

- *Serial (not vectorized, not threaded, or not parallelized in any other way) parts of the program:* In many applications, specifically in HPC ones, the actual share of codebase that runs serial may be the greatest. It does not make sense parallelizing parsing of the configuration files (which may result in a lot of extra code), validating provided input, or writing a logfile with execution progress and diagnostic information. It is fine for that entire code to remain serial as long as it does not take a significant share of the application's runtime!

At the same time, there are other sources of serialization, coming from the specific control abstractions or APIs. Some examples would be:

- *Implicit barriers,* such as the ones "hidden" at the end of OpenMP for/do or sections work-sharing constructs (if nowait clause is omitted) or many MPI library calls. Follow the recommendations in Chapter 5 to avoid superfluous synchronization and replace blocking collective operations by MPI-3 non-blocking ones. For the multithreaded applications using OpenMP, review the "Thread Synchronization and Locking" part in Chapter 6.

- *Internal synchronization APIs,* such as many kernel routines or library calls. If any of the external library calls are identified as big-time consumers in your application, study the library documentation or contact its developer to find a better alternative.

Designing for Flexibility and Performance Portability

The coding to the lowest level of abstraction aiming at the best performance is not possible in large-scale applications. The use of assembly language or low-level intrinsics is not recommended by Intel engineers, and though it is available in the Intel compilers, such low-level programming should be seen as the last resort. Code reuse is the best working approach for achieving maintainability and successful evolution of the applications. Again, the levels of abstractions in nonperformance-critical parts of the program are of no importance; choose whatever abstraction you find suitable and keep it as flexible as possible to ensure smooth code evolution.

However, ask yourself a couple of questions about parts of the programs contributing most to overall runtime:

- What are the predominant data layouts and the data access patterns inside the critical execution path?

- How is the parallelism exposed in the critical execution path?

Sometimes the use of specialized, highly optimized libraries to implement time-consuming algorithms in the program will help achieve flexibility and portability, and will define the answers to these questions. As discussed earlier, software libraries, such as Intel MKL, will offer you a useful abstraction and will hide the complexity of the implementation. But let us discuss these questions in greater details, in case you are working on an algorithm yourself.

Data Layout

The first question above is about data abstractions. Most, if not all, computer architectures benefit from sequential streaming of data accesses, and the ideal situation happens when the amount of repeatedly accessed data fits into the processor caches that are roughly 2.5MiB per core in modern Intel Core-based processors. Such behavior is a consequence of the double-data rate (DDR) dynamic random access memory (DRAM) module architecture used by modern computers. If the data access is wrapped into special containers (as often observed in C++ programs), frequent access to that data can add overhead from the "envelope" around data bits that may be higher than the actual time of computing with the values.

The data layout is very important to consider when ensuring efficient use of SIMD processing, as discussed in Chapter 7. Let's consider an example where an assemblage of three values is defined within a single structure and corresponding values from each set are to be processed simultaneously, where the pointers to that enclosing structure are passed around as function arguments. This can be, for instance, a collection of three coordinates of points in space, x, y, and z; and our application has to deal with N of such points. To store the coordinates in memory we could consider two possible definitions for structures (using C language notation) presented in Listings 8-1 and 8-2.

- *Structure of arrays (SoA)*: Where each of the coordinates is stored in a dedicated array and three of these arrays are combined into one structure.

Listing 8-1. Definition of SoA (Structure of Arrays) in C

```
#define N 1024
typedef struct _SoA {
    double x[N];
    double y[N];
    double z[N];
} SoA_coordinates;
SoA_coordinates foo;
// access i'th element of array as foo.x[i], foo.y[i], and foo.z[i]
```

- *Array of structures (AoS)*: Where three coordinates constitute one structure and then an array of these structures is defined.

Listing 8-2. Example Definition of AoS (Array of Structures) in C

```
#define N 1024
typedef struct _AoS {
    double x;
    double y;
    double z;
} AoS_coordinates;
AoS_coordinates bar[N];
// access i'th element of array as bar[i].x, bar[i].y, and bar[i].z
```

The layouts in memory for each of the options are shown in Figure 8-1.

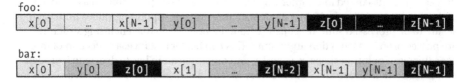

Figure 8-1. *Layout in memory for SoA and AoS options*

For an application developer, the latter case—the array of structures—will likely make more sense: the location of each point is represented by three coordinates (x, y, and z), so each point coordinate is described by one object (an instance of the structure AoS_coordinates), and then many points are put together into an array named foo.

CHAPTER 8 ■ APPLICATION DESIGN CONSIDERATIONS

However, for the performance on SIMD—capable processors, the former case—the structure of arrays-is proved to be usually better. In "A Case Study Comparing AoS (Arrays of Structures) and SoA (Structures of Arrays) Data Layouts for a Compute-intensive Loop Run on Intel Xeon Processors and Intel Xeon Phi Product Family Coprocessors,"[12] the advantages of the SoA over the AoS layout for vectorization were clearly demonstrated. The compiler is almost always able to produce better and faster running code by vectorizing the SoA data layout than the AoS data layout. So, when in doubt or unless you can prove otherwise, use SoA instead of AoS, especially on the Intel Xeon Phi coprocessor. However, the SoA data layout comes with the cost of reduced locality between accesses to multiple fields of the original structure instance, and may result in increased TLB pressure and visible costs of page-fault handling.

A data organization in memory that is beneficial for one computer architecture may end up not being the best for another. What can be done to achieve performance portability of the code, as the different data layouts may result in different observed efficiencies of the application on various computer systems? To achieve performance portability, the developer could abstract data storage and implement different access mechanisms for different machines. As an example, in the widely used Berlin Quantum ChromoDynamics application, or BQCD,[13] authors Hinnerk Stüben and Yoshifumi Nakamura allowed several data layout options in memory for the key data structures, such as the arrays representing two dimensional matrices of complex numbers.

Some of the supported layouts of arrays of complex numbers are shown in Figure 8-2.

- *Standard layout,* where each complex number is represented as a structure of two elements: the real (re) and imaginary (im) parts of the complex number, and the array is stored in a typical AoS layout.

- *Vector layout,* in which SoA is used to store the real and imaginary parts in separate arrays packed into one structure. This layout is usually more beneficial for use with vectoring instructions.

- *SIMD layout,* which is specifically optimized for the SIMD instruction sets, such as Intel SSE or Intel AVX. It is sometimes referred as "Array of Structure of Arrays" (AoSoA) and is indeed a combination of the other two approaches: several elements of real part are stored sequentially in memory to fit one SIMD register (for instance, four double-precision floating-point values in one 256-bit AVX register), followed by same number of elements storing the imaginary parts occupying another SIMD register, and so on. This layout allows a more efficient instruction stream generation for the latest Intel processors.

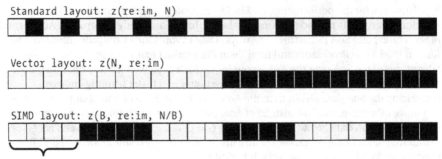

where B is the number of elements that fit into the SIMD register

Figure 8-2. *Data layouts in memory for the arrays of complex numbers available in BQCD*

The BQCD build system provides simple selection of storage layouts and also permit choosing a different code path for performance-critical sections of the application dealing with that data. The developers of BQCD invested a great effort in developing highly optimized instruction code for the several computer architectures on which BQCD is typically run.

The results obtained by the BQDC developers[14] on a server with two Intel Xeon E5-2695 v2 processors are summarized in Table 8-1 and conclude that the SIMD, or AoSoA, layout with optimized code path delivers the best performance for hot loops over vector or standard layouts.

Table 8-1. *Performance in MFLOPS/Core of BQCD Matrix-Vector Multiply Routines with Different Layouts*

Data Layout	Data in L2 Cache	Data in Memory
Standard layout	5670	880
Vector layout	1820	930
SIMD layout	9930	990

■ **Note**   Often, for memory bandwidth-bound kernels, when the dataset fits into Level 2 cache, the performance of compute kernels can be 10 times higher than when data resides in main memory.

Structured Approach to Express Parallelism

The second question asked above is how the parallelism is exposed in the application. This question embraces a better understanding of the control abstractions used. Selecting the right control abstraction for parallel processing, along with the data distribution method between processors, is key to achieving great performance and scalability of your code.

There are many ways to express parallelism. Depending on a specific algorithm, the optimal parallel implementation may employ different control and data distribution patterns, such as the ones presented in Figure 8-3.[5] These patterns can be used to express computations in a wide variety of domains, and they usually take two things into account: tasks and data decomposition. To achieve scalable parallel performance, algorithms need to be designed to respect data locality and isolation, which are important for distributed memory and NUMA system architectures.

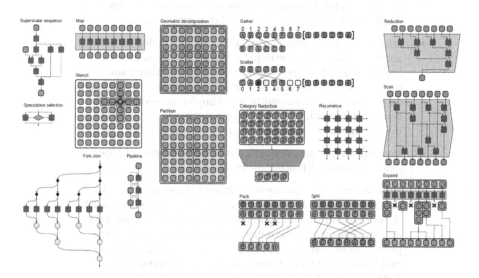

Figure 8-3. *Overview of parallel control and data management patterns (Source: Structured Parallel Programming: Patterns for Efficient Computation)*

Often found among HPC application patterns is the *partition pattern*. It provides a simple way to ensure both data locality and isolation: the data is broken down into a set of nonoverlapping regions, and then multiple instances of the same compute task are assigned to operate on the partitions. As the partitions do not overlap, the computational tasks can operate in parallel on their own working set without interfering with each other. While selecting control flow and the data layouts, the one specific issue to watch for is a load imbalance. The best application performance will be achieved when all computing elements are loaded to the maximum, and that computational load is evenly distributed among the computing elements.

Structured approaches to parallel programming and careful selection of parallel patterns are probably the best ways to achieve high performance and scalability of various parallel algorithms. For the interested reader, we recommend two great books on this topic: *Structured Parallel Programming: Patterns for Efficient Computation*[15] and *Patterns for Parallel Programming*.[16]

Understanding Bounds and Projecting Bottlenecks

Whether you are writing a new application from scratch or working on an updated, more efficient implementation of an existing program, it is a critical step to analyze the influences that hardware will bring. The detailed analysis should be done for the pieces of code consuming most of the time in the program. Some of specific questions to be addressed are:

- Will the new implementation be memory, storage, or compute bandwidth bound on the considered computer systems?

- Is there an opportunity for a different implementation of the same algorithm that will not be impacted by the bounds of current implementation and may result in greater performance and scaling? This question is related to the previous one, but focuses on research for better algorithms and implementations. As soon as a better implementation is suggested, it has to be studied and the bottlenecks identified and their impact quantified.

- How will the performance behavior of the application change with increased levels of concurrency?

- For instance, if a partition pattern is used, the more MPI ranks that are added, the less data (and work) per MPI rank there will be (in so-called strong scaling scenarios). Even if you may not have access to such a machine today, the development of manycore processors follows Moore's Law and, as a result, your application may be executed on such a machine sooner than you think. For example, in 2004 the mainstream computational nodes in a cluster had two to four processors and 4 to 8 GiB of memory. Just some eight years later, Intel Xeon Phi coprocessor chips had over 60 cores, each capable of executing four threads with wider 512-bit SIMD execution units and 8 to 16 GiB of fast local memory on the co-processor cards. So, to clarify this question:

  - At which scale will the dataset per thread fit into the cache inside the processors? This point in a scaling graph may lead to observed superlinear performance improvement for memory bandwidth bound kernels when since the cache bandwidth is dramatically higher than the memory bandwidth, as we saw in Chapter 2. (We have discussed this effect in the BQCD example earlier in this chapter).

- When can a further increase of concurrency impact vectorization and relative share of time for synchronization between the processes? If the concurrency level continues increasing, will it lead, at some point, to diminishing benefits of vectorization? For instance, the SIMD processing efficiency will drop when the loop trip count begins to approach values that are too small for vectorization to yield a positive impact.

The research and analysis in this part may end up requiring most of the time and dedication. Simulations and quantitative analysis done here should be later used to validate performance observations of running application. If the process is followed rigorously it will certainly bring a great insight into how the code performs and will give ideas for additional improvements.

Data Storage or Transfer vs. Recalculation

A more in-depth analysis of a specific parallel implementation of a selected algorithm may consider issues not often researched during single-node optimization projects. One of the areas to look at is a decision on recalculation versus storing or sending data over the network.

Imagine that you have a parallel program using many MPI ranks, and there is a single value or a small array that all MPI ranks must use at some point. One approach would be to compute required value by one of the ranks and then send it to all others ranks (i.e., broadcast the value). Another approach would be to let every rank recompute the required values independently and avoid potential wait times caused by the broadcast.

Which approach would be better? There is no universal answer to this question; it will depend on the definition of "better," as well as which inputs are required to compute the needed data and how long the calculation would take versus how much data there is to send over the network.

If by "better" we mean a lower application runtime, then in general computing the required values independently by every rank might be faster. However, the requirements of input data need to be questioned, so that the input data for the calculation must be available to all ranks. This can add time to transfer input data over the network to the time required to compute the value if all the ranks do not have access to the inputs. Also, if the code runs on a heterogeneous cluster (such as with Intel Xeon hosts and Intel Xeon Phi coprocessors), the recalculation may result in slightly different values on different ranks, because of the different processor architectures.

On the other hand, if the important value metric is power or the energy-to-solution, the best answer may end up differently. When one MPI rank is computing, all other processors are usually paused or sleeping, waiting for the result, and this enables power savings on a potentially very large number of cluster nodes. Of course, there will be some additional power needed to complete a broadcast send. But assuming the calculation takes longer than the network operation, this approach may end up resulting into a lower average power and energy-to-solution.

Total Productivity Assessment

Sometimes, optimization of an existing application requires rewriting some of its parts using a new computing paradigm or a different programming language. What will it take to implement the changes and how will the new implementation impact abstraction layers? The main question here is not how fast the application will run but, rather, what it will take to develop and optimize the application, as well as to support the code on future computational platforms. These are the final questions asked in our description, but they have to be thought through from the start. The angle to consider should be from the productivity of development, ongoing maintenance, and potentially user support. Applications are rarely written and then forgotten. Users often require extensions of functionality, increases in performance, and support of new hardware features. Thus, in a majority of cases it is not only the application's performance that matters but also the development team's efficiency and the time it takes to extend functionality or port the code to new hardware. A detailed study targeted to selecting the most suitable programming model and languages for implementation of the program may save a lot of effort in future support of the code.

Will you have all necessary resources to implement desired changes in the code? The resources will certainly include the complete suite of development tools for producing your application, debugging it, and profiling the final program and its components. Based on our own experience, if you have an established performance target, then working with the help of powerful high-productivity tools like Intel Parallel Studio XE 2015 Cluster Edition will certainly reduce your time and effort in reaching the target. We schematically summarize this observation in Figure 8-4.

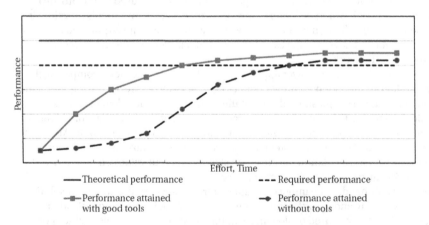

Figure 8-4. *Achieved performance vs. effort, depending on tools usage*

However, in addition to having the right tools, a successful optimization or development project will require knowledge and access to new areas of expertise and the time to learn new things. The tools, programming environments, and models based on open specifications or standards, such as OpenMP or Message Passing Interface (MPI), as we have extensively covered in this book, allow easier access to knowledge and expertise, as well as ensure portability of the code among different platforms whose vendors support the standard or specification. And since the standards and open specifications are supported by multiple vendors of hardware and middleware software, it is much easier to ensure protection of the investments made in your program development.

Summary

We discussed data and control abstractions used on computer systems today and across all hardware and software layers. Layered implementations are used to enable component-level design, increase code portability, and achieve investment protection. However, increased levels of abstractions add complexity and may impact performance. Very often the abstractions are unavoidable, as they are hidden inside implementation of components that are outside of your control. At the same time, the developers can often choose the coding abstractions used while implementing a program or improving performance of an existing application.

There is no universal way to write the best and fastest performing application. Usually the performance is a compromise that involves many points of view. To find the best balance we suggest analyzing the abstractions involved and then judging whether the tradeoffs are reasonable and acceptable. We suggested several questions to be asked in addressing scaling versus performance, flexibility versus specialty, re-computing versus storing the data in memory or transferring over the network, as well as understanding the bounds and bottlenecks, and obtaining a total productivity assessment. Answering these questions will increase your understanding of the program internals and the ecosystem around it, and may result in new ideas about how to achieve even higher performance for your application.

References

1. Intel Corporation, "Intel 64 and IA-32 Architectures Optimization Reference Manual," www.intel.com/content/www/us/en/architecture-and-technology/64-ia-32-architectures-optimization-manual.html.

2. C. L. Lawson, J. R. Hanson, D. R. Kincaid, and F. T. Krogh, "Basic Linear Algebra Subprograms for Fortran Usage," *ACM Transactions on Mathematical Software* (TOMS) 5, no. 3 (1979): 308–23.

3. E. Anderson, Z. Bai, C. Bischof, S. Blackford, J. Demmel, et al., *LAPACK Users' Guide*, 3rd ed. (Philadelphia: Society for Industrial and Applied Mathematics, 1999).

4. M. Frigo and S. Johnson, "FFTW: an adaptive software architecture for the FFT," in *Proceedings of the 1998 IEEE International Conference on Acoustics, Speech and Signal Processing*, vol. 3 (Seattle: IEEE, 1998).

5. L. Torvalds, "Linus Torvalds Blog," https://plus.google.com/+LinusTorvalds/posts/YDKRFDwHwr6.

6. Intel Corporation, "An Introduction to the Intel QuickPath Interconnect, Document Number: 320412," January 2009, www.intel.com/content/dam/doc/white-paper/quick-path-interconnect-introduction-paper.pdf.

7. ISO/IEC, "ISO/IEC International Standard 7498-1:1994 (E)," http://standards.iso.org/ittf/PubliclyAvailableStandards/s020269_ISO_IEC_7498-1_1994(E).zip.

8. Khronos Group, "OpenGL: The Industry's Foundation for High Performance Graphics," www.opengl.org/.

9. A. S. Tanenbaum, *Structured Computer Organization* (Englewood Cliffs, NJ: Prentice-Hall, 1979).

10. A. Gupta, L. V. Kale, F. M. V. Gioachin, C. H. Suen, and Bu-Sung, "The Who, What, Why and How of High Performance Computing Applications," HP Laboratories, www.hpl.hp.com/techreports/2013/HPL-2013-49.pdf.

11. M. T. Jones, "Boost Application Performance Using Asynchronous I/O," www.ibm.com/developerworks/library/l-async/.

12. P. J. Besl, "A Case Study Comparing AoS (Arrays of Structures) and SoA (Structures of Arrays) Data Layouts for a Compute-intensive Loop Run on Intel Xeon Processors and Intel Xeon Phi Product Family Coprocessors," https://software.intel.com/en-us/articles/a-case-study-comparing-aos-arrays-of-structures-and-soa-structures-of-arrays-data-layouts.

13. H. Stüben and N. Yoshifumi, "BQCD," www.rrz.uni-hamburg.de/bqcd.

14. H. Stüben, "Lattice QCD Simulations on SuperMUC," www.lrz.de/services/compute/supermuc/magazinesbooks/supermuc_results_2014/Hinnerk_Stueben_2014.pdf.

15. M. McCool, J. Reinders, and A. Robison, *Structured Parallel Programming: Patterns for Efficient Computation* (San Francisco: Morgan Kaufmann, 2012).

16. T. G. Mattson, B. A. Sanders, and B. L. Massingill, *Patterns for Parallel Programming* (Boston: Addison-Wesley Professional, 2006).

Index